THE
JOURNEY
BACK TO
SELF

A ROADMAP OF DISCOVERY

DARREN TIMMS

publishing

Chichester, England

Copyright © 2020 by Darren Timms. All rights reserved. No portion of this book, except for brief review, may be reproduced, stored in a retrieval system, or transmitted in any form or by any means—electronic, mechanical, photocopying, recording, or otherwise—without the written permission of the publisher. For information, contact Lotus Publishing.

First published in 2020 by
Lotus Publishing
Apple Tree Cottage, Inlands Road, Nutbourne, Chichester, PO18 8RJ

Text Design Medlar Publishing Solutions Pvt Ltd., India
Cover Design Chris Fulcher
Printed and Bound in India by Replika Press

British Library Cataloging-in-Publication Data
A CIP record for this book is available from the British Library
ISBN 978 1 913088 07 1

To my beautiful daughter,
who may one day know who I am

CONTENTS

———— ◆•◆ ————

PREFACE

———◆◆◆———

*On this journey you will encounter many
changes, but the biggest just may be the change
you see in yourself.*

When I first embarked on the journey of writing this book many moons ago, I had no expectations – a kind of 'suck it and see'. Writing this book has been wonderfully insightful. It became my teacher as the words came alive and resonated far more powerfully than I could have imagined. My keyboard gave life to thoughts yelling to be released. By writing them down, the messages contained within the words began to shine so brightly they were impossible to ignore, and thus became my inspiration to continue and share them with you.

I am still very much the person I was when I was growing up, yet my perspective and the understanding of things which currently define me continue to change. The platform from which I see events and circumstances ascends ever higher, and every inch of the metaphoric ladder I climb, the clearer things become. I still get stuck at times in what I call the 'blender', but through much trial and error, I know how to find my way out, quickly and efficiently, when the inevitable falling occurs.

I do not hold a host of titles, which, for some, is a necessity before the work is given any kudos or taken seriously. I am, however, a keen student at the University of Life, a school that never closes, where the teachers never go home or sleep, and where the lessons are continually presented and do not cease until our final breath.

I am qualified yet continue daily to improve my mastery of life through coaching, hypnosis, counselling, advanced NLP, timeline psychology and psychoanalysis. But I hope it is my understanding and insight, gained over two decades, in surmising why we do the things we do and what to do about them that wins your trust.

Has it been easy? Most certainly not, and at times I have doubted myself, my abilities, my beliefs, what I think I know and the need to know what I don't know, and everything in between. Many times, I asked myself: who am I writing this for and what are my true intentions? Did my ego need external validation? Was it an acknowledgement to myself that I was smart enough to write and publish a book? Was the information reliable and good enough to justify the process?

After careful deliberation with publishers, editors and other writers, it was concluded that the information represented enough value to warrant the publishing. There are, of course, elements of egoism, to appear smart or to be talked about, inside every writer, and to deny this would be both misleading and disingenuous.

By writing this book, I express personal intentions to drive the world in a particular direction, to amend other people's ideas towards the kind of world I like to engage with. No book or belief system is genuinely free of personal opinions that do not strengthen one's own confirmation bias. With that in mind, I invite you to read this with an open and curious mind, embrace that which empowers you and disregard the rest after careful consideration.

IN A NUTSHELL

This book isn't for everyone...

This book is for those who feel stuck and don't know what to do next. It is for those tired of repeating the same mistakes over and over again. It is for those willing to take full responsibility for their previous choices and every choice they make from this moment on and the consequences that arise from them. It is for those ready to ascend to the next level and become the hero of their own story.

This book is not for those who want a quick fix. It's not for those who are unwilling to dig deep and face the, at times, ugly truth about themselves. It's not for those who believe life is happening to them, not for them. It's not for those afraid of realising their full potential, and it is most definitely not for those who want only to take and not help others become the greatest version of themselves.

ACKNOWLEDGEMENTS

———◆•◆———

I would like to thank every single person who has played an instrumental part on my journey thus far. You have been and continue to be my most potent teachers.

Special thanks, however, go to Jon from Lotus Publishing, who took a chance on an unknown author and agreed within an hour of meeting me to publish the book you are now holding.

To Steve, the editor who did a wonderful job of retaining the original flavour of my work.

To my loving parents, for without them, I wouldn't be the man I became.

Lastly, to my amazing Paula – my rock, best friend, and beautiful wife – who supports and encourages everything I do: without you love, life would not be as it is.

PROLOGUE

———◆•◆———

The world is as dark and narrow as we believe
it to be, or as expansive and glorious as our
imaginations allow.

We appear more comfortable beating others over the head with a judgemental hammer, continually looking for weaknesses and flaws to shore up our fragility, than supporting and promoting love, goodness, positivity and unity. That type of thinking and how we direct our thoughts are reflected by the palettes we use to paint our unique canvases. Nothing is left untouched by the colour of our thoughts. Take, for example, the person who thinks themselves unlucky or undeserving. They are envious, fearful, suspicious and paranoid, and, sure enough, the self-portrait will reflect the dreariness supported by such thinking. Containing little joy or splendour, these individuals are incapable of seeing the happiness in others and will therefore judge everyone else to be as selfish, paranoid, insecure and unloving as they see themselves. Even acts of genuine generosity and kindness will be vigorously opposed and regarded as having impure motives, for no other reason that they paint their world according to their dark limitations.

Consider now the person whose mind is loving, generous, giving, light and cheerful. How magnificent is their world? They are conscious of the loving unity in all creatures, not just in their creed. They see themselves in others with no room for suspicion or doubtful paranoia, their canvas awash with the brightest vibrant colours that nature has to offer. They walk with a spring in their step and a tune on their lips.

Both of these types of individual live in the same world yet inhabit different realities, their thoughts and actions diametrically opposed, sharing proximity but little more. They may as well be living on separate planets, and indeed they do: one resides in heaven and the other in hell, created by their thoughts alone. Two circles that rarely overlap, or interact, and will remain so until a great effort is forthcoming. It is essential that we make an effort before the mental barriers that enslave us become ever narrower, and we experience nothing other than the unproductive and dysfunctional circles in which we find ourselves.

INTRODUCTION

*Yesterday I was clever, so I wanted to
change the world. Today I am wise,
so I am changing myself.*
– Rumi

First, let me tell you what this book isn't – a work of fiction where the storyline builds with anticipation to an appropriate crescendo. No, I have written this book the way we experience life – one moment at a time, where the trials and tribulations are forever unfolding, stimulating the behavioural responses and common emotional reactions we know all too well.

I could have written this book in such a way that there was a heavy focus on procedures, with little in the form of explanations, but after careful deliberation I decided against it. Hence, the content is more in-depth, entertaining and far-reaching than in many of the books you will find in the self-help/spiritual growth section on the shelves of today's bookstores, but not so heavy that it will weigh you down with extensive terminology and an overload of scientific jargon.

If your expectations are to read from cover to cover about how easy life can be if you were to only follow my instructions, then a heavy sigh is in order. Being human, dear reader, is no utopian dream, but neither is it a dystopian nightmare.

The secret to life is to stack the odds firmly in one's favour, at the same time accepting that while we are here, it's going to be rough occasionally... real rough in fact; therefore, anyone who tells you that they have this thing beat or that life is a permanent breeze is deluded, the returning messiah or a barefaced liar. The very nature of being human guarantees that no one, and I do mean *no one*, is leaving this place alive or unscathed not having felt the sting of immense suffering and the euphoria of wondrous joy.

We must understand the nature of planet earth. It exists within the laws of duality, where everything must have its opposing polarity. For beauty, there must be ugliness. For birth, there must be death. For positivity to exist, so too must negativity. Earth is not a utopia. It is not a paradise. It is a place of beginnings and endings. A place where we pleasure-seeking primates come to learn at a university that never closes. A place where all biological organisms decay and dissolve, and where all things must pass. Everything must and will change, of that there is no doubt. Every conceivable separation will occur. Relationships will end and your heart will ache. Your pets will come and go, and you will almost certainly bury your parents.

I don't tell you this to be morbid or to create anxiety. I tell you this so as not to sweat the small stuff but to live accordingly without wasting the most valuable commodity I know – time. Time is the most precious of all life's resources and not to be squandered or taken lightly.

Most of us live as if we are physically immortal, unwilling to acknowledge that life and death travel together. The fact is, we are not going to live forever, well not until the science cracks biological immortality. Hence, live every day with as much love, joy, forgiveness and gratitude as possible, knowing that one day, this will not be available to you.

Second, you are not lost, and neither do you need to find yourself. You are not a set of car keys left in a pair of jeans that you forgot you had worn. Your authentic self is always available – it's right there, just beneath the surface, covered only by your cultural, societal and parental conditioning, other people's opinions, and erroneous conclusions you created as a child, and thus became who you think you are. You are not your thoughts... you are infinite potential – a potential we are going to unearth as you unlearn and peel back the layers until you are once again the person you were born to be before the world got its hands on you.

That said, let's begin to enjoy the journey back to self and to cherish the first day of the rest of your life. Everything you will learn in this book will have zero value unless you first embrace the changes, and then through repetition cement them. These changes must be conditioned until they become your new standards, and nothing less than that will produce the changes you seek.

I am not a wizard, and neither can I fix you. But what I can do is introduce you to your highest potential if you are willing to apply the amount of effort needed to raise your standards. Everything we do aligns with our standards and how they reflect our self-image to the outside world. It's your self-image which will dictate every aspect of your life. Whether you believe that you can or you cannot do something, you are absolutely correct.

Self-image is everything and will dictate every facet of your life, so paying close attention to this aspect is of paramount importance. Whether you set out to lose weight and keep it off, become a better sportsman, increase your net worth, write that novel you said you would, become the next prime minister or achieve any other goal depends entirely on the qualities of your self-image. Understanding this can mean the difference between triumph and defeat. Everything you believe yourself to be will forever remain consistent with this self-image, and I do mean *forever*. In fact, one cannot act contrarian or outperform one's specific self-image. To change our self-image, we must become strategic and employ what has been demonstrated by science to work. Numerous case studies have proved that, regardless of age or gender, we are capable of making changes to our self-image through neuroplasticity.[1]

---

[1] The brain's ability to reorganise itself by forming new neural connections throughout life, allowing the neurons (nerve cells) in the brain to adjust their activities in response to new situations or to changes in their environment.

We will do anything to uphold and validate our perceived identity; hence, to fundamentally rearrange a character, it's imperative that the mechanical behaviour and the corresponding beliefs built around that behaviour be changed. For example, an overweight male who states he is unable to change his bad eating habits, is big boned, has a slow metabolism and no time to go to the gym has convinced himself that these are facts, simultaneously cementing a negative, self-fulfilling prophecy. To alter that false belief, he would have to change not only his way of thinking but his lifestyle choices too. His new thought patterns would have to include: 'I will find the time and whatever it costs to go to the gym', 'I will take that early morning stroll or bike ride', and 'I will change my food intake to reflect my new, improved choices'.

Repeated with consistency, the new behaviour will help forge a different identity. No longer will the overweight male associate himself with inactivity, lame excuses and poor dietary choices, but he will behave accordingly to align with his new self-image of someone who exercises daily and is a healthy eater. If this sounds simplistic, that's because it is. The effort and discipline required for a new self-image to arise, however, is a different proposal and very subjective.

Every minute of every day, our minds are working to make sense of what we experience, on the basis of our unique 'book of rules', but this book is a not the finished product. You can rewrite it anytime you desire, including the addition or removal of all the different characters you wish to have in your book.

You also get to apply the meaning or interpretation of the experiences and events that crop up in your life. You may not be able to control what others do, but you can, with rightful thinking, be unaffected by what others say or do, once you know that it is your thoughts that are governing your reality and not the circumstances themselves. That of course will take some effort on your part. We must train our minds to be resilient enough to brush off the opinions and judgements of others, especially when we have been raised to do the opposite.

I don't know about you, but I find it incredibly empowering to know that, as the author of my story, I can be a hero or a villain, a warrior or a coward, a giver or a taker; in fact, anything I wish to be is possible, because I get to choose at what level and how I wish to live my life. To illustrate: if mediocrity is the level at which your self-image wants to experience life, then a mediocre body, mediocre levels of achievements and mediocre relationships are the best you can expect, as you cannot outperform the self-governing restrictions of your self-image.

To be clear, dear reader, there is nothing wrong with mediocrity if that's the level you are happy to play at. But when you look in the mirror, what do you see? How do you feel when you come home from work... when you climb into bed before turning the lights off... when you wake up in the morning? Are you really content with your life? Are you living with total congruency and maximising your potential? Or are you leaving some of it on the table?

If you are not content, what are you willing to do? Will you go all in and play at the level you know you are capable of, or will you play it safe and continue as you are? I am hoping it's the latter, in which case I can help you – help you achieve healthier relationships with your partners, family, boss, work colleagues and friends, but most of all a healthier relationship with yourself.

The first stage of any new process can often be the most challenging, but every journey starts with a single step – so why shouldn't this be yours? The fact you are holding a book entitled *The Journey Back to Self* means that there are aspects of your life which need attention, but before we begin, we need to understand a few things.

There are as many differing opinions, beliefs and ideologies as there are people. To advocate a non-contestable truth, therefore, is both arrogant and futile, and to believe that your truth carries more weight than the next person's will cause you emotional upheaval, regardless of how correct you are.

To be clear: there are a multitude of ways of looking at the world, but the irony is that there are not that many proper ways in which the driving force leans towards the greater good of the earthly populace. However, if you need your truth to be accepted in order to feel a certain way about yourself, regardless of its validity, then life for you, dear reader, will be a roller coaster of extreme emotions.

We do not live in a perfect world – far from it. There are people out there who are going to upset you and push every one of your buttons, if you let them. But do you want to be right, or do you want to be happy? If your gig is running around the mountain persuading every climber to follow your lead because you know the only way to the summit, then happiness for you will be a fleeting mistress.

My advice, if you wish to be content that is, is to let those who wish to slip, slide and fall do exactly that. Those who wish to listen to you will do so of their own accord. The subjectivity of human perception means that beliefs and truths are shaped by opinions, experiences and feelings, and not by absolutes. To understand this is to appreciate the complexity of being human.

Let me be clear. Nothing, and I do mean *nothing*, exists outside of your own projection. In fact, there is no out-there until we have run an event or circumstance through our unique filtering system. We then distort, delete and generalise that information through what I like to refer to as our 'book of rules', and in that book sits our beliefs, ideologies, standards, values, shoulds and should nots, and musts and must nots.

We then project our subjective reality outwards onto the metaphoric movie screen we know as life. Everything we experience is a direct projection of what has been created in our own mind after the massive amount of filtered information has been dissected and rearranged to align with our book of rules and hence our personal reality.

Unless we open our minds, anything that challenges that book of rules, including our personal values and beliefs, will be met with stiff resistance. Frantz Fanon (20 July, 1925 – 6 December, 1961), a Martinique-born psychiatrist, philosopher and revolutionary, said:

> At times, people hold a core belief that is very strong. When they
> are presented with evidence that works against that belief, the new
> evidence cannot be accepted. It creates a feeling that is extremely

uncomfortable, which is called cognitive dissonance. Moreover, because it is so important to protect the core belief, they rationalise, ignore, and even deny anything that does not fit in with the core belief.

Don't be that person! I challenge you to become inquisitive, to broaden your horizons and to step away from any intellectual prison that halts your growth. The 'I know what I know' mantra and 'I don't wish to have my reality challenged' attitude is such a restrictive narrative, wouldn't you agree?

For me personally, I try every day to live without any rigid ideology to defend, to be always ready to learn, and to accept that I don't know what I don't know. This paradigm allows the information to flow from all angles and for me to try it on, before making a decision. That is not to say I am devoid of strong opinions or beliefs that underpin who I believe myself to be. On the contrary, our self-image and how that image interacts with the outside world is the driver of everything we think, do and say. The difference is, I am very aware that my self-image and my personal beliefs are unique to me and that my perception of the world is pure projection; moreover, I am ready to change my perception, and therefore my projected reality, in a heartbeat if empowering and acceptable information is forthcoming.

To be honest, I would be a little surprised if those reading this book had never heard before of the notion that all perception is projection. For those who haven't, welcome to a world where all things that unfold are happening *for* us and not *to* us.

In my world, being accountable is non-negotiable – where finger pointing or blaming external events for my pain cannot exist. I am under no illusion that I am shaped not by the experiences I encounter, but by the meaning I give to those encounters. Read that again. It is not the event but rather the meaning I give to the event which shapes my reality. To illustrate, it is not death, heartbreak, illness, pain, suffering or unfortunate incidents that define me, but the interpretation of those events.

Ten different people will assign ten different meanings to the same event and arrive at their idiosyncratic truth. If the event was responsible for the pain, suffering, illness or heartbreak, then everyone would experience the same reality, and we know that this is not true. It is our thoughts which create the suffering. Our suffering is taking place not out there in the external world, but as a representation of our internal world.

What you believe to be real is actually an internal representation – a creation of your amazing neurology. To understand this is to be well ahead of the curve. In fact, it's vital that you recognise this for a clearer understanding of what life is and how to use this information to your advantage.

MY STORY

Below I summarise what I believe was reason enough for me to embark on a journey of self-discovery and the driver in turning my life around from VIP bodyguard, nightclub bouncer, nightclub owner, millionaire stock trader and real estate investor, to NLP practitioner, coach, hypnotist, timeline therapist and counselling psychologist.

I have always been fascinated with self-improvement but it became an obsession more than 12 years ago, when a beautiful daughter was the end product of a dysfunctional relationship that I had gone through in my hometown of Oxford in the UK. The finer details are not necessary, but in a nutshell, the mother and my daughter left for the United States before she was three years old, and so began my intrigue into all things human psychology and why we do the things we do. I read a ton of self-help books, attended multiple workshops and even went back to college to acquire the knowledge I craved to make sense of human suffering and what to do about it.

Since using the techniques and the information I share with you in this book, my life has changed dramatically. I am more confident, able, empathic, compassionate and tolerant. But above all, I have realised that the secret to living is giving... that we are here to serve, contribute and make a difference to the lives of others if we want sustainable happiness.

My quest for deeper meaning has taken me all over the world, from the Balkans to the Balearics, and from the jungles of Brazil to Budapest. I learnt that what I sought did not exist outside of myself, and that the journey back to self is a journey of inner exploration.

Are you ready to dive deep into your own life and the journey back to self as we unearth the diamond you most definitely are?

SUBJECTIVE REALITY

———◆◆———

The image of the world around us, which we
carry in our head, is just a model.

We have all heard the words 'Well, that's their opinion' to describe how someone makes sense of the world they live in. But what does that really mean?

Have you ever contemplated how you arrive at your outcomes? How you think and why... your personal beliefs and ideology... the relationships you attract... the jobs you have or lean towards... what you eat and what you drink... your health, financial success or failure, and everything in between.

Would you agree that what you do or don't do distinguishes your outcomes? What you failed to start when you said you would... what you promised yourself and others, yet failed to deliver... what you did start and complete, and all scenarios in between.

You can point the finger at external conditions and hold any number of people responsible for your outcomes, but those are false accusations; your results are directly correlated to the actions you did or did not perform.

So, if actions are responsible for outcomes, what inspires the actions? It's your emotions and mental state that determines what you do and how you do it. Everybody knows how it feels to be in a flow state... when life meets your every step but never stands on your toes… when you walk around with a smile on your face, a spring in your step and get stuff done effortlessly.

You also know how it feels not being able to think straight or get things done… angry, agitated, distressed, disturbed. We have all been there, but for some it's their default, it's the emotional home.

What types of result would you assume those who operate from the default of procrastination and distress achieve versus those who spend the majority of their time in flow? If we are speaking in terms of majorities, which we must do when making an assessment, the answer will be obvious.

There are exceptions, yes, but those aside, we can state with confidence that folk who live with a smile on their face, have an uplifting energy and live with unblemished integrity get better results than those on the other side of the equation. Why is this? Well, you cannot access your highest intelligence or be at your resourceful best when angry, agitated, distressed and emotionally disturbed. Hence, the quality of your emotions will affect the quality of your actions and lead to either favourable or unfavourable outcomes.

So, if our actions are driven by the emotional state we are in at any given time, what stimulates the emotions? The answer is, your beliefs and childhood conditioning… or better expressed, the meaning you applied to every single experience, memory, event and circumstance that life afforded you as a young child, namely between the ages of 0 and 6, when the commanding unconscious mind was being formed.

The unconscious mind drives up to 95% of your daily behaviour, via the influential psychological programmes it created in childhood, and unless questioned and reworked, the behaviour and the meaning-making process remains the same. Sure, we are constantly changing as we age, but the fundamental beliefs which were conditioned by our early childhood experiences are the drivers of all we do. (This is a complex topic which I will cover in greater detail as we proceed.)

That, in a nutshell, is the filtering system which close to eight billion people use to make sense of the world, each using the above process to create a unique and subjective reality. That means we don't see things as *they* are; we see them as *we* are. The external world is but a mirror of our internal reality.

Looking at the equation

$$\text{Beliefs} \Rightarrow \text{Emotions} \Rightarrow \text{Actions} \Rightarrow \text{Outcomes}$$

and applying common sense, we can conclude that in order to change the outcome, we must address the root cause, where the beliefs are stored. Until we apply new meanings to our experiences, events and circumstances, and to the triggers that initiate the repeated actions, then expect more of the same. That isn't rocket science, that's plain common sense.

By changing our beliefs, our emotional responses change, which influence our actions and transform our results. All making sense? Good. But it doesn't stop there. Within the equation above sits a further filtering process which needs to be understood.

Massive amounts of information continually arouse our sensory organs and nervous systems. The numbers differ according to different sources, but the last time I checked, our nervous system and conscious awareness receive via the five senses about twenty million pieces of information per second that need processing. Some believe it's up to four billion chunks of information, so be it twenty million or four billion, the numbers are unfathomable.

That information, for all intents and purposes, is neutral until we give it a meaning. All information is unbiased until we apply a subjective definition, and this is where it gets even more interesting.

The information is narrowed down further by generalising, deleting and distorting anything that sits outside of my belief system or anything that represents a threat to my carefully constructed self-image until what remains is 'MY REALITY' – a reality which I believe in wholeheartedly and, unless I'm inspired to change it, will stay the same. To attain this reality, I must distort and delete almost all the information until I end up with less than a hundred and thirty pieces of data from the twenty million per second that are available. And this is all done instantaneously. Pretty impressive wouldn't you say? Well, let's explore a little further and see how empowering or disempowering this is before we decide.

In laymen's terms, this filtering system is designed to detect what's familiar and to prove itself correct in any given situation. We become so convinced of our truth, and what that truth means, our unique existence is as real as it gets. In fact, we rarely question it, and unless challenged, an alternative version is rarely, if ever, contemplated.

This subjective and perceived truth creates repetitive feelings and is thus responsible for the quality of our lives. We are unaware that we are not directly encountering the quality of our lives, but rather the quality of our meaning-making process through this filtering system. Unless we disturb the cycle, we will continue to get what we have always got, meaning that our comfort zone will maintain the status quo, regardless of the outcome.

To change one's reality, the filtering system must be modified to see things differently and hence apply a different meaning to the information. In order to do this, we must break the habit of being ourselves; otherwise, we will continue to seek out that which is familiar and therefore continually arrive at the same destination. All well and good, if the outcomes, dreams and desires are fulfilling; not so good, however, if the outcomes fall short of what is needed to stack the odds in favour of an enjoyable and productive existence.

The good news is that each of us can experience 'brain plasticity', which means the brain's ability to modify its connections or rewire itself. Each of us is capable and proficient, if we so desire, in the act of radical change and in the transformation of experiences which keep us stuck in life. We were not born with belief systems that cause and maintain disturbance and suffering; they were created, and that which was created can be uncreated. Similarly, that which was learnt can be unlearnt.

If that type of world resonates and makes sense, and you would like to learn more, grab a beverage of choice, get comfortable and enjoy the ride as I attempt to bridge the gaps between human behaviour, spirituality and the world we live in.

IN A NUTSHELL

As basic as this sounds, you have two options. You now know how you are creating your reality, and you can therefore continue to live as you are, a slave to your immature childhood conditioning. Alternatively, with determination, drive and purpose, you can refuse to accept the limiting belief of 'This is who I am and have always been, and who I shall remain!', and do something about it. Personally, I believe that you owe it to the world to locate and transform the traits that negatively impact you, your loved ones and anybody else infected by immature emotional behavioural patterns.

A JOURNEY OF SELF-DISCOVERY

Life is a journey that must be travelled no
matter how bad the roads and accommodations.

My philosophy is as follows. Question *everything*, regardless of where you read it or who has said it (myself included). Listen carefully to your intellect, but even more so to your intuition. Intuition, argues Gerd Geiringer, a director at the Max Planck Institute for Human Development, is less about suddenly 'knowing' the right answer and more about instinctively understanding which information is unimportant and can thus be discarded.

I encourage you to trust this process. Not blindly – but when something feels right, followed by careful calculation, go with it. Einstein said: 'The intuitive mind is a sacred gift, and the rational mind is a faithful servant. We have created a society that honours the servant and has forgotten the gift.' I will remind you of this as we proceed.

The gatekeepers of modern science may be upset with the lack of empirical evidence presented in this book. As will the unbending theologians who demand that we surrender to the will of a rewarding deity in order to live happily ever after, in this life and for an eternity after that. I aspire to neither ideology.

I have no axe to grind with science or those who believe in a personal, rewarding or punishing deity. Faith is a wonderful thing to have, and I applaud those who live with inner peace because of it. In fact, believing that there is a creating sentience which drives the universe in a particular direction is not only comforting but also essential in the quest for deeper meaning and purpose.

The human being is an amalgamation of four different parts: the soul or the spirit, the physical being, the emotional being and the mental being. To live an optimal life, all four components must be developed to their full potential, something I hope this book will assist you with. The last three parts interact and exist on the physical plane we know as life. The spirit or the soul is the energetic component that was present before physical birth and continues on after physical death. This part is connected directly to that creating sentience I speak of and is eternal. How you express that sentience in words is entirely up to you, and if you happen to be atheist, feel free to ignore and discard anything that sits outside of what you are willing to entertain.

Einstein, however, proved that all the energy of the universe is constant and that it can be neither created nor destroyed; in other words, energy (including ourselves) can only be transformed from one form to another. Where we go and what we transform into, I have no factual idea, but as an expression of energy that exists within the totality of infinity, we cannot be destroyed.

I cannot prove that beyond any doubt, and so it's a statement of personal faith. I fully support any faith or belief system that stimulates happiness, strength and hope, and supports the happiness of others. However, if your beliefs have you feeling conflicted, sad, depressed, restricted, irritated and unhappy, it's for a good reason.

Physical pain is a feedback mechanism, informing us that something is wrong. Let me explain. Pinch your arm; now twist the skin between your fingers until it's painful. What just happened? You performed an act that was met by a response in the body which suggested: 'Hey, what are you doing? It hurts... stop it!'

Emotions are also feedback mechanisms: they let us know the quality of our thoughts and actions. That is the purpose of emotions – to tell us if the path we are on is empowering or disempowering. Emotional suffering is no different to physical pain; our thoughts and actions are forever being monitored by our internal feedback machine, known as our emotions. For example, when we experience troubled relationships, jobs that cause us pain, repetitive family squabbles, or habits and rituals which hurt the body, or when we are continually having and acting on thoughts which cause emotional suffering, our bodies will let us know very clearly that our choices need careful assessment.

The longer we refuse to acknowledge these skilful and persistent messengers, the more painful life becomes. The same voice is attempting to convey a very important message: 'Hey, what you are doing is hurting me. Stop it!'

It matters not whether the pain is physical or emotional. Your higher self is always trying to communicate with you to preserve the body and maintain its optimum health, both physical and emotional. When we are born, aside from the tiniest percentage, in every cell exists a blueprint for the best possible physical and emotional health. The unconscious mind is always trying to maintain that blueprint; hence, when we go off-road and behave in ways which threaten the state of physical and emotional wellness, we are reminded repeatedly that what we are doing is hurting the body, so stop it! Yet through free will, we are permitted to act, do and say whatever we like, and every act, thought and word carry with it a corresponding consequence. This is how we humans get into so much trouble. We either don't know, don't care or are ignorant to the damage we are causing ourselves and others by our chosen behaviour.

This is also how most illness is created. Disease, or better expressed as 'dis-ease', is the result of repeatedly ignoring the warning signs. The term 'dis-ease' literally means 'a lack of ease' inside the body. It ensues when the inherent intelligence of the body is not able to achieve its optimum potential in performing its functions. This will happen whenever there is continued interference with the nervous system, negating its natural ability to maintain optimum health.

It can often take years for dis-ease to manifest. That is how resilient the human body can be, but it cannot withstand constant and indefinite emotional trauma or distress. At some point in time, this will lead to problems, emotional and physical, and often both simultaneously.

Hence, I implore you: start to pay very close attention to your thoughts, actions, words you use towards others, self-talk, emotions, aches and pains, and to anything which does not support your best self, and take evasive action before your body is unable to protect you further. It is said that someone with good health has a thousand wishes; without it, they have one. You would do well to remember that.

EPIGENETICS

You will never change your life until you change your daily routine. The secret to your success or failure is found in your daily routines.

To live optimally, one must understand the mindset that goes with optimal living. Contrary to what you may have been told, your character is not set in stone. You are neither a prisoner to your genetics or a slave to your imprinted childhood. These misdiagnosed assumptions have afforded humanity little favour, disempowering those who believe they are victims of their heredity when the latest research on epigenetics utterly repudiates these claims. In fact, the empirical evidence is so strong it's forcing the issue enough so that changes in medical-school curriculums are currently under way...

Isn't it beautiful as one narrative after another is picked apart, disproved and consigned to the trash as a new golden age of information engulfs the planet? Welcome to the science of epigenetics. This is the study of inherited changes in gene expression caused by mechanisms other than changes in the underlying DNA sequence, or, in layman terms, how we are influenced by our external environment and by our thinking processes, and how we react to them.

The excellent work in epigenetics being carried out by determined scientific researchers can help address many ailments, both physical and emotional, which humanity currently battles with. By relaying this information, I am humbly standing on the shoulders of giants, sharing knowledge that others have painstakingly discovered through many years of gruelling research. I honour each one of them, too many to mention here. I am just a messenger, but this message needs to be heard by as many people as possible, as quickly as possible.

And the message reads as follows. Stop being a victim to your genes or what you believe is your genetic destiny. Our health, both physical and emotional, is predominantly governed by our thoughts and the external environment we are repeatedly exposed to.

Dr Bruce Lipton PhD, a leading scientist and pioneer in the field, confirmed that 'only the tiniest fraction of diseases, less than 5%, can be attributed to genetic heredity' and that 'our health is not controlled by genetics'. 'This misconstrues the nature of how biology works,' Lipton went on to say.

In simplistic terms, we need to change the way we think and our external environment to help fight the ailments we currently battle with... Research shows that a combination of different elements of our lifestyle – including our diet, our beliefs and our daily habitats – has a significant influence on the genes.

This demonstrates how important it is to pay close attention to how we are living and what type of environment we expose ourselves to. Many ailments, for example, especially those caused by an auto-immune response, inflammatory conditions or allergies, are often caused by a change in social environment from the great outdoors to the not-so-great indoors. Coupled with the extra stress that can accompany these changes, it comes as no surprise we become more fragile and vulnerable to certain types of emotional and physical disorder. Our immune systems are unable to cope with the bombardment of prolonged internal and external stressors...

Needless to say, spending time in the great outdoors is far more conducive to good health than sitting behind a desk, staring into a plethora of screens surrounded by artificial light, with a phone in either ear from dusk till dawn. My dear old dad has been a tree surgeon since he was 18 years old and has never seen the inside of an office. He is now the other side of 80 yet still works five days a week, come rain, snow or sunshine, even managing to climb the trees he works on. He has his issues, but the great outdoors has been the greatest friend he ever had.

This philosophy and mindset has worked for me also. Each morning I take my laptop, books and other writing material I need, put them in my backpack, jump on my bike and head for the 'café du jour', where I write until my inspiration wanes. When it does, I jump on my bike and head for the beach, pool or gym to engage in some type of exercise. You may not have the luxury of mimicking this routine, but I would wager that your schedule, handled skilfully, would afford you time each day to enjoy the great outdoors or the use of a gym or pool.

Sadly, for many, working in the fresh air is not an available choice, which makes it more important to find time to do so. If you are spending most of your time inside an air-conditioned office or home, you are forcing your body to use stale air; by doing so, you are making it harder for your body to stay healthy and fresh.

Also, when outdoors we must consider the amount of serotonin we release in response to the amount of clean oxygen we inhale;

serotonin, the feel-good hormone, can significantly heighten our mood and promote a sense of happiness and well-being. This is neither pseudoscience nor rocket science – it is common sense. Spending extended periods in the great outdoors is imperative to achieving optimum health, so please include it in your daily routine. An easy way to do this is to remove your shoes and socks and walk barefooted on grass or sand, or in water to ground yourself.

Recent advances in environmental medicine have proved beyond doubt a correlation between human health and the immediate environment, including factors such as unclean air and dirty water and the presence of harmful chemicals, and how this is capable of causing disease.

A surprisingly simple yet beneficial global resource for health maintenance is the surface of the earth itself. It is an established, though not widely appreciated fact, that the earth's surface maintains an unlimited and renewable supply of free health-inducing energy. Mounting evidence suggests that the earth's potential for promoting better health creates a stable internal environment for the normal functioning of all our bodily systems.

There are few things left on this planet without a price tag. Grounding one's feet on Mother Earth's surface is nature's free gift to every human who is aware enough to enjoy this health-enhancing pastime. Do yourself a favour and ditch those shoes and socks at every available opportunity.

Getting back to epigenetics and what it means, let's have a closer look at the science behind it and why it's so exciting. Conventional thinking suggests that we're controlled by our genes. This is a misrepresentation of how gene biology works, according to the prominent scientist Dr Bruce Lipton, who has dedicated his adult life to human biology and behaviour. He was an associate professor of anatomy at the University of Wisconsin School of Medicine until he discovered things were not as they seemed to be. Nor were they what he'd been teaching in med school or what we've been told to believe.

Dr Lipton began experimenting with stem cells, placing them in Petri dishes for observation. He put one stem cell into a culture dish, and noticed that it divided every 10 hours. After two weeks, there were thousands of cells in the dish, and they were all genetically identical, having derived from the same parent cell. He then divided the cell population and inoculated them into three different culture dishes. In the next phase of the experiment, Dr Lipton manipulated the culture medium – the cell's equivalent of the environment – in each dish. In one dish, the cells became bone, in another, muscle, and in the last, they became fat. This demonstrated that the genes didn't determine the fate of the cells, because they all had the exact same genes; the environment determined the outcome of the cells, not the genetic pattern. Thus, Dr Lipton deduced that if the cells are in a healthy environment, they are healthy, whereas if they're in an unhealthy environment, they get sick.

With fifty trillion cells, the human body is the equivalent of a skin-covered culture dish. Moving our body from one environment to another alters the composition of the 'culture medium' – the blood. The chemistry of the blood, therefore, determines the nature of the cell's environment. The blood's chemistry is impacted by the chemicals emitted from the brain. The brain chemistry adjusts the composition of the blood on the basis of our perceptions of life, meaning that our understanding of any given thing, at any given moment, can influence the brain chemistry; this, in turn, affects the environment where the cells reside and controls their fate. In other words, our thoughts and perceptions have a direct and overwhelmingly significant effect on the behaviour of the cell.

This is life-changing information for a species that has until now believed that our health is often predetermined and if we do fall ill, prescription medicine is our only hope. Not so, according to Dr Lipton, who adds: 'Gene activity changes daily. If the understanding in our mind is reflected in the chemistry of our body, and if our nervous system reads and deciphers the environment and then controls the blood's chemistry, then we can actually alter the fate of our cells by modifying our thoughts.' Furthermore, the gene programmes are contained within the nucleus of the cell, and we can rewrite those genetic programmes by changing the blood chemistry. In a nutshell, we must change the way we think, coupled with healthier living conditions, for optimum health. This is the memorandum I promote throughout this book.

The mind adjusts the body's biology and behaviour to fit the beliefs. Stop a while and think of the possible ramifications if the brain adapts to fit the belief. For example, if you've been told by a doctor (who you consider an object of undoubted authority) that you'll die in six months, and your mind believes it, you most likely will die in six months. This is called the 'nocebo effect', the result of having a strong belief in negative thoughts, which is the opposite of the better known and scientifically proved 'placebo effect', where healing is mediated by positive thinking.

We have been programmed to believe we are hapless victims, without control over our health. We are taught that when we are sick to go immediately to the doctor because they are the absolute authority on all matters relating to health and well-being. This has facilitated an underlying neurosis, where doctors are on speed dial and called and visited far more often than they need to be. To be clear, I am not suggesting for a moment that you don't have your regular check-ups – please use common sense here.

There is a particular comical irony when certain people get better, or definitely feel better, on the way to the doctor – where the innate ability for self-healing kicks in. The comfort in knowing that you will see somebody who you believe can give calming advice or medicine to take away the suffering creates a healing environment.

I must add that pain management medicine is one of humanity's most significant discoveries and provides enormous relief to millions of people around the world. But we cannot ignore the elephant in the room.

In today's world, big pharma monopolises all things health, and doctors are encouraged to reach for the prescription pad and start scribbling before you have sat yourself down in the chair. It's by no coincidence that tens of billions of dollars are made in profits by a pharmaceutical industry that manufactures these pills and potions, which are then thrown around like cheap confetti at weddings and bar mitzvahs. I am not declaring that all medicines are unnecessary – of course not. But we are such a capable and resilient species with an innate ability to heal most of our common ills, without the constant need for prescription medicines.

Let us be the ones who make the changes we wish to see in the world. This cannot happen if we continue to look outside ourselves for solutions that often exist within. The wisest teachers, who blessed this planet with their presence, left behind this most profound but fundamental message for humanity: 'heal thyself' and then turn your attention outwards.

You can change! You can heal! You are not a slave to your genetics. By believing such indoctrinated rhetoric, you are effectively saying: 'I choose to operate via my limited childhood programming.' Believe yourself to be powerless, then powerless you will remain.

Self-defeating statements, albeit very common have been proven now scientifically to be untrue. Neuroplasticity (our brain's ability to reorganise itself by forming new neural connections as a result of further information, and therefore begin to experience something other than our past self-image and its limitations) clearly shows that via the law of exposure and repetition to new stimuli and learning, we can reinvent ourselves.

Encouragingly, a great many are changing, waking up and doing the necessary, adjusting priorities and living lives with significance and purpose while simultaneously taking control of their lives. We can transform into beings which resonate at higher frequencies – the frequencies of advanced understanding and self-healing, and, above all, the frequency of love...

'IMPRINTED BEHAVIOUR'

———◆•◆———

Children learn to smile from their parents.

'Why is life so tough?' is a question I am often asked and many times I ask myself. In a nutshell, we are born into a biological machine without an instruction manual, and raised by parents or caregivers who likewise lacked any instruction booklet and had little idea about how to manage their own operating systems effectively, let alone ours. However, and this is important, most parents do the very best they can, with the emotional and psychological toolkits they have available to them at any given time; therefore, they did what they could from their platform of limited awareness. Knowing this, it's imperative from the get-go to forgive and let go of even the tiniest amounts of resentment that is harboured towards them and anyone else for that matter. Resentment is a toxin that creates far more damage to the vessel that contains it than anything over which it is poured.

I know it's hard when a traumatic past is the truth, but letting go of the past and the resentment we hold in our bodies and minds towards others is of paramount importance. To forgive is one of the hardest but most powerful things we can do to create a healing environment in the body, and one of the most toxic and ailment-producing environments when we don't.

And if I still haven't convinced you, please forgive those who have hurt you, not because they deserve it, but you most certainly do!!!

Willingly drinking poison and then hoping the object of your resentment and hostility to suffer is a fruitless and very damaging practice, yet we do that when holding on to bitterness towards another person. Let it go, NOW!

Blaming our past and especially our family for the pain and suffering we feel is a very common and popular way to trudge through life, yet seldom do we give them credit for the pleasures we enjoy. If you have to blame your parents especially, then blame with intelligence. Everything you have become is because of what you have endured, what you have learnt from the thousands of lessons imparted to you, regardless of the intentions behind them – that resilience you have – the strength to overcome adversity.

Where do you think that came from? That's right, from the experiences you had to tolerate for you to be where you are today. Your character, your beliefs, your habits, your rituals, your moral code, your integrity, your conscience – all are fashioned on the back of your childhood experiences, specifically before the age of seven, and stored in the unconscious mind, where 95% of your beliefs, habits and patterns of behaviour reside. And no, that isn't a typo. The unconscious mind makes up 95% and the remaining 5% is what we know as the conscious mind, and both perform very different roles. And yes, you read that correctly: 95% of who you think you are was formed before the age of seven, at which point the conscious mind became involved.

Aristotle, an Ancient Greek philosopher and scientist, who is still considered one of the greatest thinkers in politics, psychology and ethics, said: 'Give me a child until he is seven and I will show you the man.' In some circles, the above statement is attributed to the Jesuit church, but let's not get lost in semantics. In other words, a child's experiences, and programming from birth to age seven, are the primary factors that determine the character of an individual's life, and so it is. That is not to say that the unconscious mind is incapable of making radical changes. On the contrary, both the conscious and unconscious mind will respond to concise directives, as long as we speak the correct language and we know what it is we wish to achieve.

So, is the unconscious mind running the entire show? Almost, and it's being run in accordance with a set of profoundly entrenched unconscious programmes that you did not consciously choose in the first place. How so, you may ask? If you have been paying attention, you will have noted that the conscious mind is nowhere to be seen until the age of seven, so you were left wide open to unverified negative messages, which were streamed into your unconscious by way of observation and instruction from your primary caretakers. In simple terms, there is no filtering system in place to question the information given to us. We are told what to do and how to do it... what we can and cannot do or achieve... and finally what we should and should not believe; and we take it all in as fact.

Above that, all events and experiences which we have encountered align with integrated emotional reactions and responses; the unconscious mind records and memorizes those responses, encoding them into cellular memory. Hence, whenever a comparable life event or experience transpires, the feelings we encountered earlier in our lives are expressed again through the cellular memories of our bodies.

All we need is the trigger – an event, a circumstance or a person – to set in motion a familiar set of feelings that have their origin in childhood experiences we seldom remember. And we continue to experience these feelings any time the original environment is replicated by a similar event, circumstance or person. Because the unconscious mind is our emotional centre, it then quickly supersedes our rational conscious mind whenever a conflict ensues.

Does that mean we are destined to be slaves to our unconscious programming? It's a great question and fortunately, no, we are not. The human mind is very plastic and can be shaped and influenced with careful attention coupled with consistency and discipline, and it's here where I will be focusing most of my attention.

To understand the unconscious mind is to understand who you are. Therefore, a thorough understanding of how it works, learns, operates, stores information and drives the machine called 'you' is damn important, and by the end of this book, I am hoping you will have a far better understanding of how it can work for or against you.

A TALE OF TWO MINDS

The function of the mind is to create coherence between our beliefs and the reality we experience.
– Dr Bruce Lipton

We only have one mind, but psychologists made a decision long ago to divide it into two parts, naming them the *unconscious mind* and the *conscious mind*; this separation was decided because they each play a different role, as well as functioning separately. To build an internal representation or mental picture of the two minds, imagine an iceberg rising 30 metres above the ocean; that represents the conscious mind. Now imagine a colossus of ice beneath the surface, at a depth of 3,000 metres; that represents the unconscious mind.

The unconscious mind is the powerhouse and operator of the machine we call 'us'; it performs thousands of actions, including regulating of our body's involuntary functions. It breathes for us, circulates blood throughout our bodies, and is in charge of digestion and elimination.

For this book, however, I want to focus on the prime directives which affect our everyday lives, and in particular on a few of them.

PRIME DIRECTIVES OF THE UNCONSCIOUS MIND

I have already mentioned this just recently but it needs repeating: 95% of daily life is controlled by the unconscious mind, while the conscious mind is activated around 5% of the time. Look at those figures again. Aside from a minimal amount of time, our lives are shaped by the habitual programmes fashioned by the unconscious mind. There is an interchange between the two but they often perform in isolation.

The interdependence of the conscious and unconscious minds is why some believe the two are the same thing. If we change our conscious thinking patterns, we can presumably change the unconscious programmes at the same time. That erroneous thinking, however, evokes numerous problems, as the way the conscious mind learns is different from that of its powerful sibling! Have you ever wondered why positive thinking (or positive affirmations) is often a haphazard affair for so many?

When the conscious mind wants something, yet the unconscious contradicts it, the conscious mind fails miserably. This is why positive thinking alone does not work unless the unconscious mind agrees with the thoughts that generate the spoken words. And the only way the spoken word makes any sense to the unconscious mind is when the feelings of those words and thoughts are in alignment. Feelings, not words, are the language of the unconscious mind.

I am not a supporter of affirmations as a standalone modality for change, because the unconscious mind fails to respond to requests that have no corresponding feelings. But affirmations used as an introductory tool for change, I fully support; they direct your focus in a specific way. When you know what types of belief you want to grow, what types of thought, standard and value you wish to entertain and embody, you start to live in alignment with the affirmed statements you have chosen to use and from which momentum is created.

Affirmations are stepping stones towards change and transformation. The brain left to its own devices will rarely support you when you are trying to change; it's designed to look out for danger and lean towards negativity. Affirmations are a creation of the conscious mind that allow us to take control over the language we use, which is either empowering or disempowering.

You cannot trust your brain to lead you to a transformative experience; it needs conditioning with specific directives. And what better way than to start with positive words, which can lead to change, as the words and the feelings that arise from your new focused behaviour begin to get ever closer, until they are assimilated into a new way of being... and voila, a new habit is born.

The conscious mind is representative of us, as individuals, including our creativity, wants, desires ambitions and aspirations, both personal and collective. It relays to the world what we want from life and who we are moment by moment. It thinks and processes information in an instant, and learns the same way from watching a documentary on TV, listening to a lecture or reading a book.

Most of the time the conscious mind is dwelling in the past or thinking about the future, and rarely is it activated in the present. We *can* control the conscious mind and with it the power to remain current, but this, like any new skill, needs learning. Hence the importance of meditation (discussed throughout this book) and its ability to teach us how to be present; with greater presence we have superior conscious control over our lives. (In the next chapter, I will introduce you to a simple hack that I use as a kind of presence reminder, which involves a bracelet or something tied around your wrist.)

The moment we lose consciousness, the more powerful sibling – the unconscious mind – takes over. Now, the primary decision maker and habit mind is in attendance, and unless we wrestle back control of our thinking, trouble potentially starts brewing.

HABITS AND CHANGING THEM

A routine mind that thrives on familiarity, the unconscious mind is a recording device of sorts that has chronicled the events in your life and plays them back whenever the same stimulus or familiar environment that initially created them arises. The unconscious mind recognises the familiar event, immediately correlates its origin and presses play on the recording device. You are now being controlled by your history, and unless you bring yourself back to conscious awareness in the present moment, the pattern will continue to play out in the same way it always has. That is precisely what a habit is... a repetitive behaviour stored in the unconscious which responds to a certain trigger the same way, over and over again. Using common sense, we can quickly assign a positive, negative or neutral tag to our habitual behaviour.

Smoking, drinking, drug taking, overeating, a need for drama or conflict, laziness, unwarranted fear, procrastination and anxiety are the end result of a decision-making process correlated to a past event (or events) that spawned specific beliefs and the meaning assigned to those beliefs. These are what most would consider 'unhealthy habits'.

Bravery, keeping fit, eating a balanced diet, compassion, pursuing worthy goals, working hard, showing kindness, confidence, and maintaining the integrity of a healthy body... these we tend to label 'healthy habits' and 'life-enhancing habits'. They were created in the same way, meaning they were assigned to past events that spawned specific beliefs and became cemented through repetition.

If we want to change habits that are considered unfavourable, we must unlearn them, not by means of any fancy process, but merely by focusing on something favourable and performing a new action until new meaning is assigned to that behaviour. This is effectively rewiring the brain to think in a different way. Dr Joe Dispenza, the author of a wonderful book called *You Are the Placebo*, used a catchy phrase to highlight the rewiring process: 'neurons that fire together, wire together'. We have more than 100 billion neurons connecting the brain to the body. To put that into perspective, 100 billion sheets of paper stacked on top of each other would be 5,000 miles high. That is how vast each human brain is.

When we pay attention and learn something new over an extended period, we create new neural connections, and new pathways are formed; this is how we develop habits. To break a habit, we must do the opposite: by avoiding familiar thoughts, feelings or actions, the electrical impulses become weaker, as do the neural connections, until the old wiring system that held those beliefs together unwires and comes apart. If 'neurons that fire together, wire together' is an easy way to remember the habit-forming process, then 'neurons that are out of sync, fail to link' is an easy way to remember how to break a habit.

Do you now understand that what you think about, you become? We are creating our reality one thought and one action at a time, either enforcing something that serves us or reinforcing that which doesn't, by centring our attention accordingly. What happens if you continue to focus on the things which don't enhance your well-being: broken relationships, alcohol, anger, frustration, the need to be right, that tub of ice cream while watching Netflix, the job you hate? The question is of course rhetorical, because you know that what we focus on, we get more of… in a nutshell, MORE OF THE SAME!

Let's get even more specific. 'I don't want that headache'… 'I don't want this relationship to end or this project to fail'… 'I hate Monday mornings'… 'I don't like living here' – by thinking about these things, you are strengthening the neural connections and fortify-ing unwanted emotional patterns. Simply put, you will continue to get that what you focus on. We must therefore focus on what we do want; that is the only way to break a bad habit while replacing it with a new one. So, what is it that you want?

Write a list of the habits which you have that serve you and another list of those that do not. You are going to look at the unwanted list only once and decide on what needs pruning from your life. If you have many unwanted habits, in order to avoid overwhelming and shocking the system, decide on one (or a maximum of two) that needs to go, and find an alternative pattern of new behaviour to replace it (or them).

Get strategic again with this and have your plan of action clearly defined. What will you do when social media urges you to grab your phone as soon as you wake up? Grab your journal instead and plan out what you need to do that day. When the urge to smoke entices you like a bee to honey? Engage in some type of deep breath work – pranayama or the Wim Hof breathing method, for example. When the desire to call or stalk your ex arises? Call a friend or a trusted family member and change direction. When you wish to give up caffeine? Replace your cup of joe with herbal tea or something you like.

If you don't enjoy the alternatives, the habits will be harder to break. Because bad habits provide some type of benefit in your life, it's very difficult to eliminate them, which is why simple advice like 'just stop doing it' rarely works. You must replace a bad habit with a new one that provides a similar benefit.

To encourage specific behaviours, the brain operates a reward system: when we enjoy something, the brain releases dopamine, a powerful feel-good hormone that we crave. Don't give up coffee and replace it with hot ginger and lemon unless you enjoy the taste. Find something you like the taste of – it will make it far easier to see it through as the old neural pathways are trimmed away, and new connections are formed in the unconscious part of the brain.

If anger or reactivity is your thing and you wish to change that aspect of yourself, start by choosing a positive phrase you could use whenever you feel that familiar emotion awakening within you; for example, 'I am a vehicle of love and tolerance' is one I have used in the past. Some days will be easier than others, sure, but with practice and repetition, your phrase of choice, said often enough with feeling, will soften those edges until no edges remain and you become that vehicle of love and tolerance, or whatever it is you have deemed important.

No matter what you wish to change, have a predetermined plan of action of what you will do instead of the destructive habit. It is important to remove all triggers from your proximity. If you frequently raid the cupboards for chocolate or your favourite cookies, then throw them in the bin and refuse to buy them again. The same goes for cigarettes. If you enjoy a cigarette with alcohol, then either don't have the wine or don't put yourself in a situation where you are reminded of this ritual. Stop going to bars and clubs for a while if giving up smoking is crucial to you. Join a gym instead, and go there in the evenings. The advantages are twofold: you will do your body the world of good and have a better chance of meeting those who align with who it is you are trying to become.

Accountability is a strong force when attempting to change anything about ourselves. I can't stress enough how critical this can be, so I encourage you to ask your trusted friends, family or those you respect to hold you accountable for the changes you wish to make in your life.

To really spice things up, add a forfeit of some kind every time you engage with a habit you wish to break. Let's say you can't stop thinking of your ex and mention him or her every chance you get to those you have assigned to be accountability sitters. To make this real, some type of pain must be attached to the forfeit. Money works well for most of us and the thought of it being removed from our purses or wallet on a regular basis could be the impetus needed to break the spell. As will be seen in the next chapter, pain is a great initiator of change: associate enough pain to anything, and the change can often be immediate.

You and your accountability circle all agree before you start that each time you talk about your ex or refer to the situation in any way, you will pay to a pre-agreed charity of choice a certain amount of money. Make it an amount that's going to sting. You want a powerful catalyst – something which makes you think seriously about what you are doing. You then honour your word by giving that money to those who have agreed to help you... Who knows, the charity of choice could become something very important to you and take the place of your ex in your heart. Remember, we can't eliminate a habit... we must instead replace it with something that brings with it similar benefits.

You can use this approach for anything you wish to stop doing... eating, drinking, smoking, swearing, moaning, shouting. Of course, it only works if your levels of congruency are impeccable, and if you have available to you new models of behaviour to replace the old. It won't work if you give yourself a pass, and your assigned friends, family or others are not strong enough to enforce the agreement, nor will it if you don't have an alternative enjoyable pastime to engage in.

To be clear, there is nothing new here. I am not reinventing the wheel, but merely bringing to your attention known methods with which real transformation is possible, and anyone can do it, regardless of genetics or social standing. Do not entertain for a moment the idea that you are hindered from any accomplishment by the lack of superior genetics or ability; that was a story told to you, supported and then upheld by repetitious ignorance. You are capable of profound changes the moment you challenge what you believe to be correct about yourself and replace it with another truth.

If you believe that transforming from overweight to fit and healthy, from weak to powerful, and from timid to confident is an impossibility, think again. It has been proved over and over again that human beings are capable of radical transformation, and you are a human being, are you not?

One facet of the unconscious mind which must not be overlooked is that it takes everything personally and is the cornerstone behind the statement that all perception is projection. To the unconscious mind, nothing exists outside of your own beliefs, meaning that everything you think, say or do corresponds personally to you. A simple example is the following.

Whenever you are being critical or judgmental of others, the unconscious mind believes you are talking about yourself. 'I hate her' or 'I hate him' are ubiquitous phrases we hear daily. How often do you use the expression 'I hate' without paying due care and attention? We use it to describe all sorts of things – food, drink, places, circumstances and people – yet the unconscious mind doesn't process anything outside of self, and therefore associates the word and the corresponding feelings with how you feel about yourself. Do I now have your attention? Good.

Therefore, choose wisely how you speak about the world and how you speak about others who share this planet with you. Vocabulary and how you use it is pivotal to your health. Words carry with them a particular frequency, as do all things that exist in an energetic universe. You don't believe me? Then allow me to introduce you to a man called Dr Masaru Emoto, who I happened upon, not by chance I would wager, while walking my path of further awareness.

Dr Masaru Emoto was a Japanese scientist who revolutionised the idea that our thoughts and intentions impact the physical realm; he was one of the most crucial water researchers the world has known. For over two decades until he passed away in 2014, he studied the scientific evidence of how the molecular structure of water transforms when it is exposed to human words, thoughts, sounds and intentions. Dr Emoto believed that water was a 'blueprint for our reality' and that emotional 'energies' and 'vibrations' could change the physical structure of water. His water crystal experiments consisted of exposing water in glasses to different intentions, words, pictures or music, and then freezing and examining the artistic properties of the resulting crystals using microscopic photography. Emoto claimed that water exposed to positive speech, or to phrases such as 'I love you', alongside empowering thoughts would result in visually 'gratifying' crystals being formed when that water was frozen, whereas contrary or detrimental intentions, such as 'I hate you', would yield 'ugly' frozen crystal formations.

Dr Masaru Emoto put water as a living consciousness on the map for the scientific world. He showed us how water is energy that is capable of more than we ever imagined. The ability that human thoughts, sounds and intentions have to empower and disempower is one of the most significant discoveries of our time.

His work begs the question, if water is affected by words, intentions and energies, what about human beings, who are composed of mostly water? The surface of our planet is 70% water... as we are, not by chance but by design, I would contend.

These are spectacular claims, I agree, and claims that I cannot confirm as being conclusive. However, we live in a mystical universe which never fails to astonish, and is forever furnishing more and more spectacular discoveries that have us rewriting the science journals.

One of the most exceptional human beings to have walked this planet was Nikola Tesla, a Croatian by birth who specialised in electromagnetism and electromechanical engineering. Tesla contributed in varying degrees to the establishment of robotics, remote control, radar and computer science, and to the expansion of ballistics, nuclear physics and theoretical physics. He was the true pioneer of the radio. He made some spectacular statements, but none more so than this: 'If you want to find the secrets of the universe, think in terms of energy, frequency and vibration.'

Tesla was a man ahead of his time, as was Dr Emoto, and both were ridiculed and labelled by modern science as 'pseudo-scientists'. They each knew and understood something which countless millions are now beginning to realise: we are energetic beings, living in an energetic universe, and our energetic signature is forever oscillating and affecting all things, as a result of what we think, say and do.

I became very conscious of how I expressed myself once I learned this and continue to watch my thoughts and how I articulate them from moment to moment. By choosing to see the world as a place of infinite potentiality, choosing to see the good in things, and verbalizing them accordingly, I am training my unconscious mind to see the same in me. I would encourage you to do the same. This is not a Pollyanna philosophy. I am aware that terrible things happen, and often. I merely choose to retain my focus, thoughts and actions on that which will serve me best.

Do I sometimes forget this and fall back into tempestuous waters? Of course I do, and so will you, more than you will care to admit, but that's ok as well. Remember, a skilled sailor did not hone his skills on a peaceful ocean.

Another prime directive of the unconscious mind is that it doesn't process negatives directly. 'Don't' and 'not' are ignored by the unconscious mind, so understanding how this works is essential.

Don't think of a green elephant with a blue monkey on its back. No really, don't think of that green elephant with a blue monkey laughing and screeching on the elephant's back. Did you think of a green elephant with a blue monkey as I described, when I told you specifically not to? Of course you did... we all do.

To be able to do a 'don't' or a 'not', your mind has to first imagine the 'scenario' and it then adds in the 'do not'. It is how the unconscious is wired. Don't play on the road, you tell your kids. Don't climb that tree. Don't hit your sister. Getting the picture? The mental images are first processed by the unconscious mind, while the negations are relegated to nothing more than footnotes. 'Don't mess up your speech today!' is translated as 'Mess up your speech!', triggering all of your autopilot scripts for visualising messing up your speech. And you can apply this same logic to any situation with 'don't' and the outcome will be the same.

Do you want your children to pay attention and do as you ask? Then be affirmative with clear directives: play in the garden... be kind to your little sister... go over there and play in the sandpit.

Do you see the difference, and how easy it is to get this wrong? Can you now see how talking and thinking about what you don't want in your own life is re-enforcing the instructions to your unconscious mind to detect more of what you don't want? Can you imagine how this habitual behaviour keeps you in an experiential loop of unwanted outcomes?

IN A NUTSHELL

If you keep thinking and talking about what you don't want and what you don't like, then that's what you will see more of in your lives. Instead, focus on and use the appropriate vocabulary to support your intentions.

THE THEORY OF PAIN AND PLEASURE

———◆•◆———

*The aim of the wise is not to secure **pleasure**,*
*but to avoid **pain**.*

The jury is out on whether focusing solely on positive psychology is the way forward when attempting to change aspects of our selves that afford us little favour. As we journey together, you will become familiar with the expression 'What you focus on, you will get more of!', and for sound reason – it's true!

Where energy flows, your reality grows, of that you can be assured, but many of my clients, friends and associates have told me that: 'to understand why we do the things we do is very important when attempting to change!' I tend to agree. There are hundreds of books out there which list ways to help you overcome life's hardships, but not so many which explain the why behind what we do.

The theory of pain and pleasure sits at the heart of everything you do and of everything you are, and yes, this too is shaped and maintained by the habits of the unconscious mind. All beliefs, values and mental habits, the decisions made, the actions taken and the patterns that define us are all based on the pain and pleasure principle. In fact, every part of a person's character is influenced and formed as a result of arising pain or pleasure in our lives.

We quickly assess what is favourable or not and busily move towards that which initiates pleasure and feverishly away from that which stimulates pain. Is it that simple? Are we, the most complex beings ever to roam this planet, controlled by the fundamental forces of pain and pleasure? The answer is a resounding yes, but the complexity of the pain and pleasure conundrum is anything but simple, so listen up.

Since birth, everything we are exposed too sits in the columns of either pain or pleasure... Now, what constitutes either will be reliant on many factors, but, effectively, that which is familiar or repetitive sits in the pleasure column, and that which is not familiar or non-repetitive sits in the painful column. All self-explanatory, but a closer look will reveal how this shapes our lives.

Let's say we grew up in a household where our parents fought continually, either emotionally or physically, or both. We repeatedly observed the making-up process, then once again witnessed how they clashed in a never-ending merry-go-round of explosive, incompatible but familiar emotions. Or, we may have grown up in an environment where one or both parents were emotionally not present, little or no affection was demonstrated, unconditional love was absent and physical touch was hard to come by.

Exposure to either of these very different, but equally damaging, environments could well be affecting your relationships today and the choices you continue to make... If you can relate to either of these scenarios, and I am sure thousands can, strong evidence suggests the unconscious programmes created in childhood are causing you to gravitate towards that which is familiar to you now as an adult; or, simpler put, causing you to seek out experiences, events, circumstances and people which remind you of your familiar childhood environment.

Let's now jump forward to the present moment and see how this may be affecting you today. We all want a loving, caring, kind and understanding partner, right? But if those emotions were absent in childhood, then any man or woman who enters our lives and expresses these unfamiliar traits with regularity is going to represent unfamiliarity and therefore confusion, on the basis of a limited or non-existent point of reference. Consequently, soon enough, after the novelty value evaporates, we often self-sabotage, reject them and gravitate back to what we found familiar as children and teenagers, and now as adults – namely, men or women who will treat us in ways that remind us of our infancy and cause us to re-enact the experiences that defined is as children.

Think of it as magnetic energy which seeks out its compatible frequency in the form of those who are often carrying their own unhealed childhood trauma. I know it's early to be discussing magnetic energy, but I am hoping, dear readers, that you are acquainted with the law of attraction and how it works? I promise I will return to this concept often as we proceed, but for now, understand that we are primarily energetic beings, transmitting and receiving energy at a certain frequency. In the very same way in which real magnets draw to them that which is agreeable and push away that which is not, we attract and repel other people.

For example, it's not by accident that many people attract detached men or women if their childhood lacked secure attachment. Neither is it by accident that exposure to, or the observing of, routine violence as a child resulted in relationships with men or women who mimicked that shared experience. In fact, unconsciously they sought them out. By dating those who can't commit, are afraid of attachment or use violence to express themselves guaranteed the familiarity needed to feel uncomfortably safe, including the sadness, emptiness and feelings of unworthiness, which defined their childhood.

Instead of understanding dysfunctional compatibility in order to learn and leave the experiences behind, they believe them to be normal because they know nothing else and have no comparison analysis to call upon. Do they look at the situation with objectivity and ask themselves: 'Why do I feel so angry, scared, fearful, jealous or mistrusting… abandoned, lonely or rejected?'. No, they don't. Instead, they believe that life this way is normal, and that the unfolding painful emotions are a natural part of their lives.

If only they could step back and realise the correlation between their childhood and the relationships they attract, they would be able to answer essential questions such as: 'What emotions and unprocessed memories are being triggered continuously by this relationship, and who or what does this remind me of?'... That look, that smirk, that contemptuous hand gesture. The silent treatment, the shouting, the aggression and the lack of self-control. The smell of cigarettes or the whiff of alcohol. Familiar traits they know so well, yet they don't put the pieces of the puzzle together and realise what they are doing – attempting to replicate their childhood encounters to feel the safety of the pleasurable familiar.

It has taken me years of deep introspection, decades of studying and research and the application of powerful healing modalities to arrive where I now find myself, and I continue to discover new things. And nowhere are those discoveries more revealing or rewarding than in the arena of personal relationships and how they reveal so much about who I was, who I am and who I am becoming.

In my own life I have had many relationships[2], but the two most painful were with emotionally unavailable older women, both absently detached, thoughtlessly consumed with their individual needs and emotionally inaccessible. It was these two relationships that forced me to look deeply into my childhood to find the common denominator, and the trigger, which was my father's inability to be emotionally accessible.

My father was my hero, and I craved his love with a burning intensity, yet it was never verbalised or confirmed with physical or emotional expression. The words 'I love you' were never stated, nor hugs and cuddles given, from the moment I started school, irrespective of the fact that he loved me immensely. He would take me everywhere

---

[2] It's by no coincidence that the two relationships which mimicked my childhood experiences hugely triggered my insecurities. Yet, it was these relationships which created what I believed to be at the time a burning desire and passion way above any other relationship I had experienced. With the power of hindsight and the understanding of how the unconscious mind works, I see now that it wasn't passion and desire for these women per se, but my inner child's burning desire to feel loved, supported, recognised and in control, none of which were available to me in these relationships.

and taught me so many things about life, and for that I am eternally grateful. But for a young boy, looking for affectionate validation, the lack of physical embrace and emotional closeness created a limiting and fallacious belief that I wasn't good enough as I was, and to be worthy of his attention I believed I must excel and outperform in sport and demonstrate physical excellence.

As an adolescent and throughout my adult life, I found myself fortifying this model, which was to look like Adonis, to be the best and nothing else, and to control every aspect of my life in order to feel safe, including the women who I dated. When I couldn't, life became unfamiliar, painful and very uncomfortable. Looking back, I am thankful for the lessons and the pain that arrived with these women, for without them, I would have never healed. And without them, I would have never met and married my amazing wife, Paula, who has helped me heal many inner child wounds. In fact, it wasn't until I healed the parts of me that I once needed did I actually heal those wounds.

In the same way, I am immensely grateful to my father for being the man he was and remains, for without him, I wouldn't be here today writing this book, and neither would I be a coach and analyst who helps thousands of people become their greatest version. I hold not an ounce of resentment to my dear old dad; he is awesome and still my hero, and I love him dearly.

Like every father, he did his best, and again, like most fathers, he replicated patterns he was exposed to by his parents and by theirs before them. I decided the evolutionary conveyor belt ends with me by being as emotionally available, peaceful, accepting, honest and vulnerable as I possibly can, and most of all by dispelling the idea of attaining perfection. This has not been easy, for each of those traits was sadly missing for the majority of my life, and I have had to, and continue to, reinvent myself through vast amounts of work, constant awareness and self-discipline.

For the record, I still get triggered, and I catch myself falling into the old patterns, but I don't allow the momentum to build. I slay the ogre when it's small, by cutting off its lifeblood at the knees – my thoughts and flow of energy! Any residue left in my system I dispense with using a number of different techniques... I breathe slowly and deeply, I do some exercise or I use a 10-second or 10-minute gap before initiating a response which I will explain further on. I also give myself permission to be angry when it's justified, but how I handle that anger is very different from how my former self handled it. Now, I am assertive and clear, but don't use intimidation or forceful expression.

I know it's difficult, but can you be honest enough to look without coloured spectacles at your own childhood to spot the familiar traits which you continue to gravitate towards and are often expressed in the form of a partner who mimics the role of your primary caregivers, however subtle? We live in a world where questioning our parents and how they raised us is a sin. Honour your mother and father at all times, the holy books of all major religions tell us.

But question you must: 'Is rewriting the faulty software governing your decision making essential to you?' I am not telling you to point the finger, disown them and say: 'You did this to me.' Absolutely not. I am telling you to be responsible and take the appropriate actions...

By taking control of your life and understanding your past, you have demonstrated an ability to respond. You have chosen to be accountable for the rest of your life by getting strategic and doing what is necessary so as not to repeat ad infinitum the patterns and rituals that cause you to suffer.

Once we come to terms with and distinguish how the psychology works, we can stop chasing the painful familiar, and lean towards that which is fulfilling and nurturing. It's hard but rewarding work, and I am hoping that you have an undeniable appetite for transformation and you will halt in its tracks the need to seek out anything other than nourishing relationships.

While reading this book, I encourage you to become not only an investigative detective but also an observational psychologist and pay very close attention to everything that's unfolding both within and around you. Remember, that which you seek is also seeking you, meaning that you will always know where you are by the company you keep, by those you are attracted to and by the events, people and circumstances that repeatedly show up in your life.

The more aware you are, the easier it will be to make the changes you seek. And the more truthful you are with yourself, the quicker you will transition away from dysfunctional behaviour that has not assisted you and continues not to do so.

IN A NUTSHELL

We attract what we think we deserve. And what we think we deserve is generally rooted in what we experienced or witnessed in our early child-hood development. With greater awareness, we can break the habit of being ourselves and start to broadcast at a higher frequency, therefore attracting more favourable people and circumstances. It's time to grow, which can be painful. 'Growing pains' got its name for good reason: growth can be damn painful as we leave behind the familiar habits that have defined us thus far and we enter into the realm of the unknown.

HOW CERTAIN ARE YOU

Doubt is not a pleasant condition,
but certainty is absurd.
– Voltaire

We live in an age where certainty can change quickly... so quickly in fact that breakfast time truths often become dinner time bullshit. Hence, if you are a believer in non-contestable truth, without room for manoeuvre, this book is going to challenge you. It takes bravery to question beliefs and ideology that define us, but challenge them we must. Dogma, in any form, restricts our ability to reach the heights we are capable of scaling.

I invite you, therefore, not to accept or look for evidence to support your own beliefs, but to have an aware, attentive and open mind to discover an ever-changing truth. Everything we hear is an opinion, not a truth. Everything we see is a viewpoint, not the truth. Who can claim, beyond doubt, a non-contestable truth? I am not talking facts, such as the existence of the sun which breathes life into this planet. The sun is a non-debatable fact; but how it got there and who or what created it remain to date unprovable by an empirical truth.

Look below and contemplate the previously believed statements that were posing as verifiable facts:

- 98% of our knowledge about the human brain has been learnt in the last 10 years!
- 80% of everything that scientists knew about the brain by 1990 has today been proved to be false!

What incredible statements. FYI, I could have filled this whole book with examples that demonstrate my point that 'what we don't know we don't know until we know it' – and that is bound to change! With modern technology it is possible for researchers today to continue way beyond what we ever thought possible before. As a result, our knowledge will continue to expand, and with it our perceptions and ever-changing truths.

My Truths

So, what are *my* truths? I have only two right now. The first is 'the present moment is all we will ever have'. Debate it, dissect it, discuss it. It matters not how smart you think you are. This moment – this now – is the only period that has existed, can exist or will ever exist.

Recall a memory from your past and relive it in your mind. The event you are remembering is unfolding right now at the present moment, and that same memory when it happened in the past also unfolded at the moment regarded as the present moment. Now go into the future, let's say tomorrow at 3pm. Can you experience that now? Of course not, but when 3pm arrives tomorrow, what period of time will the event unfold in? That's right, this one!

Life is unfolding as a continuous expression of the present moment, meaning that every minute we spend agonising about the future or bemoaning the past is a minute lost, because all we have is this moment, so please make it your primary focus. Regrettably, we miss so much because rarely are we available when life knocks on the door; we are either living in houses yet to be built in the future, or dwelling in homes vacated many years in the past.

Clinging to memories of the past or to projections into the future is mankind's nemesis alone, and no other sentient creatures, we believe, share this trait. We appear to have forgotten what nature as always known – to be totally present and alive in the only moment we hold dominion over... this one!

Life changes when mindful of the present moment. When life knocks on the door, we are there to greet it. Life does not deal with the past or the future, it deals with the moment. If you want to experience it, then you must understand this non-debatable fact, and be at home when it comes a knocking.

A simple hack I use as a reminder is the following. Take a piece of coloured cotton, or a bracelet of choice, and put it around your wrist. State a clear and concise intention as you put it on: 'Every time I notice this bracelet or piece of cotton, I will bring myself back to the present moment by breathing slowly and deeply a few times.' Breathing can only be achieved in the present moment, which makes it the best anchor I know to bring you back to the now. Bottom line: the more present you are, the greater life becomes.

With the wrist being so visible, it is almost impossible not to see it at any given moment; it can therefore serve as a constant reminder of what is needed to stay mindful and present. Simple, yet profoundly powerful.

Please modify and use the wrist reminder to align with anything you want to change. This could be an anger problem you wish to resolve, or a procrastination issue which needs attention or a commitment to yourself. In every modern city there are facilities for printing wristbands; create a statement or statements of intent for yourself, go and get a few made, and put one on.

'I will take action!' – 'I will respond, not react!' – 'I will accept that which is beyond my control!' – 'Love means freedom!' – 'Infidelity is a deal breaker' – 'I will tell the truth at all costs' – 'I will lose 5kg' – 'I will stop smoking' – 'I will not drink again' You can't imagine how powerful these small life hacks can be, so don't underestimate their ability to help facilitate huge changes in your life and to take your progress to the next level.

FYI: a new habit takes between 21 and 250 days to form, depending on the individual. If you continue to do the wrist ritual and apply the same process to any new ritual or skill you want to learn, you will literally, not figuratively, rewire your brain. You become the creator of your desired world and not a prisoner of your perceived circumstances.

My second truth is 'love is a frequency, not a feeling'. A state of being that permeates every aspect of existence... a pervasive energy, woven into the tapestry of the universe. Call it God, the universal mind, the collective consciousness – it matters not. Focusing on my finger while I point at the moon ensures that you miss the point.

Aligning with the frequency of love can help set us free, but not until we understand what it means. So, what is love? Unless we appreciate its essence, we are going to struggle, irrespective of the community or relationship we find ourselves.

If we grasp the concept of unconditional love, we will better understand who we are and what it is we are doing here. And for the record, it has nothing to do with where you were born, your gender, your religious persuasion or your sexual preference, or with the person with whom you are in a relationship.

I will revisit both of my truths regularly throughout the book when applicable.

Ignorance

People often accept the statement that ignorance is bliss, rather than examining and questioning that which affords humanity little favour. But if indeed ignorance is bliss, why aren't there more happy people in the world? I have no issue with those who embrace ignorance. The problems arise when the ignorant attempt to project what they think they know as absolute truths, without doing the research necessary to have an informed opinion or without entertaining the notion that the world they live in is forever changing, including the information at hand.

Much of the world's ignorance stems from opinions that leave little room for exploration. Illogical superstitions and mistaken beliefs are hardwired into the psychology of billions of human beings, and none are more powerful than the various religious and political systems which use robust, seductive dogma and demand that we not only tolerate but embrace it without question. The word 'ignorance' is not insulting. It's simply the state of being uninformed or lacking enough knowledge to speak from a platform of knowing. The reason we take offence is that we believe ourselves to have the appropriate information, centred around beliefs or ideology we believe to be true.

Yet, ignorance inhibits learning. A person who believes themselves knowledgeable tends not to pursue clarification of their beliefs. They automatically discard valid but contrary information, neither realising its importance nor validity. Stephen Hawking said: 'The greatest enemy of knowledge is not ignorance, it is an illusion of knowledge.' This is another way of explaining the potential pitfalls and consequences of supporting an ignorant position.

So why would I write about ignorance? What is the point? If the ignorant are not mindful of their position, why bother? The reason is, widely accepted false beliefs can hinder progress and discoveries. These false beliefs can prove fatal to a species born to evolve. The most significant obstacle to development and evolution is ignorance based on unbending beliefs without room for a contrarian perspective.

We are all ignorant to different degrees, and understanding this will go some way to addressing the problem. Interestingly, wisdom begins to expand in proportion to one's awareness of one's ignorance; therefore, knowledge of the issue is a step in the right direction. Awareness of one's ignorant position leads to improved self-enquiry and greater responsibility, which in turn leads to the necessary actions to alleviate the potential problems that can arise from ignorance. To reduce ignorance, one must continue to ask the right questions. There can be no guarantee we will find the truth, but it is imperative we continue to seek it.

Curiously, the smarter I think I become, the less I know. When we realise in the grand scheme of things that we know next to nothing, a key thing happens. There is no position to defend, and when there is no position to protect, an opportunity for new learning is created. This mentality has made me a better listener, and someone who asks meaningful questions. A quote I read long ago has stuck with me: 'Do not judge a man by his answers, but by the inquiries and issues he raises.' If you want to become a more skilful human being, then ask more questions. Engage your audience, whoever they may be, by taking a keen interest in what they have to say.

We have one mouth and two ears for a reason. How much more would we learn if we listened more and talked less? If we listened to understand, rather than speaking to convince? We have all met those who love the sound of their voice... the person who interrupts you, mid-flow, or the one not genuinely listening, just awaiting a tiny gap to deliver their opinion. Don't be that person. Develop your listening skills. It is a lost art and one very much appreciated.

No matter how wise we think we are, there is room for improvement. Addressing ignorance is a never-ending quest. Allow the information to flow from all angles, and ignorance starts to wane.

Those who state they have found 'The way' with no further need for discovery, remove themselves from the clear truth that nothing remains constant in a universe in continuous flux, which includes us!

If you have never changed your mind about a central tenet of belief or have never questioned the fundamentals, without the desire to do so, then you are ignorant. Ignorance is not blissful, contrary to what we have been told by those who were, well, merely ignorant.

There is no definitive speed at which we must learn, but we must evolve; sometimes this will occur in leaps and bounds, and other times, at a snail's pace. Do not be discouraged – this is part of the process. Growth and the dissipation of ignorance will unfold in small steps, one insight and one obstacle at a time. Remember, obstacles are put in our way to see if what we want is truly worth pursuing.

The ignorant want to be right, it's a default mechanism. But it is perfectly ok not to know. It's perfectly acceptable to answer 'I don't know', rather than using guesswork to rubber stamp a fragile ego that satiates itself with external validation. It's ok to say: 'I am not sure, but I am happy to share my opinion.' This simple statement will help in developing that easy-going approach to which people gravitate. The ultimate takeaway from this is a reminder that we are not as prodigious as we think, and we are often inaccurate in many things about which we have an opinion.

Nobody likes a smart ass, but on the other side of the coin, we do not enjoy a dumb ass either. We owe it not just to our species but to all species to develop skill sets that optimise our experiences, which means negating both aspects of that coin. Martin Luther King said: 'Nothing in all the world is more dangerous than sincere ignorance and conscientious stupidity.'

Both these traits keep humanity chained to the ground, unable to move forward. Is it any wonder we live in a world where war, cruelty, barbarism, homophobia, desperation, depression and brutality are widespread, yet love, understanding, peace and compassion are rarely expressed? We must address gross ignorance because until we do, we can expect more of the same.

The Human Journey

Before I continue, here is my statement of full disclosure. I am not fully healed, neither wise. I am very much a work in progress, and I am ok with that. When first undertaking the journey of self-discovery and self-improvement, I realised that the wiser I became, the less I knew. Yes, that sounds like a paradox, but it's not. There is so much to know, about any topic, that the best we can achieve is knowing a little about a little on the basis of what we know at that time in history.

This journey we are on, the human mission, is so full of twists and turns, so many unknowns, trials and tribulations, that to claim to have it all figured out is to be deluded. The undeniable truth is that it's both unnecessary and impossible to figure it all out, and to believe otherwise will lead you a merry dance.

Living a life of meaning, purpose and never-ending improvement, however, is a different proposition and one I strongly advocate. But know this: the more we grow, the more powerful we become as agents of change, both for ourselves and for others, and along with greater power comes greater responsibility. Once awakened from the comatose state in which most live their lives in today's society, we – as agents of positive change – become responsible for driving and moving the world towards order and away from chaos.

You are not little me, a lone voice in an infinite universe. Neither did you come here to dwell in the banality of trivial and non-rewarding pastimes. The human experience is a damn difficult one, and the suffering we all experience makes this journey anything but trivial. When we start paying attention to the painful experiences and begin to reframe and grow through them, we are paying the rightful attention to this experience called the 'human journey' and the part we are playing in driving the collective consciousness forwards.

Whether or not you understand your place in the cosmos, or you believe this life is a one-shot deal, matters not. In each of us resides an integral relationship with consciousness and the wisdom that arises from self-introspection, meaning that we are designed to question and be contemplative of our behaviour, naturally leaning with an unquenchable passion towards that which aligns with our conscience; to ignore this calling, to ignore our conscience, guarantees a life of emotional disturbance and subpar living.

We are not here just to have fun, but to grow through the fires of adversity. Seeking unending pleasures will build contempt, of that I assure you... contempt for yourself, for others and for life itself when you quickly realise that unending fun is not an option. And neither is it possible, because of the law of diminishing marginal returns, which states that as consumption increases, the marginal enjoyment derived from each additional experience declines.

Imagine eating the most expensive cheeseburger in the world. The first one may well be heavenly, the second the same, but sooner rather than later, the enjoyment from it will decline and no longer provide the satisfaction it achieved first time around. We can apply the law of diminishing returns to every enjoyable experience available to us, and the same sub-standard result will eventually ensue.

Why do you think that so many of the ultra-rich are disgruntled with life? They have all the money in the world, with access to every conceivable luxury; yet listen to their interviews or read about their lives in the daily newspapers across the world. Depression, suicides, falling foul of the law are commonplace. Despite possessing all that man has to offer, they often take pills to sleep, and drink to escape the pain of their waking life. Why is that? One would imagine, and we are led to believe, that money means happiness, but think again. Happiness cannot be purchased. Life cannot be purchased. We have been sold a lie!

There is nothing wrong with money, to be clear. Like all things in an energetic universe, money is just that – an energy system, an experienced facilitator we can use to create or exchange value. Money is not the root of all evil, as some would have you believe. It's what we will do for it, or when we place it above our loving relationships and our need to contribute, that it becomes the recipe for disaster.

Life is far more than that. Far more profound and complex. Bottom line, we are designed to serve, to contribute, to make a difference to the lives of others and never are we happier, I mean sustainably happier, and more fulfilled than when we are working towards a greater good. There is a rejuvenation of our spirit when we stop taking things for granted and start to appreciate what we do have instead of what we don't have in life, and the best way I know to feed the human spirit is to contribute – to find ways to help or do things for people who are worse off than we are.

Because, what is life all about? Surely it's about courage, it's about strength, it's about perspective, it's about love, it's about action, it's about emotion and it's about caring, not just for ourselves and immediate family but for all sentients, including animals and plant life?

Making a Difference

So many of us miss the opportunity to feel that our lives have made a difference. Don't be that person. Making a difference is not difficult – you are limited only by your imagination. The secret to living is giving, and when you embrace this, not as an idea, not as a concept but as a lifestyle, there's a spark inside you that reminds not just you but others why they are here. Be that spark! Light up your surroundings! Make a difference.

With that in mind, I challenge you to do what is right. To do what you can to make this place a little better for as many as possible before departing this earthly realm. Find out how good you can be. Challenge yourself to become your greatest version while helping others become theirs; by doing so, you will experience a level of joy and contentment way beyond that of living only for yourself.

An excellent way to make a difference is to volunteer. There are so many ways to help others worse off than you by volunteering. It has become a very popular pastime as we awaken to the fact that helping others is the most powerful way to feel good about oneself. And I don't mean that in a cottony 'feel-good' way – there is hard science behind the claim that giving improves your overall health. It can also shake things up if life has become mundane and predictable. We are amiable creatures and need variety as much as we need certainty. Volunteering can satisfy those needs: you will meet new people, face unique challenges and be given purpose, an essential ingredient for sustainable happiness.

If you're still unsure about volunteering or haven't the time or energy required, consider the five-year, multi-institutional study[3] which states that being unselfish can protect your health and prolong your life. Every day that goes by without helping another is an opportunity missed. Start today by acknowledging that others have helped you, and you now have the chance to contribute and give something back to a world that has given you so much.

THINGS DO NOT FEEL THE SAME?

Consciousness rising.

Has something stirred in you which has you questioning your reality? Are things no longer feeling the same? Have you experienced an awakening of some kind, a greater cognizance of who you are? If so, I can confidently state that consciousness or the awareness of your spirit is becoming known.

Much has been written about consciousness and the role it plays in our lives. Throughout this book, the word 'consciousness' will be repeated often, for a good reason. Consciousness is the driver behind all we are. That which gives animation to the avatar we acknowledge as the human body. The source from which all things arise and must return. A sentient, expanding intelligence that chose to manifest in each of us. Is it imperative to know this? Does it make a difference

---

[3] https://www.ncbi.nlm.nih.gov/pubmed/23327269

when trying to modify or change the psychological programmes responsible for our everyday experiences?

I believe it does. We can better put things into perspective when we know that the human journey, which is damn important and one I lay out in great detail, is just one of an infinite number of explorations we will experience as agents of eternal consciousness. To understand this, beyond an intellectual concept, is to set oneself free from the many fears that govern our behaviour, and primarily free from the most basic fear of all, the fear of physical death.

If you have recently awoken to this realisation, then life may be throwing you a curve ball or two. This can be unnerving. On the one hand, the awareness of your eternal identity brings a sense of calm, but on the other, simultaneous questions arise that can't be answered with empirical facts, and hence the confusion.

As human beings, we are creatures of habit and seek out certainty, a prime psychological need, for it keeps us safe; hence any risk to our safety is met with unease. In fact, when the predictability of an out-come is unavailable, an alert goes to the brain to pay more attention and a threat response occurs, at which point we immediately look for ways to shore up the fragility. We will then look for what's familiar, seek out the rituals and experiences which we believe help us, and take back control, not all of which is healthy. This habitual behaviour is hardwired into every human being and a primitive survival mecha-nism. Hence, awakening to a new paradigm and potentially confusing narratives often initiates strong emotions and is not always favourable.

The term 'growing pains' is not metaphoric. Growth can be damn painful, for it often leads us far from our comfort zones as we tem-porarily fall apart when questioning everything we think we know about the world and ourselves. This consciousness rising is a sure-fire way of knowing that parts of you need to perish in order for new parts to be born... that certain aspects of yourself no longer serve you and it's time to level up.

This is a transitional road that you must walk. The road less trav-elled, if you like, but walk it you must. The toothpaste is out of the tube, and no amount of wishful thinking will put it back. Once consciousness has arisen, wakefulness becomes an inherent reality and there is no going back to sleep, so the best advice I can give is to embrace what is ascending within you, march bravely forwards and step into the person you were designed to be. Any resistance to your higher calling will be met by agitation and a nagging sense of being incomplete. It'll be like an itch you just can't reach.

Some of you will relish the changes and the processes which accompany change. For others reading this now, you will want to close the book and return to how life was. However, ignorance and denying who you are becoming are not the solution to unconsciousness: *greater consciousness* is the solution to unconsciousness. Consciousness rising is rarely easy, and for most of us, it's bloody hard work. Let's face it, if moving towards an enlightened state was easy, the world would be a very different place.

Deconstructing one's reality and bravely facing the egoic constructs of the conditioned mind with a view to slaying the monsters in the closet is no mean feat. To wilfully jump into the river and swim upstream against a raging torrent challenges our very nature, which is to play it safe. How many are truly brave enough to let those demons out and wilfully do battle with them until the closet is bright and airy? Managing this hot potato is not easy... well it certainly hasn't been for me, and remains so, as my ego attempts to wrestle back control of the physical avatar that I have been afforded to experience human life.

Eternal or not, we are wrapped in a biological spacesuit with certain psychological needs which must be met. Every day, we run the gamut of human emotions and it's no easy gig. Religion, politics, world news, work life, home life, bills, sex life, kids, more bills, love, hate, envy, jealousy, problems, pains, illness, etc. A relentless barrage of things to do, deadlines to meet and goals to reach.

It is so very easy to be caught up with all things human and to forgo our spiritual practices, such as prayer and meditation, which are essential components of not only a healthy balanced life but also an awareness that we are something more than physical beings. Prayer and meditation are bridges one can cross in order to understand that there is more to life than we understand. They help feed the spirit and express an appreciation of something far greater than we can ever comprehend. Across that bridge consciousness awaits, in the space beyond the content we recognise as the human experience.

Consciousness wants to know you... it wants you to remove the limiting shackles that have defined you and connect with a creative force which wishes to express itself. It's there inside you, it's inside everyone. Consciousness not only wants you to know your transcendent identity, but also wants your human journey to be fulfilling. It wants you to live with passion, and to find your purpose – something that lights you up. You cannot fake or hide from that which genuinely interests you, that which is forever tugging at your trouser leg. Acknowledge it, listen to it... follow the sparks which make you come alive, and go out there and express it. How consciousness decides to make itself aware to you, I cannot say. What I will say is this: when it happens, you will know.

Below are some examples of experiences I have encountered.

- I no longer related as I did before to those with whom I shared my life, namely my family, friends or partners.
- Activities which once held my interest, such as drinking, night-clubbing, womanising, small talk and gossiping, lost their appeal.
- These feelings caused me a level of concern and confusion.
- I developed a desire to share my spiritual wakefulness with others, believing I could influence them if they would only listen to what I had to say. I quickly learnt I could not, and that people change only when they decide.
- I recognized the necessity to confront a range of emotional issues and past traumas which had made themselves known to me.
- Telling the truth or a need to embrace authenticity became my default, whereas before, it was far more comfortable and convenient to withhold, misdirect or straight-up lie.

- My perception was heightened. I would be fascinated by the ants, the bugs – in fact anything. The colours, the textures, the feelings, the sounds were heightened as my senses gained greater clarity.
- The simple pleasures became a joy – going for a walk barefoot across a field, cycling through the countryside, sitting alone reading a book under a tree for hours.
- I became aware of a profound sense of presence and that all things at source were connected in an infinite universe.
- The need for silence and to be away from the maddening crowds became non-negotiable.
- I acknowledged the need to contribute and serve, and that the secret to living was giving.
- Confusion and irritation became apparent if I wasn't making a difference to the lives of others.

The examples above are illustrations of what I experienced as my previous reality began to crumble – a reality in which I was the antithesis of the man I am today.

YOUR JOURNEY

Trying to explain the shift of awareness is futile at the consciousness level. Identifying and describing consciousness is akin to asking a priest to express how god looks, meaning that it cannot be quantified. Currently, we cannot take a jar of godliness and prove the existence of god, and neither can we tangibly measure consciousness. In fact, attempting to locate consciousness is similar to taking apart an mp3 player, in search of the singer.

To believe in god or consciousness or both is an act of faith – more a feeling than a knowing, but that is ok. We don't need to know everything. Trust your intuition. Can you feel within you something beyond time, something outside the limited human experience?

The religious call it the 'soul', while the spiritualists prefer the term 'infinite consciousness'. It matters not the name you give it; what matters is that you may feel, beyond words, the driving force of all things, the energy source which gives animation to the billions of different creatures chosen by consciousness to experience itself subjectively.

We are going through significant emotional and spiritual changes across the planet as the vibrational frequency accelerates, bringing confusion, uncertainty and restlessness to some and clarity and purpose to others. This will very much depend on whether you see the world as a fearful place when certainty is removed from the equation, or whether you embrace change with positive enthusiasm. Whichever camp you sit in, or if you oscillate between the two, the more aware you are of consciousness, the better you will understand what is going on within and around you.

The direction of this book is going to ebb and flow, like a river that at times meanders and doubles back on itself. The majority of the text consists of how to manage the unpredictable assignment we call life and the emotions it invokes. However, I will at times go off-road and explore spiritual ideas that I believe to be very important. If that particular rabbit hole is either too deep or of no interest, feel free to jump ahead. The book has been written in such a way that you can pick any chapter and hopefully find what it is you are looking for.

IT'S TIME FOR TRAFFIC CONTROL

Time for a break.

Espousing this advice on the basis of a former chapter may seem contradictory, but not so. Time is indeed the most priceless commodity, but it's how we spend that time which defines the quality of our lives. Rushing around like a headless chicken may appear to the watching world what a busy guy or gal you are. But stop and smell the flowers once in a while.

Life moves so quickly that we rarely find time just to be, yet being is who we are, as in *human beings*, not always *human doings*. I encourage you to use this life hack called 'traffic control'; it will help you to ground yourself when stress has you chasing your tail. It can be practised anywhere, aside from when driving or operating machinery. Try taking two-minute breaks every hour, to quiet the constant chatter in your head. You can do this lying, sitting or standing, it matters not.

Get comfortable. Bring awareness to the moment. Close your eyes and breathe deeply through your nose via the diaphragm for five seconds. Hold your breath for a count of five seconds and become aware of how it feels to focus on holding the breath. Now breathe slowly out for five seconds through the mouth as if you were blowing gently through a straw. At the bottom of the breath, hold for another five seconds, then repeat the cycle until two minutes have passed. You can extend the overall time, but make two minutes a minimum.

For a deeper experience, place your hands over your heart and visualise breathing into the heart space, while simultaneously extending gratitude for something or somebody while repeatedly stating in your mind 'I love you and I thank you'. This is immensely powerful and can shift your state from anxious to relaxed in minutes. To avoid confusion, breathe in and hold your breath while you state 'I love you and I thank you' three times, before exhaling.

Breathing is a natural doorway to presence. All life emanates and ends on the breath, and it's the singular event that connects every living thing on the planet. What is more, the breathing exercise above is a robust method of alleviating anxiety or panic-like conditions... Try it for yourself the next time you feel anxious or nervous. It's free, always available and does not need a doctor's prescription.

The importance of being aware of the breath cannot be overstated. Whether walking, driving, running or sitting, or doing any other activity, passive or energetic, focus on your breathing. This will anchor you to the only period you will ever have mastery over – this one. Understanding this is fundamental to your happiness and transformation.

Before moving on, I would encourage you to dwell a little and take your time with the content of the book as we go ahead, using this simple screening tool:

1. Let the information sit a while.
2. Revisit any material that confuses you or is contradictory to your own beliefs, before making decisions. Cross-reference the info until satisfied either way.
3. Listen to your intuition. There is nothing another can tell you but that which already rests half asleep in the dawning of your knowledge.
4. After deliberation, ignore that which does not serve you.
5. Take notes or keep a diary and refer to it often.

Everything in the universe is in constant flux, including you. You are not a fixed entity, but one capable of incredible change; yet, without an unwavering desire and an indomitable will, matched with unshakeable consistency, the changes will be temporary. Unless the changes you seek are the most critical thing in your life, the best you can hope for is a respite from the old patterns and habits that have defined you and will continue to do so.

For the record, I am not a healer, nor any type of guru; I am here to remind you of who you are. When anything you read resonates and you find yourself nodding your head, ask yourself: 'Where does this feeling come from?' I can tell you – it's from the point of reference of already knowing. Everything I state that you identify with is known already... it's known by everybody. How would you relate to it otherwise?

There lives in you, a Buddha, a Krishna, a Jesus. It's just a matter of remembering and in time, uncovering the agent of great love and wisdom that you are. Allow me to be a signpost on that journey... on the journey back to self as I help you access resources and tools needed to become the person you always wanted to be.

But what is the self? It is effectively two different parts with two distinctive roles: the finite self and the infinite self. The human self, the self we are all familiar with, is built on a collection of experiences, emotions, thoughts, actions, and memories which form the identity we believe to be us – I would define that as the 'finite self', the small self, the egoic self, which is detached from its true identity, the 'infinite self' (the 'soul' or 'infinite consciousness'). When we know who and what we are, the journey back to self becomes a voyage of exploration and excitement as we peel back the layers of the onion, one at a time, until both parts are integrated into wholeness.

WHO ARE YOU?

A spirit being having a human experience.

In the previous chapter I introduced the concept of consciousness and what it meant. I would like to extrapolate on that idea and dive a little deeper down the consciousness rabbit hole by further exploring who we are. For those not interested in consciousness, the spirit, the soul or anything that doesn't address the human part of the journey, re-join me in the next section.

If I were to ask you 'Who are you?', your answer would probably start with the words 'I am', followed by a host of content, stories and labels which you believe defines you as a human being. But content is not who you are; content is the by-product of a carefully constructed self-image that demands to make sense of who we think we are. So, from where did these labels, beliefs and stories stem? They were initially given to us by our caretakers or parents as young children, and then cemented further by our experiences, memories and emotions and the meaning we gave to them as we proceeded through adolescence into adulthood.

We created, as all humans do, an individual identity, which is then upheld and supported by a variety of belief systems that define who we believe ourselves to be from the cradle to the grave and seldom do we question this. This identity is not who we are. Every time we use the term 'I am', followed by content to qualify the experience, we move further away from our real identity, which is pure awareness having a human experience.

Try this for one minute: sit still and take a breath. Now, when I ask 'Who are you?', simply reply 'I am' and be silent awhile. Close your eyes, continue to breathe deeply and resist the need to add any quantifying labels to the experience other than repeating silently 'I am'. This knowing, this 'I am', connects every living organism to the same energy field that all things originated from and must return.

A man, a Buddhist, a Muslim, smart, sexy, intelligent, brave, jealous, rich, fearful, stubborn, ... are some of the labels we add to the 'I am' to make sense to a human mind which craves definitive structure to feel safe and secure. Yet, to experience the profundity of 'I am' is to know beyond semantics that we are not human beings having a spiritual experience, but multidimensional spirits having a human experience.

This 'I am' is the watcher of all material content that arises, but not the content itself... the stillness beyond the noise, the observer of the avatar as it engages on the five-sense dimensional plane we recognise as life but not the avatar itself. To know this, to feel this, is your ultimate destination, not by intellectualising but through direct experience. To awaken the human spirit as the divine within recognises the divine in all things.

As you begin to identify the nonstop voice in your head which pretends to be you, a subtle but very powerful disassociation arises as the unconsciousness starts to diminish. Note that I used the word 'disassociation' and not 'termination'. Our awakening experiences will be as unique as we are, so I can only describe how I felt and what happened as I began to recognise the different parts which acted out various roles.

Only the 'I am' is permanent; all other aspects of the self, i.e. the body and mind, are temporary and perform temporary actions. The body and mind are tools we use to grow, to connect and to fulfil our mission here. The 'I' is the provider of life to that being – a divine purity that transforms, but extinguished it can never be. Formless, eternal, perfect and complete.

If any of you have seen a corpse, then I am sure you will relate to the following. The body and features are the same, but the animation has gone. The first time I saw this was when a good friend was killed in a motor cycle accident. Looking at my dear friend lying there in the funeral home awoke something in me. I described it as looking at a shop mannequin – a hard shell, but nothing more. What I loved about my friend was no longer there; his soul, his energy, his frequency and his consciousness had departed and transformed. Where and into what is a mystery, but gone was the essence of this once beautiful man.

From this new level of awareness and understanding I began to look beyond the veil, where life still felt authentic but paradoxically chaotic. I felt calmer and more confident but puzzlingly more detached from the everyday reality I was used to. My heart began to open, my ideas became clearer, but above all else, there was a level of wisdom not previously experienced – a knowing that I had travelled incredible distances to get where I now was, emotionally, physically and spiritually, but, more importantly, where I was headed.

Sounds wonderful doesn't it? The Buddhists refer to this state as 'nirvana', the Hindus call it 'moksha' and the Christians call it 'bliss'.

Understanding this is one thing, continuous living within the parameters of this ancient wisdom is another. I would go as far to say it's impossible. I am of course aware that the previous statement is my perception which I am now projecting. For those living in a perpetual state of bliss, I apologise, although my apologies may well be meaningless. I very much doubt that those who have attained that level of nirvana would ever find a copy of *The Journey Back to Self* in their hands. For those who have not attained spiritual enlightenment, allow me to continue and return again to the human part of the journey.

THE HUMAN PART OF THE JOURNEY

Human life is a real gift, a miracle if you like, but will test you to your very limits. The intense, erratic and at times downright crazy emotions we must endure, minute by minute, assure that attaining a pleasurable state demands close attention.

The average human has between 60 and 70 thousand thoughts per day; according to some research, as much as 98% of these thoughts are the same as we had the day before. Even more significant, over 80% of our thoughts are negative. Can you grasp the significance or importance of knowing this information? What chance do you have of changing anything on which awareness has not shone?

You will never halt the mind's ability to produce thoughts, for that is its purpose; hence trying to stop it from thinking is like trying to prevent yourself from breathing. We can do it for a short amount of time, but soon enough, the need to breathe exceeds our ability to control it. The same thing applies to the mind and thinking. For short periods of time, we can stop the process, but nature takes over and starts it again autonomously. With practice, however, we can recognise the patterns of the mind and the thoughts that arise from a far higher vantage point. This conscious awareness allows us to take some sort of control over a process most believe to be autonomous.

We remain agitated by circumstance if we believe ourselves to be the victim of external conditions rather than of the meaning we assign, via our thinking, to them. A victim believes that they have no choice and that life is always happening to them... that someone or something is shaping their life. They therefore stop trying and refuse to be responsible, preferring instead to sit around, wallowing in self-pity and berating life and others for their hardship. This limiting belief opposes the actions needed in order to change the circumstances we believe responsible for our suffering.

We empower ourselves the moment we appreciate that how we feel arises from the thoughts we assign to the circumstances and not from the circumstances themselves. And this, my fellow seeker, is one of the toughest of all lessons to master, but master it you must if inner peace is high on your list of priorities.

To live a contented life, we must know what we want and what prevents it. What are the forces that shape us? What are the drivers that dictate our quality of life, and why do we think and do the things we do?

We all have dreams, desires and ambitions. The outcome of all those things are shaped by the decisions we make and by the actions or lack thereof. When we understand the patterns that drive us, we are in a better position to change them. Emotions are not outside of our control as some would have you believe – we *can* control our emotions. However hard that is to accept, it is a fact. Emotions do not come to us... we go to them. They are bloody difficult to control at times, but the truth is, with careful deliberation, discipline, consistency and a commitment to non-negotiable action, we can change thoughts and patterns which cause us problems.

If you regularly experience life in states of fear, anger, guilt, resentment or sadness, instead of love, compassion, gratitude, joy and excitement, you are in good company. Well... not 'good' per se, but most people fall into that category and here is why. To understand why we lean towards negativity, we must venture back into our history. We are the direct descendants of a species whose chances of surviving daily were fair at best. In other words, our DNA is hardwired to not only recognise danger but also actively seek and avoid it.

The human brain isn't designed to make us happy and fulfilled: it's designed for survival. Our brains are forever on the lookout for what's wrong, or for whatever can hurt us, so that we can either fight the problem or flee from it. That said, if we allow this prehistoric survival software to run the show, what chance do we have of enjoying life on an extended basis? A directionless mind operates naturally in survival mode, constantly finding and exaggerating any potential threat to our well-being. The result: a life filled with distress and apprehension.

It was prudent of our ancestors to pay close attention to the rustling in the bushes or to the noises coming from behind a large rock; in fact, their lives depended on their sensory acuity. Nowadays, circumstances for most of us are very different. No longer are we on the menu of any species, yet our brains are continually assessing danger or perceived risk. Once identified, real or imaginary (and most is imaginary), the brain gives explicit instructions to our emotions to match how we are thinking, which in turn correlates to how we feel at any given moment.

We must train the mind to work for and not against us, to distinguish a perceived threat from one that's real, to constantly steer the mind in the right direction, so as not to be a slave of our ancient past. Learning and training the mind to pay attention to what's happening in the present moment is a powerful way to short circuit the brain's attempts to warn you of dangers no longer applicable in our day-to-day lives.

It does not serve us to continuously wander through the catacombs of our past, seeking out illusory threats; neither is it empowering to project into an unknown future, catastrophising and predicting disempowering scenarios that have yet to unfold. By living in the now, and paying attention to our feelings, we can live at peak efficiency, not having the negative thinking that arises when we lose the connection to the present moment... This moment, this now, is where you will find inner peace and happiness. Hoping that one day life will be ok is not enough. Leaving it to chance is not a good strategy.

We must take life by the scruff of the neck and make it dance to our tune, or it will quickly pass us by. You are the DJ and you decide what sound you wish to dance to. To be clear, I am not advocating utopian optimism claiming that life is a bed of roses... not at all. Even roses have their thorns. Obviously, your issues and problems are significant, and the pain you feel is real, but once you adopt the idea that you are not experiencing life directly but the meaning-making process of your mind, the edges begin to blur as you realise you can control far more of your life than previously believed.

That in itself is progress, and progress is a state of being we must experience for life to have any meaning at all. Moreover, the brain associates progress with achievement and lights up the area associated with it. The brain then releases feel-good hormones, namely dopamine, which makes us feel happy and content, and those my friends are the favourable states each of us must experience on a regular basis for life to be agreeable.

IN A NUTSHELL

We are the classic duality, with both parts equally important. The infinite, spiritual 'I am', cannot perish, neither does it need changing. The physical you, that which interacts moment to moment with your earthly reality, is a complex amalgamation of beliefs, emotions and feelings that requires direction in order to excel. Therefore, one must learn to govern the mind, a wondrous servant, but a tyrannical master.

HUMAN BEINGS, THE ULTIMATE PARADOX

I am the wisest man alive, for I know one thing,
and that is that I know nothing.

We are the self-proclaimed alpha species on the planet, yet, puzzlingly, unable to live peacefully with ourselves or with other forms of sentient we share proximity with. It would appear that we are upside down and back to front, where hating one another is easy but loving one another, not so... where good things are difficult to achieve, yet distressing things come to us without effort.

In an earlier chapter, I argued that pain teaches us so much about who we are and what we want for ourselves and others. I stated that we do not develop contentment by being happy every day; we extend it by growing through adversity, which is true. But we must understand this in context. If we believe this consensus to be definitive, we add strength to a disempowering narrative that we are here only to suffer, where rarefied glimpses of pleasure are the exception.

Einstein said that insanity was doing the same thing repeatedly and expecting different results, yet accusations of insanity are naturally met with hostility. On closer inspection, however, we see that our behaviour patterns often match the description. How often do you have the same negative thoughts, then complain when nothing positive materialises? How often do you engage in habits and rituals that do not serve your higher good but continue unabated? How often is your daily routine a carbon copy of the previous day and the day before that? Who can debate or deny that man indulges in repetitive, non-productive behaviour, then deliberates over his suffering?

It does not have to be this way. You can steer the ship to calmer waters; you are the captain of this vessel and not just a passenger relying on the skill of others to manage your journey. We must remain mindful, continually monitoring our thoughts and steering them in the direction of love and productivity. Being the captain and not a passenger takes effort and discipline, but is far from impossible.

It's incredible, isn't it, that we experience life with such polarity? I find it fascinating and empowering to know that every moment of life on earth is defined by how we feel about ourselves, and that how we think about ourselves is directly correlated to how we perceive our world; if that be true, then we are only ever one thought away from changing our reality.

The fact we are here at all is the most startling reality. Human life is an extraordinary achievement. We rarely, if at all, stop to ponder how remarkable life is when overpopulation seems to be on the lips of people the world over. Yet, the fact we are here at all is an absolute miracle. So miraculous in fact, we lack the intelligence to comprehend it. So, let me explain in a way that makes sense to the human brain, mine included.

Imagine that there was one orange safety ring thrown somewhere in a random ocean, the kind you see on the side of rescue boats, with precisely one sea turtle in all the random seas on the planet, swimming underwater somewhere. The probability that you are reading this is the same as that of one turtle sticking its head out of the water and through the middle of that orange safety ring on his first and only attempt as it came up for air. For the mathematicians among us, that represents a 1 in 700 trillion chance.[4] To put that into perspective, the UK has a national lottery, a weekly draw of predicting six correct balls, each with its own number, from a possible 59 balls; the odds of winning this are 45 million to 1.

To add further perspective and wonderment, try this. The odds of being fatally struck by a part of a plane falling from the sky is 1 in 10 million. This means that you are four and a half times more likely to be killed by random pieces of a falling plane while waiting for the lottery numbers to be drawn than actually winning the jackpot itself.

---

[4] For the eternal sceptics and doubting Thomas's reading this astonishing factoid and shaking their heads, an article which describes in detail the odds against you being here and shaking that head of yours can be viewed online at https://www.huffingtonpost.com/dr-ali-binazir/probability-being-born_b_877853.html.

Now put the odds of making it here into perspective: a 1 in 700 trillion chance. And you don't believe in miracles?

A miracle is an event so unlikely that it is almost impossible; per that definition, I've just proved that you are a miracle. We have the good fortune to be afforded the most beautiful vehicle one could imagine to experience this planet, and for this, we ought to be eternally grateful. Consciousness chooses to express itself in a plethora of form. The fact that it has chosen you, this time around, is a miraculous gift and best not forgotten... Now go ahead and act like the miracle you are by doing the very best you are capable of.

IN A NUTSHELL

I can help you do the very best you are capable of, but I need your cooperation. Without it, the words in this book remain empty and without substance. I encourage self-development, not shelf-development, where the information sits, collecting dust on your mantlepiece. You made an effort and spent good money to buy this book; I implore you to use it.

KNOWLEDGE VS WISDOM

If you do not synthesise or experience the
knowledge for yourself, you are guessing.

Confucius, the famous Chinese philosopher, said there were three steps to learning wisdom: the first through reflection, the second through imitation, and the third through repeated meaningful experience. Without these there can be no wisdom.

Knowledge is information – philosophical or theoretical concepts or ideas that we learn intellectually. Learning is a process of discovery derived from the experiences of others; for example, books, lectures, films and documentaries, from which the information learnt stimulates the intellect. This type of learning certainly has its place, as it introduces new information, but remains just that, until we consistently integrate the knowledge acquired through direct participation, which then facilitates wisdom.

Wisdom is a very different level of understanding; it is the experience beyond words. If I tell you something, you may forget. If I teach you something, you might remember, but if I include you directly in the experience, you are going to learn, and the more you experience, the wiser you become. Please take the time to immerse yourself in the practices that I write about in this book. When I speak of practising mindfulness, meditation, grounding, affirmations or any other concept, it is imperative that you experience these, through repetition and consistency, to know what I am talking about at a level that reaches beyond the intellect.

People tell me all the time: 'Hey, I know this and that stuff.' Yet, scratch the surface and it soon becomes evident that what they think they know, in fact they do not. To understand and not to do is not to know at all. If you believe that you know something yet don't have the results to show for it, I assure you that you know it as an intellectual concept and not as a pearl of inherent wisdom. There are three levels of knowledge which capture this.

Understanding the concept is the first level of 'knowing it' – to intellectualise something... to read the words of somebody else and relate to it solely at that level.

Having an existential experience is the second level – 'to know it, know it'. For example, I can read how to play the guitar, but until the instrument is in my hands and I am playing a tune, it is not an existential experience.

Experiencing something so often it becomes an automated habit is the third level – 'know it, know it, know it'. Using the guitar again as an example, I have played it so often I own this new skill set and it has become a new habit.

Let me illustrate this further. How can you know the benefits of meditation or a yoga practice unless you have repeatedly experienced it? Can you speak a new language or learn to ride a unicycle from the words in a book? Absolutely not. You can read about it, sure – appreciate it even. But until you *feel* the experience, where the corresponding emotions correlate with the repeated action, you are presuming to know.

Knowing what to do/how to do it and doing it are poles apart. Sure, you can read a thousand books and articles on how to do it. You can relate to the pain of the poet, the genius of the philosopher or the majesty of the author, but they are just words. And not only that, they are not yours; they belong to another. In fact, any intellectual understanding not backed by direct experience often leads to potentially destructive, ignorant and deceptive states.

Unless you commit to the experience, wisdom will remain absent from your life. Sure, you will have a head full of knowledge, but wise you will never be.

IN A NUTSHELL

Knowledge is about information and ideas that we acquire through study, research and observation. Wisdom is the ability to recognise and assess which aspects of that knowledge are valid, lasting and applicable to our lives through direct experience.

THE IMPORTANCE OF TOUCH

Do not move the way fear makes you move.
Move the way love makes you move.

There are many things we don't need in life; physical touch (and the affection we receive from it) is most definitely not one of them. In fact, without loving touch we literally, not figuratively, wither and wilt, often becoming a shell of the person we were designed to be. And our need for love and nurture starts the moment we take our first breath.

Neglected babies, for example, who do not receive adequate touch, love and affection in their first year are at risk of poor brain development and social skills. Some of these ignored babies, if not held, nurtured and hugged sufficiently, actually stop growing. If the situation lasts long enough, even if they are receiving proper nutrition, the chances of infant mortality skyrockets by 30 to 40%. This was according to researchers who were trying to figure out why specific orphanages had infant mortality rates running at these very troubling rates.

Our need for loving touch is an inherent human quality and one we just cannot do without, regardless of age or gender. In fact, for us as human beings to thrive, we must be able to express and receive love freely, not only with our partners and children but with as many others as possible.

Numerous studies have shown that simple touching, let alone hugging, can trigger the release of oxytocin, aka the 'love hormone'. In today's world of religious fanaticism and PC madness, however, a platonic human touch is in danger of becoming obsolete. We must let go of the fears and overcome the programmes, prejudices and conditioning that tells us to run from a loving embrace and into the metaphoric arms of fear. It's vitally important for all of us to embrace one another and dissolve the ignorance that surrounds nonsexual affection.

The number of positive attributes of human touch is just too great to ignore. It helps calm the nervous system and reduce cardiovascular stress, and also activates the body's compassionate response mechanisms. It decreases the potential for contracting diseases and ailments by strengthening the immune system. It can even boost performance at school or college – students, when touched platonically on the shoulder by the teacher, for example, have demonstrated heightened learning. The French psychologist Nicolas Guéguen reported that students regularly patted by their teachers in a friendly manner are three times more likely to speak up in class and outperform. This isn't pseudoscience or woo-woo nonsense – this is factual.

What concerns me is the emergence of the political correctness brigade across the planet who label any form of touching as inappropriate, when the absolute opposite is true. There are billions of religious believers who are not allowed to let themselves be seen, let alone greeted by physical contact, other than by immediate blood family or partners. We are rapidly descending into a scenario where human interaction will be so forced and coerced to behave in unnatural ways that I fear for the emotional health of the next generation. This fear, this madness, must stop.

It's by no coincidence that we enjoy body-based therapies and seek out practitioners: masseurs, craniosacral therapists, reflexologists, hand masseurs, facial specialists, chiropractors, osteopaths, physical therapists, hands-on yoga instructors, martial arts instructors – in fact anyone who can provide that all-important body contact we need in order to feel safe, grounded and connected. And some will even see physicians or sit long hours in a hospital waiting room for a possible physical examination for ailments that don't exist. Why? Physical touch is the building block of human development, regardless of culture, religion or antiquated beliefs.

The growing preoccupation with restricting or outlawing platonic contact, coupled with the restrictive legislation in our schools, colleges, workplaces and pretty much anywhere else, is not a step in the right direction in my opinion. On the contrary, we must encourage and promote platonic physical touch and intimacy if humanity is to unbridle itself from this abnormal behaviour we have been forced to adopt.

Intimacy does not have to suggest sexual contact or sexual intent, the same way sexual contact can be devoid of affection, and it certainly isn't reserved exclusively for monogamous relationships.

We each know our personal boundaries without being reminded or told how to enforce them. I challenge you all to break through your cultural, religious and personal taboos and your unchallenged beliefs, and hold hands more, hug, cuddle and kiss the cheeks of your friends, consensually of course, without gender discrimination. These gestures do not have to be sexual. When done with a person's consent, there's absolutely nothing wrong with needing and sharing human affection.

In fact, I will state that platonic relationships often contain levels of organic and unconditional qualities, rarely seen in relationships that are sexually intimate, yet somehow conditioned beliefs and insecurities have convinced us otherwise. This embracing of your human family through platonic affection is a powerful way to help shift the stale and rigid belief systems of ignorant oppression. Yet, until we are able to let go of the fear, shame and guilt associated with platonic touch and affection, the system will remain unimpaired.

So, what is it going to be? Love or fear? Affection or isolation? As the great Bill Hicks, an American comedian, so eloquently said: 'It's only a choice. No effort, no work, no job, no savings. Just a simple choice, right now, between fear and love. The eyes of fear want you to put bigger locks on your doors, buy guns, close yourself off. The eyes of love instead see all of us as one, without separation.'

Love and fear share the same space, but they resonate at different frequencies. According to quantum scientists, everything in both the known and the unknown universe is energy resonating at a specific frequency. Love is the highest form of energy, and fear, the lowest; they co-exist, yet each has its own vibrational signature. All emotions vibrate at different speeds, for emotions are expressions of energy: E = motion, meaning energy in motion. How we think and what we do at any given time dictates our energetic signature and thus the quality of our lives.

When we experience life at the frequency of love, it works, it flows... a smile, never far from the lips... a spring in the step, shoulders back, the breath deep and free. We cultivate like-minded energy that draws favourable events and others to us. Things that need to be done are performed efficiently. There is gratitude, not just for our life, but for all life.

In contrast, let's look at the recognisable traits associated with fear: a tight jaw, a furrowed brow, a dense head and hunched shoulders… shallow and rapid breathing patterns. Events and people who mimic our fears and frequency show up. We repel from us people whose light shines brightly. A fearful demeanour exudes a definitive statement that suggests: 'Stay away.' Things to do become heavy and burdensome, and life is a struggle, not a gift.

During our entire lives, whether conscious of it or not, we are either moving towards love and away from fear, or towards fear and away from love. Understanding this is damn important. Why? Because where our focus goes our reality grows, and what we focus on we get more of. Hence, when attempting to change a part of your life that is not working it's imperative to keep your eyes firmly on the prize and retain a focus on what it is you want.

Don't repeat the mistake I did of focusing on that which I no longer wanted instead of on that which I was trying to achieve. Or better said, stop focusing on the fearful aspects of life you wish to transcend, and concentrate on that which brings you joy and closer to love. Why? And I will repeat: 'What you focus on you will get more of.' For example, I suffered total deafness in my left ear in 2014 after a free-diving accident and quickly developed very intrusive tinnitus; this filled my whole head with an assortment of high and low squeals, hisses and a constant electrical buzz 24 hours a day, which had me at times doubting my sanity.

For over two years I battled with this debilitating intrusion into my life, yet it was the battle which sustained the condition. I was obsessed with getting rid of it, to eliminate the enemy within, not realising that my motivation to do so was not only maintaining it but also increasing the intensity. Everything I did was in the attempt to silence the phantom sounds that would not shut up. Then it finally dawned on me. Rather than continually monitoring the levels of intrusion and living my life in fear of angering it further, I began to focus on what I wanted and not on what I did not. I began to do things I enjoyed: I wrote more, I played more golf, I did daily gym sessions, I swam more and I cycled every day while listening to podcasts or uplifting music, which shifted my attention. I was now moving towards greater peace through shifting my attention away from the noise in my head. You see, moving away from what you don't want is different from moving towards what you do want. Let me give you an example.

Imagine driving on an icy road, and something causes you to brake hard, and you find yourself sliding towards a lamp post. Do you retain focus on the lamp post and on not wanting to hit it, or do you divert your attention to where you need to direct the car for a more favourable outcome? Those who choose the latter are going to understand the metaphor without further need for expansion. In simple terms, consciously guide with a keen focus your human vehicle in the direction you wish to go.

I started to visualise my life as I favoured and continued to enjoy pleasures and pastimes I had put on hold for fear of angering the neurons in my brain that were partying 24/7... That's not to say I engaged with life in such a way that would guarantee an elevation in the intensity of the buzzing and hissing, which I had learnt through painstaking trial and error. Instead, I began to accept it as part of me, rather than fight with it, and I chose to direct my focus on things in life which made me happy and which I could control. This sent a very different message to the brain, which took the tinnitus off high priority as the noise very slowly began to back off; the more I gave my mind new instructions, the more the tinnitus let go. I found this fascinating and suddenly realised, through direct experience and not just empty words, the process behind the science of changing programmes that do not serve us.

It took many repeated cycles, mind you, of checking back in on the noise to grade it in the pursuit of progress, which backfired time and time again before I got it. Remember, I had hardwired a very destructive habit into my psychology, having obsessed about it for two years, day and night; hence the neurons had been firing and wiring together, building a fortress of unhealthy mind activity. Breaking that fortress was not going to be easy. It takes between 21 and 250 days of repetitive behaviour to hardwire a habit, and I had trained this obsession for well over 750 days without a moment's rest. Can you imagine how strong the neural connections became? Only through constant effort and engaging with new behaviours that consumed my mind was I slowly able to dissolve the old toxic patterns and fire and wire new favourable emotions that arose from new and exciting models of behaviour.

The tinnitus is still there, but it no longer consumes my every thought, and above that (and this may resonate with you or it may not), it was and still remains my most powerful teacher. Why is that, you may ask? Well, the last seven years of my life have been the most challenging thus far; as well as deafness and tinnitus, other powerful tests have turned up in my life.

For me, it is no coincidence that my exponential emotional growth arose from the ashes of the sternest adversity. That growth has facilitated within me a far greater ability to empathise with the suffering of my clients and in fact with the suffering of anybody and anything. I can now, through the experience of severe torment, understand how my clients feel when they come to me sad, downtrodden and desperate for some kind of relief. No longer do I trivialise anybody's pain. If they are hurting, then it's real for them, regardless of how futile it may appear to the external world... Having said that, once I have built good rapport with my clients and earned their trust, I quickly guide them to states which are beneficial for healing and towards circumstances that will change their lives.

It is said that the universe presents its toughest tests to its most resilient fighters, and I now believe that. I have also come to the conclusion that the universe, or God, or whoever you feel is behind this thing called the human journey, needed to know that I was capable of understanding suffering at a level way beyond semantics or as an intellectual concept.

I don't believe for a second that my real tests began as a coincidence the moment I became a therapist and coach and began to write this book. The life coach and author combination gives rise to a very powerful position, and with great power comes great responsibility. If I wished to be an authority on the pain and suffering of others, then I would need to feel it myself... and, boy, I felt it.

As always, feel free to discount that theory, but it makes sense to me and has helped me come to terms with what most believe are random events.

I hope this authentic example of how we can change bad habits or destructive thought processes will inspire you to use the same methodology to eradicate fearful experiences that cause suffering and enable you to fall back into the arms of love and positivity. I hope also that you will assimilate that powerful information to make sense of your own lives when trouble knocks at your door. Love is who and what we are. Love is our birthright, and our default is to resonate at the frequency of love. Sadly, that default is not a permanent state of being and will need your consideration to reinforce it.

So, if our default is love and we are born that way, what happened? In brief, we took on the psychology of our care givers, which stemmed from their worries, fears, beliefs and struggles; before long, we adopted the same dogmas, including the irrational fears that plague us to this day.

Fear, therefore, is learnt and not a hardwired trait. Sure, fear is at times a useful emotion to call upon; it keeps us safe and out of harm's way. It's this fear that stops us wandering into the tiger pen at the zoo or taking our surfboards into the sea where great white sharks are breeding. This type of concern is healthy, and most of us call upon it to navigate safely and successfully through the tricky waters of life.

All emotions are expressions of either love or fear. Love or fear is the driving force behind everything we think and do; it may not appear so, but from an informed perspective, this becomes obvious. Think of the emotions, namely freedom, gratitude, humility, forgiveness, joy, happiness, empathy, compassion, hope, serenity, tolerance, confidence, satisfaction, inspiration, enjoyment, kindness and contentment. They are all extensions of love, and I would wager that reading the words and the corresponding internal representations instigated a favourable emotional response.

Contrarily, pay attention to how it makes you feel and the internal representations created when you read the words oppression, rage, jealousy, anger, envy, greed, selfishness, sadness, doubt, suffering, disturbance, conflict, worry, over-cautiousness, approval-seeking, low self-esteem, procrastination, anxiety and depression. Now ask yourself, when have you experienced happiness while experiencing any of the fearful emotions mentioned above? Unless you have an antisocial personality disorder, the answer will be a resounding 'Never!' Compare that with how you felt or feel when experiencing the feelings of love and their corresponding emotions.

For where love is light, free, open and expressive, fear keeps us locked in our heads, which limits our potential, and we struggle to be happy when our potential is limited. In fact, fear disables our ability to connect with our higher intelligence, which we must do so in order to be at our resourceful best. Fear cuts us off from accessing these resources, whereas love enables them. That said, here is the caveat which leads on from my own experiences above: nothing that arises in our lives is without purpose, including fear-based events. Every event in life, fearful or loving, is either a lesson or a blessing.

If we pay attention, our fears can highlight how certain beliefs are out of configuration with our loving selves. We can then use that as a guidepost for challenging those beliefs, and adjust the way we look at circumstances to see them through the lens of love. That often leads to a transformation of the dread we once held towards the object of fear as we reframe and retain the necessary learning. This is a challenging, but ultimately compelling and cathartic, process and one we must experience for emotional growth.

It's ironic that the things we once feared the most often become our greatest pleasure when we walk this path. I have no doubt you have heard the cliché that pain is the best teacher, and for good reason – it is!

By paying attention to our fears, we can discover our bliss. The worry that fear often creates urges us to find out why it is there and how to transform it. Fear makes us feel uncomfortable, and to resolve this we need to pay close attention to what is going on in our lives. Sadly, by choosing to ignore this process, we are resigned to making the same mistakes repeatedly. If we are awake to the process, however, the pain can help us to see life from a new perspective. It offers us the chance to grow and evolve. Pain presents to us a beautiful opportunity to transform from caterpillar into butterfly.

Learn to better understand your pain and the lessons that arise from it. You could be making the same repetitive choices when dating, for instance, when you continually attract partners who share the same, or very similar, emotional traits. Or, you might be pursuing similar jobs that do not serve you or repetitive behavioural patterns that do more harm than good.

Letting go of fear is a process. I believe that the majority of people in today's society operate from a learnt default of fear; this can be summed up as a fear that we're not going to get what we desire, which strengthens the belief in a lack of something or other. This results in grasping at straws or in a fear that we'll lose something we already have, which promotes scarcity, leading to hoarding and clinginess.

Once we become aware and acknowledge that we're repeatedly acting in fear, we can make a conscious choice to live another way. When self-introspection and the need for change arise, it's vital you have a practice (or practices) that supports reform. Be kind and treat yourself with compassion as you realise the old ways of living no longer serve you. I say 'be kind', because we tend to be very harsh on ourselves when we lack self-love, and the lack of self-love is always born out of fear.

Understand that you had to experience these things to become the person currently undergoing a powerful metamorphosis.

You have finally learnt the lessons and can climb another rung on the ladder and move closer to the resonance of love. Now ask yourself this question: 'What can I do now?' You may be surprised. Previously unacknowledged possibilities for change present themselves in many ways, as they did for me:

- Joining a yoga school.
- Learning a new language.
- Enrolling in new empowering courses.
- Beginning a meditation practice.
- Reading new energising books.
- Watching inspiring YouTube channels and listening to powerful Ted talks daily.
- Beginning to set goals and committing to them, barring emergencies.
- Asking myself: 'Are my tribe resonating on my desired vibe? Are my friends helping me grow or holding me back?'
- Realising that who I spend time with is who I become.
- Getting belligerent with the process and appreciating that my time is valuable, and that the world was treating me the way I treated myself. (If you don't value your time, then don't expect others to either!)

Asking a further question – 'What more can I do?' – revealed something very powerful. It inspired me to obtain honest feedback about myself, and I would encourage you to do the same. Forget mutual admiration clubs and seek out feedback from friends who will give it to you straight. In my opinion, a true friend doesn't support a life of subpar mediocrity; they hold you accountable for being the very best version of yourself.

When we start to treat ourselves lovingly, new doors open for us. We begin to build momentum through enhanced self-esteem as the motivation behind our behaviours shifts from fear-based thinking to being motivated by self-love and self-surety. We still experience moments of fear, but its power diminishes as we continue towards a path of love and transformation.

Every choice made carries with it a consequence. Being accountable and responsible for your decisions means leaving behind the role of a victim. No longer will you see others or experiences as a source of your fears and suffering, but as teachers or lessons of growth. Obviously, this does not mean hoping for pain or fearful experiences in your life. But when they do show up, as they must, recognise the message instead of avoiding it or apportioning the blame on events, circumstances or people you wish to hold responsible.

Pain, like any emotional messenger, will not leave until you have acknowledged its presence and the lesson has been fully learnt. Until you grasp what has happened, you cannot avoid doing it again. Until the light of awareness has illuminated the problem, can any issue in fact be acknowledged? I would say, *absolutely not*.

Some people have a tough time admitting failure[5]; all too quick, they point the finger at the external world, but that does not help you re-examine what happened in order to do better next time. In life, there is satisfactory feedback and there is unsatisfactory feedback. By paying close attention to your choices and the ensuing consequences, you can see what worked and what did not.

You now know what it is you do not want in life, and it's time to focus on that which you do. As you think, you become, with your external reality mirroring the thoughts that create it. Everything we do is directed by our thoughts and choices. You may not be consciously aware of this, and at times it may have seemed like external factors beyond your control were responsible.

The truth, I believe, is that everything in our lives, and I do mean *everything*, is a result of our choices. From the moment of birth, we are shaping our reality from one minute to the next and one thought

---

[5] I prefer not to use the word 'failure', as it disempowers and suggests negativity. I favour the word 'feedback'.

at a time, meaning that we are here today by the sum total of all thoughts, decisions and choices made.

To change anything about your life, you must first change the interpretation of what's happening in your world. Please be aware that you see the world not as it is, but as you are, or as you are conditioned to see it. By going inside and changing your perspective, the world changes for you. Change the perspective, and the meaning changes. Change the meaning, and the emotional responses change alongside them.

IN A NUTSHELL

If you desire to take charge of your life, you must realise you are the creator of your reality. You must discipline yourself, or you will continue to get what you have always got. Discipline yourself to do what you must do when you need to do it, whether you feel like it or not.

AN INTRODUCTION TO LOVE?

*Love **is** life. And if you miss love, you miss life.*

We struggle with the term 'unconditional love', often confusing it with the powerful yet harmful combination of addiction and attachment. It is the most misunderstood concept, bringing untold misery and hardship to so many, especially those in personal relationships. But why is this?

The fear of loss drives unhealthy behaviour. Losing the feeling of love is comparable to jealousy in that it smothers the other person; it creates an immense pressure to be the only thing in their life that conveys happiness. Ironically, then, the more fearful you are of losing your lover, the more your neediness will push a healthy person away from you.

Love never was, is or can be a business contract; neither can it be forced or coerced. Love is not something you do, but something you are… freedom, the energy that lives in everything, not something destroyed by fickle feelings and emotions that come and go like an autumn breeze.

In today's world unconditional, or absolute, love is very much misrepresented. First, there are no conditions associated with the qualifier 'absolute'. When we introduce conditions into the equation, we enter the realm of transactions and arrangements. Conditions work fine when things are going well, and both sides of the partnership are receiving what they need in order to feel fulfilled; like any business arrangement, it is considered favourable.

The problems start when the arrangement falls foul of the expectations placed upon it. So, how may we differentiate between a real love affair and a business transaction? We were taught, and believe, that love exists between living things, or, specifically, between people; to chase and desire the feeling of wanting and being wanted meant that love was on its way. But that has nothing to do with love and is more akin to satisfying insecurities and fears. We obsess over and declare ownership rights the moment the sweetening of emotions reaches a tipping point.

We impose rules and regulations on what is and what is not acceptable, inflicting a reflective image of ourselves on the partner, based on ideas and beliefs dear to us. It is this model that has trapped (and continues to trap) couples across the world, regardless of religion or belief system. Do not be fooled here. Just because the clear majority engage in this type of relationship does not make it right… it makes it more insane. If humankind wishes to evolve, then letting go of the excessive control mechanisms within personal relationships is a wonderful place to start. Love has zero to do with ownership. Love is not jealous – insecure human beings are. Please note the difference.

A real love affair is the relationship we have with life itself and not necessarily with another person. It happens within. The clearer this is, the more joyful life will be. When we connect to our inner being, the infinite loving entity that we are, no longer will we assume that love is exclusively the way one feels towards another person, or what another must give to feel secure.

When we look at everything lovingly, the world becomes magnificent... the birds, the trees, the plant life, and all the other creatures who share this space. When we can look at everything and see ourselves, life begins to exist through us and not through something external, something separate from ourselves.

Your relationship with others and life itself can only ever be as good as the relationship you have with yourself.

Print this quote and place it in the house, car or office, or anywhere that is highly visible. How quickly you understand and embrace this fact determines your future happiness. Contest it, and life will remain difficult. If you believe that happiness is an external event and that others are the source of your ultimate contentment, then buckle up, it is going to be a bumpy ride.

Do you want to love others and long for others to love you unconditionally? Then you must learn to love yourself unconditionally. That means raising your vibrational signature. It means raising your standards through better decisions, choices and actions. Each thought you have is an opportunity for raising or lowering your vibration, moving you towards or away from love.

Do you want to know where you are? Look at the people you are energetically pulled towards and the types of people that are attracted to you. 'Your vibe attracts your tribe' is a catchy way of remembering this.

The bottom line is this: you will continue to get what you deserve, because you will get what you tolerate. This may sound harsh, especially if you are suffering right now. If so, my heart goes out to you, but that said, if you continue to vibrate at the same energetic frequency, you will attract the same experiences over and over again.

Imagine yourself as a radio station that is broadcasting on a frequency of 99.8 FM, and from your radio station you broadcast a very specific message and repeatedly play the same type of music which attracts a very specific type of person. Unless you adjust your frequency and broadcast on a different channel, your audience will remain the same. To change your audience, you must change your channel – move your dial upwards, to let's say 102.6 FM, and broadcast a different message and play a different style of music. This is how you know what frequency you are resonating at... by the types of people who tune into your channel and are seduced by the songs you play.

Unlike the words we use at times to manipulate or fool, energy is very pure and doesn't negotiate, and neither does it play a role; it merely receives and transmits. We are energy primarily and hence we also receive and transmit.

Why is it that you find yourself attracted to someone from the moment you see them, and find others a complete turn off? Why is it that when you walk into a room, you can feel the atmosphere without a word being spoken? Because everything is frequency, everything is energy and your magnetic resonance is always seeking out that which aligns with its own vibrational signature.

The style of films, documentaries and series you are drawn to... the books and magazines you read... the hobbies and pastimes you engage in... the types of animal you like. These all represent magnetic energy resonating at a frequency that aligns with your own. Know it, recognise it and evolve by understanding how it works.

On awakening tomorrow morning, I want you to make a decision... to see the world through the eyes of fear or through the eyes of love. It is all a matter of perspective and you do get to choose.

Some days will naturally be harder than others. Some days, regardless of how hard you try, you will feel low, blue and disconnected.

On such days, especially if not working, treat yourself to some much-needed rest and recovery. Call it your nothing day, where you stay in bed and gorge yourself on a favourite Netflix special, or you read a book, do some light stretching or meditate. Just don't attempt to do anything that taxes your emotional or physical body. When you genuinely need to rest, honour that. Now, let's be clear here. I don't want you using this as a blanket statement for never leaving the house, paralysed by fear, indecision or depression or through being overwhelmed, and refusing to make important decisions.

Be sensible about this and use these low energy days to recharge, recuperate and recover, before resuming the upward curve you are on. Listen carefully to what your body is telling you and where your energy stores are currently sitting, and act accordingly.

You will also have days when people test you to your limits, pushing every button and triggering a plethora of emotions. When these days come, and they will, then be mindful to respond, not react... and, yes, there is a difference. Remember, emotions that continually demand your attention are those that need working on. The situations and people which ignite your fuse are the very ones that you must become fully aware of in order to carry out the work on yourself which needs to be done.

MIND THE GAP

---◆•◆---

When you react, you let others control you.
When you respond, you are in control.

To believe that our lives are meaningful, we must strive for constant improvement. In fact, the unconscious mind is programmed to continually seek more and more. Of course, growth is not a linear phenomenon, and we are going to stutter, fall down and appear at times to be in reverse, but that's ok. Losing our way is inevitable and an essential element of further growth. Accept this, be aware, and without judgement meet every new challenge with vigour and joyful anticipation on the road to continuous and never-ending progress, for progress is the goal, not perfection.

Progress is easily hindered if you are reactive or take yourself too seriously. Reactivity is a nemesis to growth. Look out for this in your everyday life. How do you cope with criticism? How do you react to any type of negativity or perceived sleight of your character? Do you take an open, curious stance or do you immediately react with an aggressive, defensive attitude? Reactivity is something we can use to grade our emotional well-being and gauge whether we are progressing.

See how often you catch yourself becoming reactive to external stimuli, and see how quickly you can catch it before the intensity escalates. This internal barometer of emotional wellness is a very valuable tool to have at one's disposal, and I encourage you to tune into it as often as possible. I know it is not easy, especially when we feel aggrieved, slighted or wronged for any number of reasons; I promise you, however, if you can catch the gap between thought and reaction, and there is always a gap, you will save yourself an awful lot of emotional disturbance.

There exists a small window of opportunity between every thought and reaction, which may be the single-most crucial period you will ever control. This moment in time, this gap, if harnessed correctly, permits us to respond, rather than react.

We have all been there – the situation where an instantaneous reaction has caused remorse or regret. The time you told the boss to shove his job where the sun can never shine, and suddenly you were unemployed. That fight you had with your friend, sibling, mother or father, which resulted in months of resentful silence for all parties. Or when you decided to spit venom and vitriol at your spouse/partner... saying the most hurtful things because you had a bad day and he or she pressed the wrong buttons at the wrong time. And now you are bitterly sorry for the deep hurt you caused, because you were unable to catch the gap between a thought and a reaction.

Ask any number of inmates serving long jail sentences for spontaneous outbursts of violence how their lives are currently working out for them because of their lack of discipline. The saying 'Act in haste and repent at your leisure' is perfect for describing those who react without applying the gap between thought and action.

We can use this gap in a layering process, depending on the severity of the situation. Let's start with a 10-second gap, which should be enough for almost any situation you find yourself in. That space between thought and implementation is one of the most precious segments of time you will encounter in life. Once you become aware of its power, you can use it to your advantage for the rest of your life. So much in life hinges on defining moments, those seconds and minutes that can make or break us. For example, before reacting, ask yourself:

- Are the actions I am about to take, reflect who I am and my highest values?
- Will they serve my greater good and the greater good of the current situation?
- Will they add value or create uplift in the other person?
- Will my efforts contribute to the overall health and well-being of myself and others?
- And finally, is my reaction necessary?

A quick appraisal of the above will no doubt produce a few 'No's, and for every 'No', it would be beneficial to your life and the lives of others if you can step away and think carefully for a few minutes longer, before making a decision.

I stated earlier that it takes no effort to be reactive – it's autonomous. But it takes an effort to respond with careful deliberation. This simple technique will defuse almost any situation and potentially save you from a host of potential regrets. The magic word here is 'respond'; there is a colossal difference between responding and reacting. One is instantaneous, an egoic retort; the other is delivered after the 10-second rule has been applied, and the content, therefore, comes from a place of greater awareness. Not only will this help you become a more productive and pleasant human being to be around, but you will also diffuse inflammatory situations; therefore, by the extension of increased awareness and discipline, you will help others, which is terrific.

One can further harness and increase the wisdom of this gap by extending the period in situations that need more contemplation, or when more complex cases in life present themselves. The 10-second gap will change your way of life and the way you communicate, but the wisdom gleaned from extending the period to, let's say, 10 minutes for more difficult situations will work miracles. A period of 10 minutes gives us more than enough time to calm down, interrupting impulsive decision making; it will be long enough to think through alternatives that are better aligned to your best version of yourself.

This method will not always be perfect, and I cannot promise that some decisions made, even after 10 minutes, won't prevent you from misguided actions. But I do guarantee this: with regular implementation, you will make better choices, preventing you from doing or saying things you will later regret. If either period appears insufficient, read this beautiful parable, which is both profound and enhancing.

When the father of Russian mystic George Gurdjieff was dying, he called for his boy. Gurdjieff was just nine, and he remembered the incident all his life. The father said: 'I am so poor. I cannot give you anything my son. But one thing which my father gave to me I can give you. You may not even be able to understand what it means now, but you will as you grow and it proved to be the most precious thing in my life, so I am giving it to you.'

So, young Gurdjieff listened as his father continued: 'Whenever you feel angry, never reply before 24 hours. Reply by all means, but first, let there be a gap of 24 hours.'

Gurdjieff followed his dying father's advice; it became deeply impressed in his mind the very day his father died. Years later, Gurdjieff said: 'I have practised many, many, many spiritual exercises, but that was the best. I never retained the anger during those 24 hours, and that changed the whole flow, the whole current because I had to stick to the promise.

'Whenever someone would insult me or create an uncomfortable situation I did not care for, I would just tell them that I would come back after 24 hours to reply. Guess what? I never replied because it proved such nonsense to reply.'

Only a gap was needed to realise that the emotion he was feeling at the time was alive with ego, with reactivity, but very little, if any at all, was based on emotional intelligence. And the whole life of Gurdjieff became something different from that moment, as it can and will for you if you embrace this form of contemplation... Use it, understand it and grow with it. It will be, as it was for this brilliant man, one of the most important lessons you will ever learn.

TIME TO BE RESPONS-ABLE

As hard as it is at times to be responsible, we must be just that, guiding out thoughts and actions in a favourable direction and interrupting the negative patterns, if need be, with definitive and strategic interventions.

I must distinguish clearly what I mean when I tell you to take responsibility. 'Responsibility' is a much-misunderstood term. It does not mean taking on the burdens of the world... it does not mean accepting blame for things you have or have not done. 'Respons-ability' means your 'ability to respond'.

I am not suggesting that you adopt the approach that everything is your fault, rather I want you to adopt the mindset that everything is your responsibility. When you say to yourself 'I am responsible', it doesn't have to mean shouldering the blame for the current situation. You are stating to yourself that you are able to respond... that you are choosing to be 'respons-able'.

By stating 'I am not respons-able', you will not have the ability to respond and with it the choices that can help you move forwards. Respons-ability is consciously choosing to have the 'ability to respond' to life. Rather than blaming others for your situation, you acknowledge your personal power.

Response-ability is the capacity to choose. You have decided that out of the many responses you have available, you can choose the one you want. Do you see how empowering this is, when compared with the alternative? Responsibility creates choice... blaming others not so. Better choices lead to better actions which contribute towards a higher vibration; the higher you resonate, the closer to love you feel, and the closer you are to love, the more blissful you become. Love is the highest of all frequencies and your mission is to broadcast from that station as often as possible.

One needs only to seek out loving pastimes, to practise loving thoughts, and to spend time with those who are loving and speak from a place of loving intention in order to experience it for oneself. Your task is therefore to find the barriers within – barriers that you have built against love, including primarily the lack of love you have for yourself, and to remove them.

LOVE IS ALWAYS THE ANSWER

In today's reality, love is a commodity like any other, given or received on the basis of the premise of 'What's in it for me?' We have learnt to associate love with things – material possessions of minimal value – yet we were born to be loved and items are intended to be used. However, the world is detached and inverted, because things are being loved and people are being used.

True, unconditional love permeates all, and nothing is immune from this undeniable truth. To understand this is to transform your lives. But what is unconditional love? The word itself conjures up more confusion than any other, irrespective of the language used to express it. Love needs no learning or understanding, but until we strip away the disinformation, it stays a misunderstood concept.

'What is love' is the most searched phrase on Google, which highlights the amount of confusion that accompanies the word. To be loved is an inherent need of every human being on the planet, and without it, we deteriorate. Yet, it's our erroneous beliefs and common misconceptions which lead us a merry dance and down a road that ends more in torment than in bliss.

We sit and ponder on the puzzle of what love means. If we can figure out how to be kind enough, pretty enough, funny enough, smart enough, sexy enough, rich enough or simply just enough, life will reward us with the perfect loving relationship we deserve and crave.

We all have an underlying desire to be wanted. We are so starved of true love that when we catch a glimpse of what could be just that, we cling to it like dirt to a blanket. So how do we get it so wrong? What are we missing here?

The planet's greatest minds, both past and present, have debated this subject and attempted to answer this most elusive of questions, never coming to a definitive conclusion. From my perspective, I believe they go at it from the wrong angle.

We are told that love is something which is demonstrated, something we do towards another, yet love cannot be done. Acts of contribution are expressions of love, but not love itself. The giving, serving and helping of others are actions that raise one's vibratory signature and thus closer to the frequency at which love resonates; hence the absolute necessity of giving and serving. The more we give, the closer to home we feel, and home being that place of love we all came from and must return.

When we are at our best, which means when we are happy and content, our vibrational signature resonates at a very high frequency. It's this frequency which makes us feel alive, full of energy and as happy as can be. That feeling you experience is the frequency of love or being in harmony with *God*, oneness or however you wish to language God and what that means to you.

There are many ways you can elevate your frequency, but none are more popular than choosing another human being to do it for you. But this avenue has limited returns. Human beings are relational creatures; we were designed for that and are at our best when interacting. The problems arise when we expect or demand that one significant other can satisfy all our needs. Placing that amount of responsibility on the shoulders of another flawed human being is folly indeed.

Why? The moment the object you have deemed responsible for your happiness no longer satisfies your criteria, which must happen by the very nature of being human, your vibrational signature declines, and if you have no other methods of increasing it, life becomes a battle. Please see this. By focusing solely on a specific human being to generate your happiness, without other human beings, pastimes or habits that can do the same, your human journey will be arduous at best.

Love is not dependent on how somebody treats you, and neither is it the sole responsibility of another to elevate your frequency. That responsibility belongs to you. I am not saying that relationships cannot enhance your energetic, physical and emotional states – of course not. They *can*, and they do, but if your only form of sustainable happiness flows from a significant other, then prepare for hardship, for nobody outside of yourself has this ability to sustain happiness other than you.

One of the most erroneous statements I continually see on relationship or dating websites is that somebody completes you. Internet forums are full of statements such as:

- 'This man completes me.'
- 'He was the final piece missing in my jigsaw.'
- 'I didn't realise how empty I was until he arrived and completed me.'
- 'I feel so incomplete when not in a relationship.'

Sorry to burst your bubble ladies, and to a lesser degree gentleman, but holding on to false theatrical ideas of completion will not help you dispel this unhealthy illusion that you cannot be complete on your own. Yes, we are happier when in healthy relationships, but the operative word here is 'healthy'. It's by no coincidence that the divorce rate is so high, and that relationships the world over are ever more tenuous. The reason for this is that our expectations that we place on our partners to make us happy are just impossible and unsustainable.

A healthy couple is two individuals who already feel complete and who come together and mutually support and enhance each other, without the high levels of expectations that arise in couples where massive insecurities and unprocessed childhood wounds are present, which in my experience represent the largest of majorities.

Be assured, you are not a puzzle with pieces missing in the form of potential partners you have yet to meet, ready to make you whole again. This type of thinking is very disempowering, and points towards co-dependency, where an over-reliance on your partner to feel complete is not only demanded but non-negotiable as well. By promoting such beliefs, you are saying aloud: 'I am unable to function, be happy or feel complete without a partner at my side who can make all my pain and suffering go away.' Now, there are men or women out there who will play that role for you; in my experience, however, the sheer amount of emotional underpinning needed to maintain this unsustainable position quickly leads to resentment or exhaustion and often both.

Some men, much to their own detriment, may not say it aloud but are attracted to women who can be self-sufficient and happy with or without their partners around. Desperation and neediness are often the worst smelling perfumes and will undermine, not enhance, relationships.

Until you can generate genuine strength and happiness in yourself, then providing power and joy for another is impossible; your attempts will be transparent and without substance, and will leave both partners feeling empty. In contrast, if you are a person who is comfortable and confident in their own skin, a very different message is sent out... a message that states: 'I am in control of my emotions and my state of completeness. I do enjoy, and being in, enhancing relationships, but they don't define who I am.' The bottom line is this: we don't need completion; rather, we need others to enhance, enrich and complement who we are and the journey we are on.

FISH LOVE

The term 'fish love' went viral in 2017 when a Rabbi, named Abraham Tversky, spoke of the difference between unconditional love and selfish desire. He asked a young man: 'Why are you eating that fish?'

The young man replied: 'Because I love fish.' The Rabbi said: 'Oh. You love fish. That's why you took it out of the water, killed it, cooked it and ate it.' He went on to say: 'Don't tell me you love fish. You love yourself, and because the fish tastes good and makes you feel good, you killed it.'

So much of what is love is fish love. A couple falls in love. What does that mean? It means that he saw in this woman someone who he felt could provide him with all his physical and emotional needs, and she thought this man was somebody who would make her happy for the same reasons, but they are each looking out for their own needs. The other person becomes a vehicle for their personal gratification.

At this juncture, you may be thinking that I am against relationships and I am advocating that you are better off alone. If so, you are wrong. Relationships can be richly rewarding, but not when they are based on insecurities and emotional instability. Relationships built on flimsy foundations become wars of attrition and are anything but wholesome and fulfilling. For the record, any relationship can be testing, even the best, for that is how we grow, but let's not fool ourselves. A healthy dynamic is complementary, enhancing, and respectful.

Notice I used the word 'complement' and not 'complete', which many believe a significant other should bring – completion. As previously stated, to feel or need to be completed by someone else is a guaranteed recipe for disaster. Love complements those who already feel whole, yet those who are not are left continually seeking out validation from their partners. The romantic notion that another completes us is wonderfully poetic, but it's anything but.

The movie industry churns out the continual dross, promoting the notion we remain half a person until that special 'one' enters our lives and we become assimilated into a single being, existing solely for the other. The shelves are also full of books advocating the same co-dependent rhetoric... the music industry the same.

I am certain you have heard others talk about their partners and themselves as being two halves of a whole... about life feeling empty until Mr or Mrs Right appeared. It sounds wonderfully romantic, yet

I wonder if we believe this, or if we have simply bought into this idealistic fantasy shaped by a society that knows how we yearn to feel whole. There is nothing wrong or unnatural in feeling or wanting to feel whole. What we do to achieve it, however, is a different thing.

We do need each other collectively... we rarely thrive on extended separation. We are social creatures, metaphorically finding our homes in one another. It is human nature to spend time together. That may sound contradictory to the earlier message I attempted to convey, but bear with me.

The polarity between healthy interdependence and co-dependence cannot be measured. We flourish in healthy relationships, and that's why when we are alone for too long, we crave someone to share our hearts and experiences. Without others to inspire or bring out the best in us, we remain emotionally hungry and subdued.

In healthy relationships, we automatically feel happier – our vibration is raised and our well-being enhanced. I will concede that a moderate amount of struggling within the relationship dynamic could be considered healthy; it generates a tension, a resistance which facilitates emotional growth, the same way that working out creates physical resistance, which in turn creates a stronger physical body. How much struggling, of course, will be subjective, so careful consideration must be paid.

It is said that behind every good man there is a good woman, and that behind every good woman there is a good man. No argument there. But how many personal relationships are 'good'? It takes a lot of skill, determination, emotional intelligence and nurturing to build a partnership that meets the criterion of 'good'.

And this is where the rubber meets the road... Only a healthy, independent person, with heightened levels of self-esteem, can support mutual dependence. That's because only a mature, emotionally aware human being, who understands the need for healthy independence, can be dependable for another.

Why is interdependency so healthy? Well, paradoxically, interdependency requires a couple where each person is capable of sturdy independence and an ability to function autonomously of the other. It's marvellous for couples to love each other, to feel protected and to share intimacy while supporting one another and their needs. However, the power must be shared equally, and each half of the couple must take responsibility for their own feelings and actions within the relationship. When self-esteem levels are high, one manages thoughts and feelings without the desire to control others in order to feel good, safe or empowered.

Each respects the other's separateness without the need to inflict their will. Thus, they're not afraid to be honest, and can listen to their partner's feelings and needs without becoming reactive, dismissive or, worst of all, contemptuous. There's emotional maturity, giving rise to reciprocal respect and support while committed to the relationship, without possessiveness or ownership rights. They are both aware that two individual human beings can never be a singular entity, however dreamy that sounds to the needy ear or aching heart.

A healthy personal relationship consists of two unique individuals sharing innermost proximity, with an advanced level of intimacy over that of other relationships. When two whole beings come together, co-dependency does not exist, for they both led independent and satisfying lives before they met, and they would do so again if the journey were to end.

There can be no debate that the right partner adds a beautiful dimension, a complement to one's existence, but to expect another to complete you is to live in a dream world. A dream that turns quickly into a nightmare when the cold, hard truth dawns. Your partner cannot fulfil all your needs and is therefore going to disappoint you. And why will your partner disappoint you? Because they cannot enter your head and change how you feel about yourself and how you uniquely believe life should be, including the ideals you have created about your personal relationship.

Let me ask you a question: 'Would dating the perfect partner allow you to be happy?' Before you answer that, please allow me to ask you a further question: 'What creates your happiness?'

If you have been paying attention thus far to the content in this book, you will know that happiness is directly correlated to the quality of one's thoughts and the meaning we assign them. Our thoughts create our emotions, and therefore it's our thoughts and their interpretations that create happiness, misery, joy or suffering. And if that be the case, which it is, do you wrongly assume that the perfect partner is able to dispel all the negative thoughts and beliefs in your head, and has the power to transform all adverse thoughts you have about yourself into positive thoughts about yourself?

A loving supportive partner will certainly help you grow in confidence and give you a stronger platform to face those destructive thoughts and common patterns which have defined your life. But eradicate them? Not a chance. Nobody, other than you, can change the thoughts you have about yourself. You may have been told or invented an idea that a man or woman would enter your life and take away all the pain, self-doubts, worry and lack of self-love. That, however, is a cruel and deceptive narrative that modern society has told you.

Our feelings of shame or of being unlovable or just not good enough stem from deeply ingrained psychological programmes created in our formative years, specifically the years between birth and seven. And we must work hard to neutralise those emotional programmes by unhooking the automatic responses, initiated by events that remind us of the initial experiences that created them. Later on, I will outline exactly the process I use to achieve this.

You may believe that if you just found someone to truly love you and treat you accordingly, the feelings of shame and unworthiness should dissipate. But, no matter how much someone tells us or shows us, it's seldom enough to convince us that we are lovable and worthy unless we truly believe it about ourselves. No one except you has the power to eliminate all the negative thoughts about yourself, notably those which trigger strong emotional responses.

In my profession, I see a cross section of relationships extending across a diverse range of multicultural backgrounds, and rarely do

I recognise one that embraces the unconditional in equal parts. What I see are those who believe themselves to be in relationships which conform with the definition of unconditional, but often what they have in common is this: an attachment or an addiction to each other which, for the majority, tends to be unhealthy. Jealousy, possessiveness, anger, ownership rights, unreasonable demands, reduced freedoms... these are some of the more common emotional frailties that define the majority of relationships. Such qualities are believed to be entirely plausible by the protagonists and seen as acceptable. Most relationships work this way, and consider this state of affairs to be 'normal'. But, is it normal to suffer? In a world that verges on emotional insanity, the answer would be a resounding 'yes', but that reflects just how far we have veered off course.

The Indian mystic Krishnamurti had this to say about humanity: 'It is no measure of normality or sound emotional health to be well adjusted to an extremely sick society'. This sums up what is going on today as we promote insecurities and instability yet shy away from serenity and freedom of choice. And until we readdress the balance, emotional stability and sustainable contentment will be transitory.

A significant reason why so many people in our society are miserable and stressed is that they desire to control others but are unable to do so at a level which satisfies their insecurities.

Can you recognise that your needs, demands and desires are coming from a place that has little to do with the unconditional? If so, congratulations – the first step to change is awareness of the problem. Moreover, can you reduce the desire to control? Letting go of controlling others or outcomes beyond your influence are two of the most critical and hardest lessons you will ever learn in life.

Control, attachment and addiction are all about 'me' and what 'I' can get from the situation, event or others, and are entirely self-serving, as I described in more detail a little further back. 'If you give me this, I will love you.' 'If you treat me a certain way, I will love you more.' Yet statements like these have no business whatsoever being associated with love. I grant you, the emotions will be sweetened when your partner or life is following the rules you have decreed in order to be happy – that's a given.

But can you maintain that level of contentment when life throws you a curve ball or your partner is not dancing in tune with the song you are singing? We have all faced this dilemma. So, what sets us apart? How we deal with it, of course. Can you look with total honesty at your partner and your relationship and know where the deal breakers are? Once these deal breakers have been established, are you strong enough to walk away if they continually arise? Can you love yourself enough, or do you fear the unknown or being alone more than staying in a relationship that no longer works and one that makes you feel alone?

That is why the waiting rooms of the medical fraternity are full, and the relationship counsellors get ever busier. The psychologist's couches are worn out. We know something is very wrong and we need the advice of an expert to help us out.

How successful, statistically, would you say the marriages of relationship experts are? I will not bore you with stats, but can reliably inform you that the percentage of divorces among therapists, doctors and relationship councillors is higher than average. That is not to discourage you from looking for guidance or professional help when life has put you in a headlock. I share this to show you how we are all in this together... the messiness and difficulty of being a human being... the emotional hardships that can and do arise in personal relationships, regardless of how smart or well-trained one is in the art of human behaviour. Teaching it and doing it can be far apart, it would seem.

Healthy amounts of self-love and loving without conditions for most seems out of reach. To think of enjoying your partner without conditions appears alien in a world that demands you take what you need when you need it in order to feel safe.

So, how can 'unconditional' in relationship terms be best described? The Dalai Lama said that the best relationship is one in which your love for each other exceeds your need for each other. Dwell on that a while and notice what arises within you.

From this elevated perspective, you may become aware of the emotional frailties that accompany your unique conditioning and see them for what they are: malfunctioning programmes that need your careful attention. Both partners, of course, must understand the meaning of unconditional love for it to be healthy and productive, unless one of them is happy to love the other without conditions while not receiving the same in return. If you are content with this arrangement and it fashions no emotional disturbance, then knock yourselves out. But this is where radical honesty is essential.

If you are suffering and know the relationship is over, please, please love and respect yourself enough to walk away to continue your journey and to fulfil your God-given potential. So many of us leave this place without having made a difference. By embracing and sharing our gifts, we are honouring and giving thanks to the architect of the matrix for experiencing life as a human being. Next time, we may not be so lucky. Please see the difference between a relationship that enhances your life, and one that is damaging or holding you back. If your relationship is not helping you grow, I can assure you it's not the type of relationship you need to be in. We are not bad people for being in and remaining in toxic relationships for longer than we should. It takes time to recognise one's own self-worth. It's imperative to forgive our younger, more inexperienced selves for putting up with less than we deserve. But, now it's time to start loving and honouring who you are, totally aware of your value; this will allow you to walk away from anything and anyone who doesn't see it.

Unconditional love and freedom are intrinsically linked: unconditional love is absolute freedom, and for that love to be authentic, it must be free of possession. Watch how birds take to the sky; isn't it beautiful to see them glide, effortlessly overhead? But put these same birds in a cage, and they cease to be what you love about them; now that they have been incarcerated their freedom has been stolen and with it their spirit. Whether the cage is gold, encrusted with diamonds or the size of a football pitch, it matters not – it's still a cage, a restriction, a prison.

The same thing applies when flowers are picked from the garden or field, taken home and put in a vase; their freedom has been destroyed, their life force terminated and with it their wild nature. One moment, they are living free as creation intended; the next, they are uprooted and stuck in a jar for our selfish pleasures.

We may not realise it but we do the same to each other: we construct emotional cages, born out of insecurity, idealism, obsession and a variety of supplementary neuroses which we use to control and dictate, according to the terms and conditions we set. Such fragility we have... such fear. Crushing the spirit of the other, repressed by the weight of overbearing expectancy through lack of self-confidence.

The need to control others is one of the principal problems on the planet today, both on a macro level and on a micro level. Ironically, those who do not control themselves are the most prominent controllers of others. Their need for a positive reflection of self in others is the primary driver of the problem, which is based on fears – fears we conquer by managing our own emotions and feelings of self-worth while simultaneously giving others back, by extension, their freedom, their autonomy, their birthright.

Without healthy, emotional autonomy[6] life is a struggle, where your happiness continually hinges on the compliance of your partner (or partners) and how they treat or serve you at any given moment. If you recognise this pattern, also recognise the destructive nature of controlling or the need to control others. Human beings are hardwired to lean towards autonomy and freedom, and run from oppression, repressive regimes and dictatorial doctrines, which stifle freedom of choice.

Autonomy is the ability to make choices according to one's own free will. If we feel coerced by external pressures, our independence vanishes, and this is very important. As it happens, a lack of

---

[6] 'Emotional autonomy' is defined as a sense of individuation from parents and relinquishing dependence on them, and implies changing conceptions of the relationship with parents from childhood, through adolescence, to adulthood. Adults who have claustrophobic relationships with their parents and who have not developed emotional autonomy often project this neediness onto their partners until such time the damaging nature of the condition is realised.

autonomy, according to psychologists, may lie at the heart of a great deal of our unhappiness. That rang true for me when I first began to study emotional autonomy at the Institute of Counselling Psychology. I had often wondered why the feeling of being hurried or coerced created such resistance.

I never acted favourably when being forced to do things against my will or things which I felt impeded my free will – even things I would choose to do if I weren't being forced to do them. That may sound childish or selfish, but not so. Studies show that even the most fervent altruist will fail to produce good feelings when they are strong-armed or forced by others. That is damn important to understand, because the ramifications of oppressed autonomy can be catastrophic in relationships if not clearly understood.

Think a while and remember a time (or times) when your mood was negatively altered by demands put on you by your partner/parents/siblings or work colleagues. It matters not that the requests are healthy; if your reaction is one of continued resistance, you will have an active programme that responds negatively to compromised autonomy.

As previously stated, human beings are hardwired to resist threats to autonomy. The key is to know when the programme is triggered, take a breath and act accordingly. Recognising my need for autonomy has improved my relationships, as it helps me realise that when I have an adverse reaction which seems out of proportion, it often means my sense of independence has been compromised or, better expressed, my perception of it. Once I reframe the event and change that perception, the meaning changes, which generates different emotions and consequently a different outcome. I urge you to do the same. If you feel your emotions stirring in response to a request, then stop, breathe and recognise the automatic response pattern; identifying with it in this way will prevent you from saying or doing something unnecessarily detrimental.

Can you imagine how many relationships suffer or end because of the failure to understand autonomy and how it affects us? If we could recognise our response to a perceived obstacle to freedoms for what it is, we would be better able to act accordingly. We would realise the arising thoughts and responses are our problem and not anyone else's. From this lofty perspective, it's far easier to associate choices which align with our inherent need for autonomy alongside the requests of others, without losing our cool or perceived loss of freedoms.

Take, for example, your partner asking you to do something against your will or to do things that interfere with your schedule regularly. Assess how vital the relationship is to you, and whether you are unreasonable or too rigid. If, after deliberation, the relationship is worth it, you can reaffirm your autonomy by placing the relationship needs and the happiness it brings you ahead of the self-serving agenda, by willingly choosing to adhere to the requests of your lover. That is a win–win, as it affirms your need for autonomy while serving and upholding the needs of your partner. And let's be honest, as appealing as it is to do what you want on your terms, the relationship dynamic requires many sacrifices, from both parties, if you want the relationship to succeed.

You can and may say no, whenever you like – that is, and will always be, your choice. But know this: every action provokes a reaction, with consequences that arise from it. With that cautionary note in mind, you should be wary of playing perpetual hardball and begin to compromise a little more, especially if the relationship you are in is healthy.

IN A NUTSHELL

We work better in teams and are at our best in good company, but to expect another imperfect human being to be the provider of all things at all times for you to feel loved is not just unrealistic, it's impossible. We must do the work necessary to mend the childhood wounds we bear. If we don't, the pain and injuries of the past will continue to bleed all over our present lives and on those who didn't cut us.

REINVENTION

As human beings, we are capable of conscious and unconscious behaviour... of acts of kindness and cruelty... of productivity and non-productivity. I explained in a previous chapter how our conditioning is responsible for the way we show up in the world and the beliefs which drive our behaviour, which unless challenged remain unaltered. So, how do we develop and court emotions and behavioural traits that are more favourable not only to ourselves but to our collective human family?

Let me remind you that the human mind has on average between 12,000 and 60,000 thoughts per day, and that over 95% of them are the same thoughts as yesterday, the day before that, the week before that and on it goes. These are not random figures pulled out of the air for sensationalism: they are based on sound scientific research conducted in 2005 by the National Science Foundation, who published an article on the number of human thoughts per day. Furthermore, up to 80% of those thoughts were deemed negative.

As you can see, the collective mindset of humanity lends itself not only to repetitive thinking, but also to negative thinking. Breaking the habit of being oneself is therefore no mean feat; in fact, it can be very overwhelming when looking at it in its entirety. When we get strategic and break it down, however, things take on a different appearance. Instead of looking at the whole forest, let's start with one tree at a time. We cannot own this thing called 'life', but with care and attention we can start by owning the day and building positive momentum.

In the next section, we will look at what I call the 'seven virtues', a mind map of sorts that, if practised with consistency, will change your life.

The Seven Virtues

1. Align Your Words with Your Actions

We will do anything to uphold our perceived identity... the rules we live by... our values, beliefs and morals. The trouble starts when we are not congruent with whom we claim to be. It is emotionally disturbing when we know what we should do, yet do something else. Do you claim to love animals, for example, yet fail to practise vegetarianism? Do you claim to be reliable and efficient, yet cannot arrive on time for anything? Since we set these rules and values, sticking to them is vital; if we do so, we will be satisfied with our actions, without any regret. When we align our thoughts, words and actions, life becomes far more harmonious.

Remember, others are constantly watching and assessing who we are. By not aligning words and actions states clearly that we are not to be trusted or relied upon. Be passionate in your desire to change. Walk the walk if you talk the talk. We gain respect, not with words alone, but with actions that align with the language we use. Do you want more genuine respect? Then correlate your morals, words and actions.

Say something and stick to it, barring an emergency. It's by no coincidence that those who plan and execute on that plan are the pioneers and leaders, not just in the work space but also in life itself. Seeming to do, however pure the intention, is not doing. Our actions state with greater accuracy more about our future than words or promises ever can.

2. Follow Your Purpose

Spending time doing things without purpose will drain the very life force from you; hence the importance of engaging with purposeful intent. Purpose is the precursor of momentum. Momentum leads to enthusiasm. Enthusiasm leads to inspiration, and from there, anything is possible.

Accomplishment without fulfilment means one thing: failure. Read that again. Accomplishment without fulfilment equates to failure. Fulfilment comes from living a healthy and purposeful life, upholding values that supersede just selfish pleasures.

I know many multimillionaires, tycoons and captains of industry whose lined faces are etched with constant tension and disgruntlement. Money will not buy you happiness but living with purpose will. Take a closer look to see if how you live complies with your values and principles.

Often when considering whether our life is attuned to our personal values, we can spot conflict. Until we identify and remedy the disconnect, life will be average at best, and the average is not what we signed up for, or at least I hope not.

We each have something or many things to offer the world that will enhance and satisfy the undeniable need to contribute. It is essential that you figure out what your gifts are and share them generously. Here are some questions that may help you home in on your purpose:

- If money was no object and I knew I could not fail, what would I choose as a career?
- If I was going to die within a month, what would be my biggest regret?
- What would I like to have inscribed on my tombstone and have people say about me at my wake? ('Here lies Cathy, she loved the Kardashians'? Or 'Here lies Cathy, she made a difference and touched lives wherever she went'?)
- What can I do to make the world a better place?
- How can I contribute and serve others?
- Who am I when I feel most alive, most of use and most awake?
- When during the past 12 months did I feel most alive and invigorated? What was I doing and who was I being?

- What would I do if I didn't need to work?
- From my deepest understanding of love, what would I like others to receive from me?

By answering these questions, you will get some ideas of the core values which define you as a human being and therefore your purpose. From the answers gleaned, you should have a list of things which point the way towards a life of greater meaning. Spend some time with your list until a picture of how you want your life to be appears in your mind's eye, then set sail on a course of action that brings your purpose and life in accord with one another.

3. Be Thankful

The one emotion that enables us to get out of our heads is gratitude. This wisdom cannot be ignored. Zig Ziglar (November 6, 1926 – November 28, 2012), an American author and motivational speaker, stated: 'Gratitude is the healthiest of all human emotions. The more you express gratitude for what you have, the more likely you will have even more to express gratitude for.'

The simple act of saying thank you is transformative. We don't need the incredible, or the miraculous, not when we are genuinely grateful for what we have in the present moment. If I asked you to write a list of things to be grateful for right now, with imagination and clarity, the list would be longer than you think. Try it! Take a piece of paper and start writing all the things you can be grateful for.

There are hundreds of things to express gratitude for... the air you breathe... the food in the freezer... the water you drink... the comfortable mattress and bed sheets you sleep on... the AC on a hot summer's day... the money in your pocket and the shoes on your feet... the smile from a loved one... all green lights on the way to work... the plants, the trees, the rivers and the lakes... the birds, the bees, a good cup of coffee. Your gratitude list is limited only by your imagination. Gratitude lessens the weight of life while adding a dimension of majesty, and it allows us to discover serenity, even in moments of misfortune.

Now look at your list and say 'thank you', together with a smile, for each entry. I would be amazed if by doing this, a change in emotion and attitude has not taken place. Even when life is difficult, even when you have given your all, yet things still appear lousy, there will be things to be grateful for. Keep this gratitude list with you and read it whenever life is testing. The more often you read the list, the shorter time you will spend in emotional states that do not serve you, as the old patterns of negative thinking begin to dissolve. I have friends who make these gratitude lists and place them in highly visible places around the house, in the car or next to the pc or laptop at work, and swear it has made tangible differences to their lives. I suggest you do the same.

Practising gratitude can revolutionise your life. Every night before bed write down three things you can be grateful for. On awakening, grab your pen and paper and jot down three more. Every other day, return to your lists to remind you of the simple pleasures which bring joy and contentment to life, and continue to build upon a growing appreciation of what's good in your life. Remember to remain grateful for what you already have while pursuing a new direction. If you lack gratitude for what you already have, what makes you think you will be happy when you have more?

4. Be Positive

Even when things are terrible, even when you have given everything and still the pain remains, find the positive by asking yourself: 'What can I learn from this experience?' Every event is either a lesson or a blessing. However traumatic or painful, there is always a lesson we can learn and grow from. Physical, emotional or mental trauma are authentic experiences we all go through; how we respond to them, defines us as human beings. You cannot always control the events or circumstances, but you can choose how you want to acknowledge and give meaning to them.

If you live with a partner, you are still at home or you share your house with someone, the first thing you must do when entering your home is share something positive. I don't care what it is, the first words that come out of your mouth should be words of positivity in the form of the best thing that happened to you that day. Insist that your partner, family, housemate(s) or friends do the same. You will be surprised how this breaks the habitual need to moan and groan about life, as well as adding a completely new perspective to how you communicate and view the world.

5. Contribute

Here is a suggestion for those who have everything yet can't find peace or contentment: find a worthy cause and get involved, hands on. Contribution is one of the most powerful things we can do that empowers both yourself and those you contribute to.

Pick a problem and do your bit to make this world a better place. There are so many charities and worthy causes you can affiliate yourself with. Whatever you are passionate about can be edifying; for example, social policy, government corruption, sexual equality, the underprivileged, mental health care, violence in the home, animal cruelty. There are so many to choose from – pick one that resonates with you and commit at a level that makes a difference. You may not solve the world's problems alone, but you don't have to. Your contribution makes a difference, and making a difference contributes to improved well-being for all concerned.

When we contribute over and above that of serving ourselves, we meet one of the essential psychological needs that every human must satisfy daily in order to feel that their lives mean something.

Get your psychology right, and the world will be a better place. Get that psychology working for you, and, I assure you, the growth you are seeking will find you. Growth leads to progress, which primes your emotional state for greater contentment. Moreover, bonds made through contribution heighten the connection to others, which dissolves separation, a major cause of conflict across the planet.

Contribution is the surest way I know of growing spiritually and emotionally. Serving others, I guarantee you, will bring joy to your life. Reach out to friends and family or colleagues and ask if they need help with anything. How you wish to contribute, like gratitude, is only diminished by a lack of imagination or care. If you really want to grow, then a contribution is the vehicle to achieve it. Without contribution, growth comes very slowly, if at all.

6. Don't Compare

Comparison is a thief of joy and an act of violence against the self. When we compare, we fail to recognise our individual beauty, as we are too busy comparing ourselves to others. From cradle to grave, comparison is rife. We were taught as children to do so by our parents, who were taught the same way by their parents, and theirs before them, yet it doesn't serve you. Life stays a bittersweet affair if we continue to run comparison software. When we compare, the saplings of jealousy and envy are close to hand, neither of which produce healthy fruit.

Learn to run this race at your own pace. You are unique, like no other being ever created since the beginning of time. You really are incomparable to anything or anybody. Isn't it time you realised?

Comparison programmes uphold the illusion of separation, of superiority and inferiority. Neither are you superior nor inferior to anybody else. Furthermore, the comparative standards we use to compare our lives are based on illusion. Do you really believe that those you aspire to be like, on the basis of their social media accounts, are reflective of their authentic everyday lives? Not a chance! And by comparing ourselves to manufactured identities is massively unfair, because those standards we are trying to stack up against don't exist.

Be the best version you can be. Spending your life comparing health, wealth and aesthetics with the outside world will wear you out. Be better than the person you were yesterday; that is the only competition you need engage in. Jealousy, by comparison, is a poison that eradicates happiness and erodes self-esteem. Being the best person you can be, and appreciating what you do have going for you, will help you experience far more joy and happiness in everyday life.

7. Tell the Truth

Nothing liberates and clears the air like honesty. Telling the truth is not easy but has incredible power, and is a necessary component of a fulfilling life. It is helpful not only for the person who is telling the truth but also for the recipient of it.

Truthfulness clears the air, removes the bullshit and allows authenticity to flourish; without it, we remain bit-part actors performing on a stage. Lying or withholding the truth is always self-serving, manipulative and born out of fear. I encourage you to tell the truth, especially to your partner. By withholding, you are doing them an injustice, a chance to grow.

Telling the truth is one way of rebalancing the scales towards the positive. It takes less time to process the truth and speak it than to manufacture or deceive through lying. This extra clarity enables one to think more clearly, and less likely to be caught up in shenanigans of the mind, looking for the perceived right words to say, but not words that are truthful.

I have told many lies for many reasons: to swell my self-worth, to inflate my ego, to hide indiscretions, to gain an advantage, to manipulate. The list is endless. But, since embracing the truth, life has been so much smoother.

There will be an uncomfortable period as you transition from lying to telling the truth. Upsetting a few people is inevitable and goes with the territory, I'm afraid. But, be assured, you will quickly get used to it as the heavy burden of storytelling, exaggeration or outright deliberate lying departs and is replaced by genuine authenticity. You will look in the mirror and like what you see. You will lie in your bed at night with a clear conscience and a deep-felt contentment.

The truth fears no trial. Telling lies requires extra layers of thinking, whereas the facts can only ever be facts and need no fabrication. To fabricate takes effort, a wasted exertion. When we lie, we must remember what we told each person. We must think about what the different reactions might be... from there, we start manipulating information to control the outcome. The truth, on the other hand, requires no forced effort.

Stop lying to yourself and others, and see how liberating it can be to tell the truth. Start by sharing things with your partner that you would usually withhold; this may be a little intense at first, but I guarantee you that the more you practise an honest approach to life, the greater the increase in levels of intimacy.

It is possible that you may lose a few so-called 'friends', but those who don't run from you will be the ones who love and respect you for who you are, rather than for any number of false archetypes previously created. Try it and see for yourself.

A Map for Mastering the Body

Now that we have a map for mastering the mind to practise and follow, we need a map for the body. Most people believe that the mind governs the body with instructions and the body obeys and performs accordingly, but that's not entirely true. The body responds in the same way to habitual behaviour as the mind; in fact, the body, through excessive repetition, knows how to do something better than the mind.

Think about it. When you wake up, the first thing you do is grab your phone and either turn the alarm off or immediately check your social media content. Is that a mental action or a physical action? I will wager that your phone sits in the same position on the same side of the bed and goes off at the same time every day. You will reach for it without thinking from your side of the bed and perform the same routine day in, day out.

Both your body and your mind have become so accustomed to this ritual it has become a hardwired autonomous response. It is these responses and daily routines which have imprisoned you, and breaking out of this prison is a must. Keep doing what you have always done, and you will get what you have always got. To build on and illustrate further how the body and mind are slaves to ritualistic behaviour, let's look at a typical day and see how this may be working against you.

You wake up at the same time, to the same alarm tone on the same side of the bed, thinking the same thoughts you did yesterday, the day before and the day before that – right? You check your phone for social media interaction or emails before getting up to visit the bathroom.

You take a shower for the same length of time, using the same products. You brush your teeth the same way, look in the mirror the same way and head to the kitchen for your preferred drink of choice. Breakfast, if you take it, will be a combination of your usual foodstuffs as you watch or listen to the gloom and doom being piped into your home, courtesy of media companies that promote a specific agenda.

You drive to work the same way, in the same car, arrive at the office at the same time and interact with your colleagues the same way. You think more or less the same things, and therefore arrive at more or less the same conclusions. You eat or take a break at the same time and share conversations of a similar ilk with the same people. You check your social media accounts and allow certain events or circumstances to push your buttons, as they always have, yet you continue to do it.

Finally, you take the same route home, then do the same things until it's time to go to bed, which may or may not include working out, Skype calls, more work and social chatting.

Now, look again at the itinerary above: it will not be your exact routine, but for many, semantics aside, it will be close. So, I ask you: if you continue to ponder on and do the same things, driven by the same emotions, which produce the same outcomes, how are you ever going to change? This question of course is rhetorical – you cannot. You have hardwired the brain and body to think, act and feel in such a specific manner that it runs autonomously.

You know that change is necessary, yet you continue to think, act and perform in the same way – true? How are you ever going to change your circumstances if life is embodied by routines that do not support change?

The way to break the habitual chain is to change as many things as possible with regard to how you lead your life. Reinvention starts from the moment you open your eyes tomorrow morning. So, today, I want that you grab a pen and notepad, sit down somewhere quiet and think of the customs or behavioural traits that need attention.

Any non-enhancing habits need immediate attention. These include conversations and with whom, the places you regularly visit, the people you hang out with, repetitive thought processes, the food that you eat, what you drink and what material you read, watch or listen to, and even what time you go to bed. Once you have established a list of recognisable behaviours and habits, it is time to get creative.

Now is the time to change that daily routine and give the brain something new to ponder... additional information to chew on... fresh experiences, new thought patterns and different hobbies. The new experiences will lead to new emotions, which, if practised with enough repetition, will become new habits.

Below is a sample routine I have used – you are welcome to try it. Feel free to play around with the different elements of this schedule, but try to change as many things as possible from your own everyday agenda.

Keep a Journal

Buy a small diary or a daily journal and keep it with you at all times. I keep mine next to my bed when I sleep, so it's instantly available on awakening. I encourage you to keep a small journal with you always, the reason being that goals and aspirations written down have a far greater meaning than those just thought about.

Studies have shown that specific types of journaling have been shown to increase happiness after just one week. One particular example is to keep a gratitude journal and write down what you are grateful for every day. Another is to reflect on a positive experience that day.

Wake Up Earlier

Set your alarm for one hour earlier than usual; it will be a tad uncomfortable initially, but you will thank me for it soon enough. Waking up earlier is already an accomplishment in itself! It gives a sense of achievement, progress[7] and satisfaction, which is damn important when trying to rewire the brain by breaking old habits.

Keep Electronic Devices Well Away from the Bed

Leave the phone at least 2 metres from the bed, with Wi-Fi and Bluetooth switched off and airplane mode on if you need it for an alarm. Better still, get a cheap alarm clock and leave the phone out of the bedroom altogether.

---

[7] The brain associates progress with achievement and lights up the area associated with it. The brain then releases feel-good hormones, namely dopamine, which makes us feel happy and content.

Electromagnetic field (EMFs) from mobile phones and laptops are powerful transmitters of radiation which affect the quality of one's sleep.[8] No matter what you do, or what is happening in your life, sleep *is* important, so leave devices which emit false light out of the bedroom.

It is much better to read something which doesn't stimulate the nervous system, using a reading lamp behind you that you can switch off easily as your eyes begin to drop. Even better still, get a cheap book light which attaches to the book for reading in bed.

On Awakening...

When your alarm goes off an hour earlier, do not snooze or reach for the phone or laptop. Take three slow and deliberate deep breaths, followed by a genuine expression of appreciation. You made it through the night, when 140,000 people did not.

I know I have mentioned this previously, but it's so important it needs repeating. Before leaving the bedroom, think of three things to be grateful for and write them down in your daily journal... your health which is priceless, the bed that cradles you, the sheets that keep you warm, the blinds that keep the light out, the heating system that keeps the house welcoming, the roof over your head that keeps the rain out, the water in your fridge or the food in the cupboards, your children, family and friends, your car, your clothes, your choices!!!

Gratitude, like all emotions is a positive mindset we cultivate by directing our focus in a specific direction. The more we practise gratitude, the more grateful we become.

---

[8] A study conducted by the Department of Electrical and Electronic Engineering at the University of Melbourne showed that EMFs impede the body's production of melatonin, a hormone that regulates sleep and wakefulness. Interestingly, this happens because the pineal gland (where the melatonin is produced) senses the EMFs as light, and therefore slows the melatonin production. The symptoms of EMF exposure are: sleep disturbances (including insomnia), headaches, depression and depressive symptoms, tiredness and fatigue, dysesthesia (a painful, often itchy sensation), lack of concentration, changes in memory, and dizziness.

Meditate or Pray

Finding time for either or both of these activities is vitally important. We must find time to slow down and control our stress hormones. Our brains are always working, often far too hard, causing stress and anxiety. Meditation and prayer help to calm down your system and put you in a peaceful state of mind. I will be expanding on the absolute necessity for meditation and prayer in our lives as I continue.

Sit up straight, with the spine erect, close your eyes and meditate or pray (or do both) for just 10 minutes. For those who claim they have not got time, if you haven't got 10 minutes, then you don't have a life. Use this time for expressing gratitude to something greater than yourself, for the miraculous gift of life... to God, the universe, the stillness, or however you wish to give thanks.

Journaling and Visualising

Now use the next 10 minutes journaling and visualising how you want your life to be and how you can actively achieve the goals that will get you there. Start easy by planning for the day ahead; then, as you get better at not only writing down your goals but also sticking to them, create longer-term goals and spend some time each morning visualising the successful conclusion of those dreams. Visualising is so important that I have dedicated a whole chapter to it a little later.

Move That Body

Remember, we are energetic beings that vibrate at different frequencies, and vibration needs movement. The more we move, the higher the frequency at which our bodies vibrate, and the better we feel. After writing your gratitude list, get out of bed and move: run on the spot, do some stretches or, better still, dance. Put on some upbeat music, close your eyes, feel the rhythm and move for at least 10 minutes.

Science has shown that changing the physiology in the body through exercise directly affects the brain in a positive manner. Further studies have revealed that those who exercise first thing in the morning are more likely to do it regularly than those who schedule exercise later in the day; this is because our daily activities often run late, eating into exercise time.

As you become more accustomed to exercising, feel free to get out in the fresh air and enjoy some walking, running or cycling. Alternatively, join a gym and bloody use it! I know it is hard to get out of bed early at times, but make the effort. By the time others wake up, the adrenaline, endorphins and serotonin in your system are creating a joyful experience.

The morning is so important for priming oneself for the day ahead. Do you want the day to be great? Then, you must start it in a positive way. Granted, some days, regardless of what we do, are difficult. But be assured: giving the body a boost of feel-good hormones will enhance your emotional state, which helps tremendously when coping with the trials and tribulations that life affords us. A problem faced when you are emotionally enhanced carries far less intensity or worry than the same problem experienced with poor emotions.

Take a Cold Shower

Yes, that's right, a cold shower. We are used to our warm showers, but if you want that body to vibrate at a higher frequency, turn that shower control to real cold for at least five minutes for maximum benefits. Among other things, a cold shower improves immunity and circulation, promotes better alertness, stimulates weight loss, aids in muscle soreness and recovery, and eases stress. But, most importantly, it combats depressive feelings as a result of the impact of cold receptors in the skin, which send copious numbers of electrical impulses from the peripheral nerve endings to the brain.

Thus, a cold shower produces an antidepressant effect, boosting your mood. Start by turning the temperature down at the end of your warm shower if it's too shocking to start with cold water, but continue to reduce the warm water and increase the cold exposure until the whole time is spent under a cold shower. Cold water has a potent anti-inflammatory effect, and inflammation is one of the major causes of diseases that we humans do battle with.

Once comfortable with a cold shower, graduate to a cold bath as often as needed – 10 minutes minimum and the colder the better. What I do is get out of an ice bath after 10 minutes and immediately do some press-ups or free-standing squats, or simply run on the spot. Try it for yourself and if you don't feel invigorated afterwards, check your pulse for signs of life.

Breakfast

Start with a large glass of water or two as you prepare for breakfast. Pay attention to how much quality water you drink each day; I recommend up to three litres, but no less than two, per day in order to aid your body in flushing out toxins. I like to add cider vinegar, a small spoon of bicarbonate of soda and lemon to my water for an extra boost to deal with the pollutants which impact upon our physical and emotional health and affect our energy.

Eat nutritious and life-enhancing foods that vibrate at high frequencies. Leafy green vegetables – especially kale, watercress, spinach and broccoli for example – are high-frequency foods. Certain fruits – such as blueberries, blackberries and apricots – are also high-frequency foods. Get creative and blend a smoothie with all of the above for a wonderful way to start the day Be mindful of how many calories you ingest in any given meal or drink. Don't overload the system: two or three regular meals throughout the day are better for you than one huge dinner when you get in from work.

Breakfast cereals, fruit juices, white breads, pastries, fast convenient foods, fizzy drinks and anything with artificial sweeteners may taste good, but the majority are toxic, full of fast-acting sugars that overstress the pancreas and have zero vibrational frequency. If you can afford to eat organic, then do so, as pesticide-treated and genetically modified foods or foods wrapped in plastic have little or no goodness.

Pay attention to how food appears to you. I know which foods are right for me by how they look and how they make me feel. We all have an inherent intelligence that alerts us to what serves us and to that which does not. So, pay close attention and eat and drink more of what aligns on the basis of that principle.

This is not a nutrition book, so I won't overly lecture you on what to eat or when to eat it. Some people prefer to skip breakfast and have lunch as their first meal. What I will tell you, and I hope you pay attention, is that the food and liquids you consume become you, so choose wisely. We live in an age where information is readily available; therefore, if you are eating and drinking poorly, that is your choice and your choices produce consequences.

Think of your body as a highly tuned piece of priceless engineering, for that is what it is – a billion-dollar super computer. Like any vehicle, the better we look after it, the better it will serve us. A Ferrari, for example, is an expensive car; if you fail to service it regularly or you put the wrong fuel in it, before long it will begin to break down and not perform the way it was designed. But if you respect it, use high octane fuel and service it when applicable, this beautiful car will give you immense pleasure and reliability, as will your body if you treat it with the same care and attention. This metaphor is clear: feed your body with the right nutrients, service it regularly with exercise and it will perform at optimum levels, and like the car it will give you a lifetime of fun and excitement, allowing you to enjoy to the maximum what life has to offer. So, treat your body lovingly and make it your best friend.

The Commute

The total time for completing the above routine is less than 50 minutes, hence the necessity to wake an hour earlier than usual. With breakfast out of the way, you are now ready to leave the house if you commute to work, or you are prepared for facing the day at your laptop etc. if you work from home.

Driving or commuting to work is a drag for most people who I speak to, but it doesn't need to be so. For some unknown reason, the moment we get in our cars and start that familiar journey to work, the combative part of who we are comes alive. Honking the horn, giving people the finger, miming rude words to other drivers who have pissed you off, tailgating, slowing down to irritate those trying to get past, full-blown shouting matches with windows down with equally angry commuters... the list is endless, and it's barely 8 am. Road rage – we have all had it or been the recipient of it, but either way, it's a waste of bloody time and does your body and mind no good whatsoever. Isn't it time you realised and addressed this?

Of course, not everyone is a middle-finger-flipping foul-mouthed hooligan on their daily commute, but I would wager that there are far better ways to be spending that time than are currently employed. How often do we get to be with ourselves in a fast-moving and demanding world? Perhaps the daily drive into and out of work could well be it? Why not utilise this precious time to broaden your knowledge or practise some kind of mindfulness?

Time is so damn precious, yet we seldom appreciate it until it's too late. Why would we wish time away like we do when saying things such as: 'I can't wait for the day to end so I can do X, Y or Z' or 'I can't wait until next month so I can go on holiday' or words to that effect. Unless you are in considerable pain right now which might be alleviated by time, what you are doing is wishing your life away. Is it really that painful? Isn't it better to be productive with what little time we have to ourselves? I learnt to love spending time in the car for the reasons outlined above – precious time alone, which I used to further my personal development.

You can continue to waste valuable time, or you can use it to expand your awareness, your knowledge and your mindfulness. Allow me to explain. Let's start with awareness and how to improve upon it. Most of us, when focusing on anything, tend to zoom in intently on what's immediately in front of us; we tend to have little or no awareness and ignore what is happening around us. This is called our 'foveal vision', which means focusing on something where the line of sight is a virtual line in front of us.

You may have heard the term 'tunnel vision', as in 'he or she has tunnel vision' to describe someone totally transfixed on something or other. 'Foveal vision' is the fancy term for tunnel vision, and it doesn't always serve us. As the name suggests, entering into a tunnelled state indicates becoming fixated or obsessed, where we become preoccupied and lose context, and with it the stimulation of the central nervous system. Once the central nervous system has been activated, we experience all the effects of excitatory hormones, such as adrenaline and other stress hormones. From here, it doesn't take much for the fuse to be lit, and before you know it you are wound up like a clockwork mouse on amphetamines, awaiting the slightest of aggravation to justify your state of arousal.

Now, the way to avoid this when driving, or in fact in any situation, is to take advantage of a different type of focus, called 'peripheral vision', which means, in simple terms, paying attention to what's happening at the edges of your field of view. For example, lift your arms to the sides at a right angle while looking straight ahead; you may or may not be aware in your peripheral sight of the presence of your hands. Now wiggle your fingers; I am sure that now you can see them moving. Start to take in as much detail as possible of your surroundings by keeping your head straight and looking forwards but with a far softer gaze, allowing more information to enter your awareness through the eyes. Practise this wherever you are and take in as much information as possible. This state has been practised by some of the most ancient cultures to accelerate learning through altered states of consciousness, in order to combat anxiety and stress and to induce calm.

Try it now for yourself while simultaneously breathing slowly and deeply, and really pay attention to what you become aware of. Look directly ahead and slightly up, and fix your eyes on a specific spot, concentrating your point of focus for 10 seconds. Now relax your gaze, bring your eyes back to parallel and engage your peripheral vision and notice everything. Heighten all your senses: the sounds, the smells, the things you touch... everything. That feeling you are now experiencing is mindfulness. Feels good, doesn't it?

The next time you get in the car, do what you have to do for the first few minutes, and then drop into the peripheral vision and start breathing and performing the exercise as explained. And no, it's not dangerous; on the contrary, your senses are heightened. You will see and be aware of far more: children walking between parked cars, animals crossing the road, etc. You can avoid dangerous drivers far more quickly, all the while feeling relaxed and peaceful. Start with 10 minutes each day alongside the slow and deep breathing, and enjoy this state of enhanced mindfulness. Let your mind relax, free from the stresses of other drivers who don't know what you know. Be kind to yourself and don't strain or worry if after a few minutes concentrating this way becomes difficult. It's ok... you are human, and this type of mindfulness, like all practices, must be harnessed through repetition.

What I don't want you to do is fall into the old routine of reacting to the commute as you usually would. There are many ways to further your learning and enhance your time while driving. You have the local radio stations or your favourite recording artists to listen or sing along to, which is a far superior option to shouting obscenities or bemoaning the traffic lights which don't care about your complaining or have any idea that you exist at all. But something far more beneficial and educational is available to you – something that can take your life to the next level.

Road School

I know for many of you the word 'school' conjures up images of tyrannical teachers, playground bullies, dreadful school dinners and a place you had to be rather than wanted to be. But that was then, and this is now. You are no longer an obedient child. Now you get to choose the topics and subject matter that garner your interest.

Think of the car as your very own classroom, with the world's best teachers sitting beside you. Every journey is an opportunity to sit with the game changers – those who have what you want and, moreover, the knowledge required for you to have the same.

Audiobooks, podcasts, YouTube tutorials... Ted talks... The world's best artists, authors, motivational speakers and pioneers of change. These are all available to you with the slightest of index finger pressure on your touchscreen phone. What an incredible time to be alive, when we can access this level of information at will, with the majority of it being free of charge.

But why would you listen to what Donald Trump is doing at Kim Jong Il's birthday bash? Or listen to the details of the scandal that has arisen from his latest twitter rant? How much joy and happiness will you feel knowing that Iran is the next country earmarked for democracy by the Western coalition, or that Hilary Clinton takes medication for a balance problem and wears a wig?

Think about it. Do you want to learn a new language? Then start in your car today. Fancy spending half an hour getting up close and personal with the world's best self-help gurus and motivational speakers, or listening to how Oprah Winfrey took over the world from her very humble roots and troubled childhood? They are all just the press of a finger away. You really are only curtailed by your own imagination. Write down a list of the people in the world you respect, who make you laugh, who can teach you cool stuff. Then see if they do a podcast or have material you can listen to.

Alternatively, immerse yourself in the doom and gloom of world news, deliberately designed to confuse and frighten you, which produces stress hormones in your body, such as cortisol and adrenaline. If you think I am scaremongering and a paid-up member of the tinfoil-hat-wearing conspiracy theorists brigade, then think again.

The world news is a blanket of fear-induced disasters that are over and done with, ongoing or soon to happen. In fact, journalists are told to locate and exaggerate the most-stress-releasing stories imaginable. There are thousands of journalists out there competing with each other, trying their hardest to produce the most sensational and hard-hitting pieces of news that will grab the attention of an already stressed-out public.

In a world where billions of perpetual smartphone users have become war correspondents and political analysts, we have become paranoid, glum, fearful and insecure, which brings me back to stress hormones and their effects. Science has known forever that a raised cortisol level hinders learning and memory, lowers immune system function, plays a significant role in body weight increase, plays havoc with blood pressure, increases cholesterol, contributes to heart disease, and much, much more. Prolonged stress and elevated cortisol levels are also linked to depression, mental illness and lower life expectancy.

Stress hormones are released by the adrenal glands in response to worry, either real or perceived, as part of the fight-or-flight mechanism, which I spoke of earlier. Once this reaction is triggered, the body is mobilised and ready for battle; without the necessary release through fighting or running away, high levels of stress hormones build up in the system, wreaking havoc on the mind and body.

Most of us have heard of 'fight or flight', but there is a third component in the equation, called the 'freeze response'; this is where we become paralysed in response to fearful stimuli. Sitting in our cars listening to stories of woe, gore and tragedy, we have no way to move those stress hormones around or out of the body, and hence they are stored in the cells.

And here it becomes interesting. The neural pathways in the brain have become so profoundly efficient at recognising incoming stress that it takes less and less stress to trigger a harmful response. Think about that and the implications for your mental and physical health through repeatedly tuning in to stress-inducing stories or watching or reading anything that induces fear, anxiety, anger or apprehension.

I could go on, but I am hoping by now, you have got the message.

If you do choose to continue to watch, listen and indulge yourself with stress and cortisol-releasing stories, events and circumstances, then please be sure to perform some mild exercise for 20 minutes as close to the event as possible. That way, you will at least burn up the cortisol and adrenaline and minimise the damage to your system. So, what's it going to be? The intense and stress-inducing journey to work? Or some mindful expanded vision work and a healthy dose of inspirational and life-changing directive from those who are maybe where you would like to be?

The law of attraction, which I explain in the next chapter, states: what we focus on, we tend to attract by way of a vibratory signature. In my world, if you focus on the murkier side of life, fear-inducing news stories or anything that creates strong negativity, then circumstances, events and people which share that particular frequency band and vibratory signature are going to show up in your life.

Do you want to know the world's best kept secret? Something that the greatest scholars have finally realised, when trying to figure out what sets the happy apart from the unhappy? Positive and happy people do more of what makes them happy on a daily basis, whereas sad, negative and fearful people focus on things which sustain that particular narrative. Profound, I know, and worthy of deeper exploration, which I will get to in due course.

My advice is to think carefully and use your time as productively as possible. Which brings me back to the underlying equation and message of the book: choices and consequences – whatever you choose to do, know that corresponding consequences are sure to follow.

IN A NUTSHELL

From where I am sitting it would appear a no brainer, but perhaps we don't value time the same way? Time, for me at least, as previously stated, is a precious commodity and one that I don't get back at any price, so I guard it well. I can't make you do anything you don't care for. However, if you are fed up with arriving at work already stressed out, then you know what to do, starting with the journey home.

REFRAMING

———— ◆●◆ ————

*If a problem can't be solved within the frame
it was conceived, the solution lies in reframing
the problem.*

E arlier, I mentioned the importance of emotions and the role
they play in our physical and emotional health. I explained
how they teach us to pay attention by offering ongoing information correlated to our thoughts and actions. If listened to carefully
and acted upon, they become our own internal doctor, on hand to
give us feedback on the choices and decisions we have made.

With that in mind, for the rest of your day and every day that follows, I want you to pay close attention to how you react and respond
to external events, other people and various circumstances. Become
curious about the emotions that arise and the triggers that initiate
them. Log these in your journal as you go about your day, and use your
coffee breaks or quiet time to go over them and try to spot recurring
patterns. Get strategic and enjoy this new role of existential detective, where the clues to your betterment need acknowledging before
any chance of solving the case is possible.

What emotions are regularly triggered? Anger, resentment, jealousy, rage, bitterness, anxiety, judgement, a lack of worthiness? Keep
in mind that repetitive feelings want your attention – that is their
purpose. As the senior detective helping out with this case, I must be
clear: it is not the people, events or circumstances which are guilty of

inducing the emotions and feelings within you, but the meanings you assign to them. The sentient genius behind the ongoing case we call 'in search of evolvement' decreed that the one place we rarely look for the answers to the riddles presented is found inside of us, and that is the puzzle this genius wants us to figure out if we're ever going to solve the mystery.

Emotions that continue to crop up are those we need to pay close attention to. If we are continually angry or react with anger to the usual stimuli, then know this: it is not the person, event or circumstance we must concentrate on, but the anger itself. In simple terms, we have an anger issue that warrants further consideration, and if ignored, nothing will change.

This applies not just to anger but also to all recurring emotions. The triggers, therefore, become our best teacher if we are able to learn the apparent lesson contained within the experience, reframe the event and unhook the negative charge. Sounds great, right? But how can we do this? To be honest, there are many modalities used in client sessions that can yield positive results. Details of one technique that I used recently are outlined below.

GETTING STRATEGIC

All emotions were created at some point in our distant past as a reaction to an event; that emotion was positive, neutral or negative, depending – of course – on the meaning we assigned to it at the moment of inception. It only takes the experience to be repeated three or four times for a personal generalisation to become a fact.

In the case of extreme trauma, where the event is massively intense, a belief can be hardwired in an instant and, unless reframed and better understood, it will continue to trigger the same automatic response every time a reminder of the event is present. I spend most of my time with clients doing precisely that – locating past events and neutralising the charge attached to them, so that when unhooked, the clients will no longer react as they have done their whole lives. The memory and the event remain intact, but through a better understanding and a positive reframing of the old story, decisive new learnings are recognised, and hence an emotional release from the original event ensues.

To give you an example of how this works, a client came to me with a recurring issue which she believed was triggered by external circumstances at any given time. In simple terms, she blamed everything and anyone for her reactions and had not looked inside herself to find the solutions. We started the session with a general chat to build rapport between us; this is a very important part of any therapeutic process because it builds confidence and trust. As the client spoke, I would note and write down any limiting beliefs, feelings and emotions that didn't fully support her. I noticed a few things and asked her to focus on an area in her life where she felt dissatisfied.

I continued by asking her to notice her inability to manifest what she wanted in life and what emotions arose when thinking about it. Frustration and anger were her reply, and she added that she could feel them in her throat and chest as she thought about it. I asked her which emotion was the strongest of the two. Anger, she replied. I then proceeded to ask her if the feeling of anger had a size, shape or colour. The unconscious mind thinks in pictures, feelings and emotions and it's the unconscious mind where the deep-rooted psychological programmes are created and therefore must be accessed in order to reprogramme them. By asking her this question, I encouraged her to see an internal representation of what was bothering her. Her answer was a large black jagged object swirling around in her stomach.

I asked her: 'Was it solid or hollow, cold or warm?' She replied: 'It was solid and hot.'

I then asked her to notice the sensation inside the black jagged object. Her answer came back: 'Its raging; like a Tasmanian devil!'

Rage is the most aggressive form of anger and hence I was not surprised why this woman had reacted and suffered as she did.

Now that I had her internal picture, and she was having an authentic experience of it, I asked her to drift back in time – to go as far back into her childhood past as she could remember, between the ages of one and eight, and find an event which replicated how she felt. She closed her eyes and began to travel back in time until she happened upon an event she had entirely forgotten until now.

I asked her where she was and with whom. She replied: 'With my mother and older brother in a shoe shop. I'm seven and he's ten.' I asked: 'Is there something not happening that you want, or something you don't want to happen, that is?' My client replied: 'I wanted a pair of school shoes that my cousin had, but my mum said they were too expensive, and I couldn't have them. I remember crying and saying please, but mum was adamant and gave me another, cheaper, pair to try on. To make matters worse, my brother was laughing at the shoes I had on, and although mum told him to stop it, she had a smirk on her face. I was so angry and frustrated, but worse than that, I felt I wasn't good enough, and certainly not as good as my cousin.' 'I remember,' she continued, 'thinking that my mother didn't love me enough to buy me those shoes and that their laughing at me completely negated how I felt.'

I asked her what limiting belief was created at that very moment, an idea that still holds true today. Her answer was: 'I'm not good enough. People are always laughing and making fun of me, and I don't deserve the best of anything!' A secondary thought was: 'If I don't get my way, I become angry and aggressive.'

She was crying at this point, but they were not tears of sadness or anger, but tears of awareness – a relief of sorts, but we were not finished yet. I asked her to centre herself with a few deep breaths as I invited her to imagine going back in time to meet her seven-year-old inner child and to have a chat. What wisdom could she impart? What knowledge had she learnt on her journey from that incident with the shoes to now? What could she say to help her better understand that it wasn't personal and that these feelings were created on the back of an experience that seemed cruel and unfair and how that made her feel about herself?

I gave her a framework to guide her. I suggested that perhaps the scars from this past event were the reason for the compassion and tolerance she offers her own daughters. I instructed her to tell her seven-year-old self all the things she would tell her own daughter of five, faced with the same situation. She was silent for a while and then began addressing her seven-year-old self:

'It's ok, you were and are totally loved.'
'Mum and dad always did the best they could with the resources available.'
'Money was a lot tighter in our house than in your cousins.'
'What you wear on your feet has nothing to do with who you are as a person.'
'If people laugh at you, it's because they are hiding their own insecurities and it has nothing to do with your self-worth.'
'You are supported entirely and loved unconditionally by your father and me.'
'I will never abandon you, nor reject you.'
'You are safe, seen and recognised at all times.'
'I've got you.'

She then stopped and said nothing else was coming up, so I encouraged her while her eyes were still closed to forgive her mum and anyone else for her pain, and to let go of any lingering resentment she had left in her body. This was an emotional process and one that was deep and involved, with lots of dialogue with me playing the part of her mother. Role playing is an excellent procedure for letting clients see themselves in action and helps them establish and assimilate powerful insights achieved in the exchange.

We moved on to the final part of the procedure by my telling her to come out of the past and into the future, where she was now a

75-year-old woman, full of experience, knowledge and wisdom. I asked her: 'What type of advice would you give to the person you are today about this anger and rage that has plagued your life, through the eyes of this sage and calm woman? See yourself sitting in a comfy chair opposite who you are today, where the two of you can have a chat.'

Ask her what advice she has for you and what she needs to know about life that has evaded her thus far, from the perspective of her 75-year-old self. Again, there was a pause before my client began to recite the vast amount of words from her wise and informed elder self, which left me shocked. One never knows how much content will arise, but this was a real surprise and totally unexpected:

- Self-love is the most important love of all.
- Tell your children you love them daily and that love is unconditional.
- Kindness and compassion to yourself and to others will set you free.
- The idea of separation is a myth. We are all one family.
- External validation, although comforting, is not as important as the love and validation you give to yourself.
- Your worthiness is not based on what you wear or the car you drive or the home you live in.
- Be patient with life because it's going to test you endlessly.
- Life is both beautiful and chaotic and to understand this is to appreciate it.
- Life is very short and not to be wasted hung up on the opinions and actions of others, so use your time more productively.
- Take care of your loved ones and those who love you.
- Set yourself higher objectives.
- Take more risks.
- Stay healthy and respect your body.
- Enjoy yourself whenever possible.
- Make the most of what life has to offer.

- Choose to feel more relaxed and confident.
- Aim to make better decisions.
- Trust yourself and don't worry too much about the future and enjoy the present moment more.
- Have a healthier relationship with money. Cover all your needs and your loved ones', and what is left is a bonus.
- Enjoy your parents while you can.
- Engage and appreciate your siblings while you can.
- Impact more people through greater contribution, and leave a positive impact on the world.
- Relax more, enjoy the journey, savour every experience and take yourself less seriously, because nobody is getting out of this thing called 'life' alive.

At this point, we both started laughing, which was ideal because I needed her to break the trance-like state she was in to finish the session. Once she had stopped laughing, I asked her to be aware of where she was and take a moment to reflect on what was felt, what she had learnt and how to apply it to her life today, as well as on what actions she might take and how she may think differently about things.

To say she was relieved was an understatement. The lightness of her body language and the air of contentment in her face reminded me why I do this work. To facilitate and guide another human being towards more peace and understanding is a beautiful gift, and I thank the creator for blessing me with these abilities to help others.

Recognition of past events and an understanding of the intention behind them are critical when attempting to move beyond limiting beliefs and repetitive emotional patterns which hold us in captivity. Once the events and the emotions have been identified, a healthy reframing can be applied. This reframing alters the perspective from which the client previously experienced the event, and they are now able to see it through the eyes of an adult and not the eyes of a child. If we change the perspective, we reverse the meaning. Change the meaning, and the emotional reaction changes. Change the emotions, and the feelings change, and voila, the old charge has gone and no longer triggered as it has been since the event happened way back in early childhood.

Is reframing always a success? Does every client get full relief from this healing modality? No, is the honest answer to both. The sheer diversity of human nature and the character traits contained within that diversity guarantee a certain failure rate. There are also other factors at play here; a secondary gain, for example, where the client wishes to hold on to their predicament, can be a roadblock to any progress. 'Secondary gain' is where a negative or problematic behaviour actually provides a positive or beneficial end result in some way. For example, smoking may help a person to relax or interact socially with a group of friends who meet up regularly for a glass of wine and a chat. The post-double-espresso cigarette sitting outside a favourite coffee shop in the sun with your buddies is another powerful ritual that sabotages the good intentions of the wannabe non-smoker. And it's not just cigarettes.

A person who gets the recognition they crave when unwell has a vested interest in holding on to whatever facilitates the attention needed to feel wanted or loved. Feigning and maintaining illness is a favourite way to acquire and uphold a reliance on prescription medicines. As you can see, a secondary gain is a potent motivator of people's behaviour and cannot be spotted easily in therapy unless the client practises full disclosure; even then, underlying programmes which sabotage any attempts to change can be subtle and at times vigorously denied. Having said that, the positive effects attributed to this and other techniques I use are genuinely pleasing and can be tested in the field quickly.

Continuing with my client, I asked her after the procedure was finished to check back in with her emotions, thoughts and internal representations. All had changed, and no longer did they cause her any disturbance. The charge was now neutral, and the internal images were no longer dark or had any shape at all... For me at least,

NLP[9] techniques like these can be used alone with good results. If you want to use the above technique on its own, run through the list of questions I asked my client and write everything down, paying close attention to the lessons of wisdom imparted to your inner child and later by your wise older self.

But for the best results, I suggest working with a professional NLP practitioner in your area if you can afford it, or reach out across the world to any practitioner who ticks your boxes and you feel comfortable working with. With VOIP providers as they are, the world is your oyster.

THE JOURNEY CONTINUES

On my own journey, I found that working on myself became the most critical part of my life. What I read, who I spent time with, what movies I watched, how I spent my leisure time… in fact, no aspect of my life remained unaffected. No longer was I content with mediocrity. Spending hours wasting time in the company of those not interested in transformation was soon discarded, and I highly recommend you follow my lead.

Life's too short to be wasting valuable time on anything that offers you limited value. Getting strategic for some represents an intensity, a seriousness, that takes the fun out of life. I beg to differ: when we know what we want, where we are going and how to get it, life becomes a marvellous challenge. I want *you* to know where you are going and what *you* want. This includes the company you keep; where

---

[9] NLP stands for 'neuro-linguistic programming' and, in simple terms, means this: practical techniques, skills and strategies that are easy to understand and which can lead to profound changes in one's life. It is a modality based on proven methods that show how the mind thinks and how behaviour and the way we use language can be positively modified to improve all aspects of your life. It really is a wonderful gift to humanity and more powerful than traditional talk therapy techniques alone, but when these are combined with NLP, the compound effect is considerable.

and with whom we spend our time is who we become, and most of us lower our standards when it comes to the places and the company we choose to keep.

Imagine the following scene. You need to use the WC in a public area, bar, club, garage, shopping mall, etc., and when you enter the cubicle, the smell is horrendous. The toilet is dirty, and the previous visitor was, let's say, having obvious digestion issues. However, you really need to go and have no choice but to use what's available.

Having endured most of the experience by holding your breath, you quickly do the necessary and prepare to leave. Then horror of horrors: the lock is broken, and you are stuck and can no longer hold your breath. You call out, but nobody is around, so you berate your lousy luck, complain about the disgusting smell and ask yourself 'Why me?'

Ten minutes go by and someone finally enters the WC, whereupon you call out for help. The person assures you that they will tell someone who can come to your aid. Twenty minutes go by, and now you are sitting on the toilet lid as the janitor begins to remove the cubicle door. No longer does the smell or location have any significance on your mood; in fact, both have lost their impact on you. However, the dreadful conditions and the offensive odour remain just as potent. The difference is, your focus has shifted and you have forgotten about all other things apart from escaping your temporary confinement.

The moral of this story is the following. We quickly adjust to our surroundings, even when those surroundings are anything but healthy, including the inhalation of the smell of other people's shit. Be very mindful of the places you choose to frequent and whom you spend your quality time with. Exposing yourself to toxic environments, let alone breathing in them, is not a healthy practice. Yet you do precisely that by lowering your standards and getting used to places and people who pollute your surroundings.

It's time to set your life ablaze, to level up... to seek out individuals who fan your flames, and to develop those relationships. Ask yourself: 'Is my current tribe adding fuel to my fire or are they raining on my parade?' Get your microscope out and detective's hat back on and carefully check your last 50 interactions across your social media platforms. Who is nourishing, feeding and supporting your growth, and who is killing it? Who of your friends are sharing articles, studies or news items that align with where you want to go? And who are filling your time and inbox with rubbish? Who are gossiping, judging and putting others down? And which friends speak lovingly and compassionately about others?

Defend your light with your life; hence, the pessimists and the naysayers must understand that you no longer wish to engage on that level and must respect your choices. Write down all the people you choose to spend your quality time with, and decide who stays and who goes. That may sound mercenary, but if you wish to scale that wall, you need those who are willing to help you over it, and not those who are pulling you back from the ankles. Misery really does enjoy company and if left unchecked will infect you the same way.

The world takes its cue from how we value who we are. By wasting time with people who do not enhance or complement our lives, we are sending a powerful message to the outside world. 'I do not value my time, so why should anyone else!' This incredible world we live in appears to turn on unwritten rules that teach us what we need in order to grow.

She – and yes, I will forever address the earth as female – cares not for debate, nor for our whining, but continues to fill our lives with those who match our vibrational signature. Beyond this dynamic matchmaking process lies an incredible intelligence. This 'knowing' continues to deliver to us what is needed to evolve, and the supply, like the lessons, is endless. How we perceive these, or what we learn from them, *we* decide, but the experience won't stop until we know, beyond an intellectual concept, their true meaning and take the appropriate action to transcend them.

THE LAW OF ATTRACTION

———◆•◆———

What you think, you create. What you feel,
you attract. What you imagine, you become.

Raising one's energetic frequency is not difficult. Every choice and thought affects our physiology, as each thought carries with it a chemical and energetic counterpart. A loving thought or definite idea creates an internal environment ideal for a higher vibratory signature. Fearful, angry, deceitful or jealous feelings, for example, will produce the polar opposite. So, my question is: 'Where are you living – what's your emotional and vibratory home?'

We all have a default emotional home. Sure, we are all capable of being angry, scared, agitated or just pissed off. I sure do, but I don't live there: I fall down but I jump right back up again, brush the dust off and move forward.

If your default is to see life half empty, with danger lurking around every corner, or to believe that most people can't be trusted, are out to get you, turn you over or rip you off, then expect life to deliver into your proximity precisely the types of people who epitomise those archetypes and situations.

Consider a man who thinks himself unlucky or undeserving. He is envious, fearful, suspicious and paranoid. Consequently, the self-portrait will sure enough reflect the dreariness supported by such thinking. Containing little joy or splendour, he is incapable of seeing the joy in another, and he will therefore judge all others to be as selfish and unloving as he sees himself. Even acts of genuine kindness will be violently opposed as they are seen by this man to have impure motives, not for any other reason than he paints his world according to his own dark limitations.

If you think yourself not worthy of love, then you will undoubtedly find somebody who confirms those thoughts! Are you convinced that you cannot get a decent job or make money? Life will conspire to present to you those circumstance which reinforce those limiting beliefs.

Knowing this, how do you apply the law of attraction to make your life better? Is it as easy as stating a repeated affirmation and then sitting back while the universe delivers into your lap your every whim and indulgence? Of course not, and to indicate otherwise is both ignorant and deliberately misleading.

I am not for a second suggesting that all you need to do is think positive, send your order out into the cosmos and await your quantum reward. If life really was that easy, the human experience wouldn't be so damn difficult. In fact, I believe that those who promote and encourage this type of thinking are doing humanity no favours. Take, for example, authors, self-help coaches or speakers who try to convince an audience that wishing hard enough for a red Ferrari, a Fabergé egg or a fistful of diamonds will manifest the same. I would go a little further and suggest that this approach, at worst, deliberately and disingenuously attempts to sell them a lie and, at best, unforgivably misleads them.

That said, in order to change we must imagine ourselves as something different. We do have choices and we do not have to live our lives as victims of circumstance. We do attract what we repeatedly focus on.

If you focus on health, love, positivity, giving, sharing, fun, activity and laughter, for example, the odds become more favourable for a contented life. Focusing on anger, conflict, drama, selfishness, greed, envy and suffering, on the other hand, stacks the odds against you.

Resonance, vibration, quantum fields and the law of attraction may sound complicated, but it is straightforward in practical terms.

Raising one's vibration is not woo woo, rocket science or witchcraft... not for me at least.

The law of attraction gained momentum in 2006, after a documentary film swept the world, changing millions of lives and igniting a global movement. Later that year, a book entitled *The Secret* hit the bookshelves. In this book, author Rhonda Byrne revealed information known only to a select few: she stated that 'the secret' of obtaining what we desire (and confirmed by prominent physicists, authors and philosophers) was based on the law of attraction. And the good news was, anyone could access its power to bring themselves health, wealth and happiness. Many new-age concepts come and go, but this belief remains as popular as ever. The law of attraction and *The Secret* have enjoyed phenomenal success; the book has been translated into over fifty languages and remains one of the longest-running best-sellers for sound reasons – it works... but not at a level which most positive thinkers believe.

Writing out a cosmic shopping list and putting it on a refrigerator, or on a vision board hanging up in the bedroom, is just the start. If you want any chance at all of manifesting into your life desirous outcomes, then prepare to put the work in. You see, what we say as an affirmation and what we believe are often two extreme opposing positions. Energy is not fooled as we are. First, you must be convinced of what it is that you want, and then align your thoughts, intentions, actions and, above all, your feelings. You must be able to see the desired action of the future already completed in the present moment, and the body must feel and act as if it is happening or has already happened. That is the biggest secret of all – to actually feel it at a cellular level while thinking about what you are trying to achieve in the future.

In his book *The Isiah Effect: Decoding the Lost Science of Prayer and Prophecy*, multiple New York Times bestselling author Greg Braden speculates that in order to create in our world we must first have the feelings of our creation already fulfilled. Our prayer, meditation or visualisation practice then originates from an entirely new perspective. Rather than asking for a specific outcome to pass, we acknowledge our role to take an active part in creation and to give thanks and gratitude for that we are confident of having created.

Braden goes on to state that whether or not we see immediate results, our thanks acknowledge that somewhere in creation our prayers, desires and ambitions have already been fulfilled. Now, our practice has become an affirmative invocation of gratitude, fuelling our production, allowing it to blossom into its most significant potential. It doesn't stop there of course. Actively working towards what you want is paramount, and no amount of wishful thinking, no matter how convinced you are of achieving this goal, will yield favourable results.

Standing in your garden saying repeatedly 'there are no weeds, there are no weeds, there are no weeds' is futile if the flower beds are overrun with them. No amount of affirmation will change the fact. Neither will you fool your unconscious mind by repeating over and over 'I love myself, I love myself, I love myself' in the bathroom mirror each morning, when the truth is you can't stand your thighs, eye bags, sagging chin or any number of things. To rid your garden of weeds, or change how you feel about yourself, you must work hard until you complete your objectives, coupled with the use of a visualisation process that aligns your words with your feelings.

Similarly, writing yourself a cheque for a million dollars and a picture of a Ferrari next to it on the fridge is wasting time, unless you believe it first and then have a strategy to actuate those desires. Otherwise, the only way a Ferrari will adorn your driveway is if a Ferrari owner lives at the top of a hill and you at the bottom, and they forget to engage the handbrake. Getting the picture?

VISUALISING CHANGE

————— ◆●◆ —————

*The only thing limiting your goals is your
imagination and hard work.*

We have control over three things in life: our thoughts, the images we visualise and the actions we take. I have explained the need for extensive action alongside the requirement for changing thinking processes that do not serve your greater good. I have not yet described in detail, however, how the visualisation process works and how that can help us.

Visualisation has been used by successful people in all levels of society to envisage their wanted outcomes, helping them, in turn, fashion ideal lives. You too can practise the proven techniques for changing negative self-images and eliminating negative self-talk. There is nothing complicated, or anything to learn, other than allowing your creative imagination to work for you.

Visualisation is a productive method for bringing positive energy into your mind, body and spirit, expanding your ability for creativity. It will take some time, as most things do, to master the process, but visualisation and meditation have been proved, beyond a concept, to bring positive results to the practitioner. Try not to run before you can walk, and start off with something simple. For example, find a quiet place away from disturbances, sit or lie down and begin to breathe deeply in through the nose until the lungs are full; then, as you slowly exhale through the mouth, relax your mind and body. Do this sequence six times, then start the visualisation process.

I want you to imagine a scenario in the future where you feel happy. See yourself smiling and happy as you breathe slowly and rhythmically. What makes you happy only you know, but the idea is to create a real experience at a cellular level, where your body encounters the feelings of happiness on the basis of a future projection.

The mind cannot distinguish between what is real and what is not; it only knows how to react to incoming stimuli and act accordingly. If it feels real, and the chemical reactions to this experience are genuine, the body and mind believe it to be real. Repetitive encounters of any kind, imagined or not, will initiate the forming of neurological pathways which become our habits. As you know, we have habits that empower and habits that hinder. I would encourage you to focus on those that help you grow, such as positive visualisation.

Give it some time. Enjoy the process and embrace the learning of a new skill. For the record, I found visualisation difficult at the start, especially when jumping in at the deep end, trying to manifest in my mind's eye and feel in my body a whole theatre of content.

Start simple with the above, and increase the content as you become used to the process. Once you are comfortable and able to produce happy feelings by thought alone, get more strategic with it by writing out what it is you wish to achieve, down to the last detail. Use all of your senses to create desired outcomes, and see them clearly unfolding in your mind's eye while sitting in meditation... the colours, the sights, the sounds, the smells and what you can taste. Remember, the language of the unconscious mind is symbolic and sentiment based, hence creating an internal representation, with objects that generate feelings speaking directly to the unconscious mind, the powerhouse that dictates our mechanical and ritualistic behaviour.

To reap the most significant benefits, develop a daily practice to reinforce the communication between your mind and body; a daily visualisation of your aspirations as being already complete can rapidly accelerate your accomplishment of those ambitions.

Using visualisation practices to focus on your ambitions and wishes does three essential things:

1. It stimulates the creative subconscious, which will start producing creative ideas to help achieve your aspirations.
2. It programmes your brain to more willingly notice and recognise the resources needed to achieve your dreams.
3. It shapes your core motivation to take the necessary actions to realise your goals.

There is no precise time to practise visualisation, but I would recommend doing it on awakening and before bed. It is especially effective before sleeping, since it sends particular messages to the subconscious as the suggestions and desires marinate overnight.

VISUALISATION TECHNIQUE FOR IMPROVING SELF-IMAGE

I am going to outline a well-loved and well-used visualisation technique for improving self-image, counteracting negative self-talk and creating your best self. Feel free to discard or modify this particular example if it doesn't resonate with you.

Step 1

Imagine sitting in a theatre, and your most fabulous version of who you are walks on stage and begins to talk to the audience with clarity and confidence about a subject of your choice. See yourself with as much detail as possible, including your clothing, your facial expressions, the way you hold yourself and your levels of confidence, as well as the way you breathe, smile, laugh and engage with the audience as you continue to speak. Add in any sounds you can hear – background music or other people talking, laughing and cheering – as you delight the watching crowd. Now, try to recreate in your body the emotional state you think you would feel as you engage in this activity; be patient with this if it proves difficult. Try retrieving a memory when you felt great and experience how it feels. Then go back to the practice and see if you can recreate that same feeling.

Step 2

Now get up and walk around the stage and up the steps, and approach your greatest version from behind. Step at once into him or her without pausing. Observe what they see, feel what they feel and experience as much as possible what is going on, including the sounds, environment and anything else that appeals to you. How are you breathing? How does it feel to be on stage with the whole audience appreciating and enjoying what you have to say? How does it feel to express yourself with clarity, humour, kindness and wisdom? This is you at your best, sharing with the world your amazing gifts and talents with calmness, surety and confidence, which is neither egoic nor needy. Enjoy this moment for as long as you wish and then move on to the next step.

Step 3

Step out of yourself and return to your seat and at once take a high-definition coloured snapshot of your best self, standing on stage with a cheering receptive audience. Now shrink the image down to the size of a biscuit and eat it. As you begin to chew and swallow, imagine that each tiny piece, just like a hologram, holds the full scene of you captivating the audience and performing well. Imagine these little 'screens' travelling down into your stomach and out through the bloodstream into every cell of your body. Then imagine that every cell of your body is lit up with you stood on stage performing flawlessly. It is like one of those superstore windows where hundreds of televisions are all tuned to the same channel. Stay with that feeling until the feel-good factor begins to fade, and then open your eyes and go about your day, coming back to that feeling whenever you need to…

Practising this three-step visualisation technique twice a day can produce remarkable results if applied with regularity. The brain needs at least 30 days, but more accurately two months, of persistence before a new habit is hardwired in the subconscious. Hence, doing this once or twice may help, but in my experience (with which neuroscience agrees) a new healthy habit needs extended consistency, repetition and persistence. Ambition and aspiration are said to be the paths to success, but persistence is the vehicle you arrive in, and without it, victory is unlikely. Bear this in mind when using any new technique to change something in your life that is not working.

This process can be used not just for creating an ideal you, but also for anything you wish to have more of. A common issue presented to me daily when seeing clients is the lack of a compatible partner or no partner at all. I will tell you what I tell them.

We are easily fooled by the words and actions of others, especially at the beginning of a new relationship, when creating a good impression is vital. Humans, if nothing else, are experts at playing roles, storytelling and creating a plethora of different archetypes to hoodwink and fool. Energy, however, is not easily fooled. Our energetic signature is clear to see and feel if you dare to look and are confident enough to trust your intuition. We really could save ourselves an awful lot of time and effort if only strong enough to believe that intuitive sense we have access to.

SEEKING A SUITABLE PARTNER

Leaving intuition aside for a while, if finding a suitable partner is the most essential thing in your life, and it appears to be for most, then being at your best is crucial. Rather than focusing on what's out there, start with yourself by raising your vibratory signature, with better thoughts, words and actions. Remember, that which you seek is seeking you!

Rule Number 1

Learn to genuinely love and appreciate yourself by visualising who you want to be and holding yourself accountable to those standards. You can only meet someone at the level you have met yourself; or better said, your relationship with others can only be as good as the relationship you have with yourself.

Rule Number 2

Practise compassion and kindness... starting with yourself. These heartfelt emotions are essential, and people can feel the authenticity of who you are through an open heart.

Rule Number 3

Remember, we are energy first. Every thought, choice, action and decision made is shaping your world. *Be* the energy you wish to attract.

Rule Number 4

Know what you want and focus on it. Move towards what you do want and move away from what you do not. Where your attention goes, your reality grows.

Rule Number 5

Don't sell yourself short and settle for less than you deserve. Know your value and your worth. You don't value yourself? Then prepare to meet those who will affirm that belief.

Rule Number 6

Tell the truth and be vulnerable. Let people see the real you; that way, there can be no nasty surprises or shocks as the masks fall away one by one as familiarity grows.

Rule Number 7

Be sure that a loving partner is coming. Visualise your ideal man or woman and enjoy having fun with the process.

Rule Number 8

Practise sending loving thoughts. Thoughts of love and positivity have a meaningful influence, not just on ourselves but also on those to whom we are directing those feelings. Try this simple exercise. Look at a stranger the next time you are on a bus, train, plane, having a coffee or sitting in the park... it matters not where you are. Then repeat this a few times: 'I wish you genuine happiness and abundance, I honestly do'. Follow this by repeating 'I love you' at least 10 times.

Do this exercise when you have 30 seconds to spare. It's quick and easy and it changes your body physiology and emotional state. Positivism expressed in loving gestures towards others is remarkably influential, with healing properties that raise your vibrational signature. You may wish to do it, however, when the object of your intent is unaware, or they may feel uneasy. I practise this when the person's profile is visible; I focus on their heart and silently repeat this mantra a few times.

As you see, the list of rules above suggests that you are responsible for who and what arrives, stays and leaves your life. By affirming this, you take back your power. Being accountable ushers in an entirely new level of emotional maturity. No longer can you point your finger at the world and say: 'You did this me.' Being responsible means leaving childhood behind. Are you ready for that? Are you ready to stop apportioning blame to external parties and events for your pain and suffering?

APPLYING EFFORT AND DETERMINATION

It matters not what it is you want more of, be it a person, a job, a dream vacation, a car, a boat or a plane. You will stand or fall, succeed or not, depending on the amount of effort and determination that *you* apply in life.

Once you have decided that you are in control, remember to practise with regularity until the sensation of having these things is felt at a cellular level. Feel the experience of driving your dream car or trekking through the rain forest with your own Tarzan or Jane. Feel the power and hear the noise of that engine rumbling beneath you as you take the car out for that first drive. Feel the rain that is falling all around you and the cacophony of wildlife that accompanies every bare footstep upon the lush green and dense rainforest floor.

See and feel yourself engaging with anything that you wish to manifest... Then go about it with vigour and purpose, until your dreams begin to take shape. Remain curious and receptive to the unknown. If you don't believe in what you are doing, it's going to be difficult to change anything at the level of the unconscious mind, and it's at that level that the most profound changes occur.

Remember, the whole point of a new way of thinking and acting is to give the brain new things to focus on. Around 95% of our daily thoughts are carbon copies of yesterday's thoughts and last week's, and on it goes. The reason why change is so tricky is that the unconscious mind is the habit mind – it likes to take the path of least resistance and seeks out the familiar. Hence, it takes considerable and consistent effort to break the habit of being oneself.

Continue to learn new skills or enrol in further courses, for example. Learn a new language, or to play that instrument you promised yourself. Try to change as many things about your daily routine as possible. Change your shampoo, your brand of coffee. Brush your teeth with your weaker hand. Take the bus instead of the car to work, but if you do drive, take a different route if possible. Go to bed an hour earlier or later, and sleep on the opposite side you are used to. You may smile at these suggestions, but I can assure you, the reason you are not changing is familiarity.

By changing your automatic patterns of behaviour, you start the process of rewiring the brain and at the same time step outside the confines of familiarity and habits that dominate your thinking, actions and consequences. Psychological change demands that you resist unproductive habitual reflexes and wilfully choose healthier alternatives – choices which differ from the automatic reflex you have been conditioned to accept. This can be scary at times, relearning new skill sets.

We are creatures of habit; hence, we crave familiarity and comfort, which is fine if the habitual behaviours we embrace are enhancing, but often they are not. Moreover, there is no growth in the familiar, in certainty; growth arises from *uncertainty* and from meeting head on the fears that result from it.

Chance does not afford change. Conscious awareness coupled with challenging work and discipline is the recipe needed to create lasting change over a period of time… 66 days to be exact, according to the latest studies done on the science of creating new habits. The ballpark figure of 21 days, although appealing, is in fact a very broad and loose time frame, just long enough to sound feasible but short enough to willingly embark on a quest for change.

Contrary to public opinion, however, a new automated habit takes on average more than two months to achieve, according to Philippa Lally, a health psychology researcher at University College London. In a study published in the *European Journal of Social Psychology*, Lally and her research team decided to figure out just how long it actually takes to form a habit; they concluded that it took anywhere from 18 days to 254 days, with the majority of the people involved taking more than 60 days to produce new and automated behaviour patterns. In other words, if you want to make lasting changes then set your expectations appropriately. The fact is that, to build a new behaviour into your life, it will take you anywhere from two months to eight months of daily application, and not the 21 days, which must not go unnoticed.

Look at New Year's resolutions – a great example of how we try to drop habits that don't serve us. We attempt to quit smoking... to eat healthier food and lose weight... to exercise... to change jobs... to change a relationship status. How long do you think they last? According to US news sources, approximately 92% of resolutions fail, and 80% fail by the beginning of February, meaning that in no time, the old patterns are back in control, as the new resolutions drift into obscurity. Why is this?

- Most people don't employ or can't afford to employ skilful coaches or therapists who can help them achieve the desired changes by changing their mindset and holding them accountable for extended periods of time.
- Their goals aren't clear and have no real plan of action. If you can't measure it, it's not a very good resolution, because vague goals produce vague resolutions.
- The time it takes to make permanent change has not been adhered to.
- The pleasure associated with the familiarity of old habits outweighs the suffering or the desire to change them, as explained earlier in this book by the notion of secondary gain.

The decision to change can happen in an instant, but the work necessary to support and uphold the change requires effort and time. And as basic as that is, and as well you know, you must condition yourself through continued application or risk going back to the programmed state in which most people live their lives.

Get specific and write down what needs to be done, one step at a time, then muster up the courage to put your plan into action! Words are empty without an action that accompanies them... Be realistic and don't expect miracles overnight; we are aiming for progress, not perfection. Start small and focus on one thing at a time, rather than on a single overwhelming goal. Remember, it is not the degree of the change that matters, but the act of distinguishing that change in your life and working towards it that is important.

Ambition can be fun and inspiring, especially at the beginning, when the novelty value is high. But your elation can quickly give way to frustration when the trials and tribulations of life trigger you left right and centre, and you find yourself reaching for a bottle of red and a family bar of Cadbury's Fruit and Nut.

Changing the habits of a lifetime is no easy quest. It's bloody difficult to be objective with regard to our own suffering; being too close to the action clouds our better judgement. We must therefore become strategic in the pursuit of change. If a coach or therapist is out of the question, then at least look for a role model... learn from the best. Find someone who has already achieved what you pursue, and replicate the formula; this can subtract years of trial and error.

Standing on the shoulders of giants, for me at least, is the most powerful way to initiate change. Remember, we are not trying to reinvent the wheel here. As unique as we are, paradoxically we are remarkably similar. We all know and experience pain and suffering. We all have parents, partners, jobs, hobbies, habits and (most of us) children which instigate familiar emotions. However, some manage these emotions more skilfully than others.

Those wanting the best results learn from other people's mistakes, and so they can shorten their learning curves. Nothing will make a bigger impact on your future than the people you associate with daily. Maybe you know somebody who turned their life around against the odds: they overcame a toxic relationship, lost 20 kilogrammes of weight, left behind a dead-end job... Become curious and, with their permission, find out how they did it, down to the last detail, and copy their formula. If you don't know anybody personally who meets your criteria, then go online and find the inspiration from the thousands of people who have been where you are and have succeeded. Buy their books, enrol in their courses, listen to their podcasts, do all three, but *do it*!

If role modelling is not your thing, then getting leverage over yourself with some skilful questions is a smart way of initiating change. It's time to don the detective's cap once again. With your trusted journal and pen, your healthy drink of choice and a place to concentrate, write down what you stand to lose by continuing to engage in any unhealthy habits that are creating problems in your own life or in the lives of your loved ones. Start with your most pressing issue, the problem that causes you more suffering than any other, and ask yourself:

1. Where will I be in one, two, three, five or ten years from now if the current patterns continue?
2. Who suffers the most if this continues?
3. How will my life unfold if I don't commit to changing that which no longer serves me?

If you cannot get enough leverage over yourself, then perhaps focus on your children, wife or partner. You claim to love your spouse? ... and would do anything for your kids, including being the role model they need to feel proud, safe, loved and secure? Then show them, by eradicating the habits that cast a shadow over those claims. A very powerful meme was sent to me recently that stated: 'Most parents would die for their kids, yet less than 30% will live a healthy lifestyle for them'. Don't be one of them!

Set difficult but attainable goals and work towards them. For some, taking giant leaps will work beautifully, while for others, baby steps from A to Z are just what the doctor ordered. There is no race, but I do need your cooperation. If you want to win the lottery, the least you can do is buy a ticket.

Please note the term used here is 'difficult but attainable goals' and not goals that have their origin and completion in terms of perfection. The deceptive prerequisite for perfection is one of mankind's greatest burdens and weighs heavily around the necks of billions of human beings. When I ask you to be yourself and to become your best version, please put away any ideas of a perfect self, for that is impossible and the striving for it will undoubtedly end in frustration and disappointment.

IN A NUTSHELL

If your current rituals and habits are disagreeable or do not serve, you owe it to yourself to choose better options through hard work and discipline.

BE YOURSELF

———◆●●————

... not a perfect self, but your higher self.

We feel unhappy at times because of the unnatural and counter-intuitive things we are programmed to do. We live in a world where different is rarely encouraged, and so we often profess that this is the life we wanted for ourselves. How frequently do you cross paths with people who enjoy their work, are genuinely comfortable in their skin, engage with open honesty, have real self-belief and are absent of duplicitous archetypes? Is that another projection, you may well ask? Yes, of course it is. How can I be aware of this, unless my point of reference stems from the direct experience of role playing, dissatisfaction with work and the entertaining of mindless small talk while simultaneously telling lies?

Does this mean I am being fraudulent by espousing a system for healthy living, physically, emotionally and spiritually? Absolutely not. To first recognise our flaws is to become aware of the need to discard them, and as with all things in life, there are various levels. The level of authenticity I have reached thus far is satisfactory for where I am right now. Do I want more self-belief and legitimacy? Sure... I am a work in progress, just like yourself. Am I happy where I am? Yes... I can honestly say I am, but the growth or thirst for more significant improvement does not decrease.

To grow emotionally and to become a self-governing thinking human being, one must be, above all things, authentic; this is non-negotiable. The 'trying to fit in' mindset has contributed to the bludgeoning increase in emotional and mental illnesses which have swept through the Western World and are on the rise. To be authentic in a world continually trying to make you something else is a great success, but not to strive for authenticity is to create a life of irritation.

There is nothing worse when sat alone or lying in bed knowing that so much of what you believe never gets said, or that the person you want to be remains hidden behind the variety of masks gathered on life's highways. Being something on the outside while feeling something completely different on the inside may work for a while and may fool some of the people some of the time, and if role playing provides you with a life you really want, then more power to you. My one question would be this: 'Do you wish to be right for the world, or right for yourself?' Answering that, at least, with complete congruency will give you an honest and insightful acknowledgement of what you want. If you can indeed be yourself, then originality is a given, because there's no one like you. My advice is therefore to nurture and expand your uniqueness, not your averageness or ability to perfect your acting skills.

We have become a species of settlers... and nowhere is this more glaringly obvious than in our personal relationships. Why do we endure, suffer and prolong relationships that are in no way enhancing, but convince ourselves otherwise? We do brain-numbing jobs that do not align in any way with our purpose, or align with our gifts and God-given talents. We willingly give up our freedoms and embrace passivity so as not to rock the boat, simultaneously convincing ourselves and others that a life of mediocrity is what we signed up for.

There is an imaginary need to project to an external audience that everything is perfect in our homes, with our kids, in our jobs and with our partners. Yet perfection never can, never has and never will exist, and it's this powerful and inconvenient truth which generates the necessity to avoid perceived failure in the eyes of an external audience whose opinions are deemed more important than our own.

THE PERILS OF COMPARISON

We look at others and appraise our success or failure on the basis of what we see. We regularly compare, yet seldom realise how unhealthy it is. A comparison, out of context, to another person is an act of violence against the self. We look at others and appraise our success or failure on the basis of what we believe is valid, but seldom do we have any idea of what is going on inside the head of the person we are scrutinising. We make the same mistake when appraising the relationship dynamics of friends or acquaintances. I have lost count of the number of times I have told a client that, unless they are sitting in a chair in the living room of someone they hold themselves up against, they are assuming something to be true that is really unknown! Yet, on we go, comparing ourselves to anyone and anything, seldom realising how unhealthy it is.

I was asked by a client recently if making a comparison was ever healthy. It's a good question, and I had to think for a fair while before offering my opinion. I replied that it is almost impossible for us not to compare ourselves to others, and it appears part of our nature on the basis that we all seem to do it. I added that comparison is therefore a natural but doubled-edged behavioural trait, which, for some (albeit a small minority), facilitates growth.

One could successfully debate that comparison can be the catalyst one needs to take one's potential to the next level, and I have no opposing retort to counter. Using a yardstick higher than that of others in order to attain superior performance is fine, as long as you don't lose sight of what it is you are trying to achieve – to be the best human being you can be!

Unfortunately, the majority of comparison is not contextual and therefore wholly unreasonable, and without the proper comparison analysis, we quickly lose sight of reality, and with it our self-esteem. I could argue that those already performing close to or at the peak of their natural ability may find inspiration in the methodologies of the elite performers in their respective disciplines. Sadly, it's not the already established high achievers who are prone to the disease of comparison, but your average Joe and Joanna who indulge in senseless comparisons.

But how does one define success? What does it mean to be successful? That is also subjective. Is success having a seven-figure bank account? Does having a perceived superior IQ do it for you? Could it be that success hinges on your children's achievements? There is no definitive recipe for success. Einstein said: 'Everyone is a genius. But if you judge a fish by its ability to climb a tree, it will live its whole life believing that it is stupid.'

It's futile to compare yourself, as a beginner, to the champions. This type of unrealistic expectation will leave you feeling empty and alert that inner critic to remind you again that you're not good enough, and it's that voice which torpedoes any chance of success. It's the same voice which has been dictating proceedings your whole life... a voice that was born out of ignorance and over-expectation when the unconscious mind was busy forming and attempting to make sense of the world in which you found yourself.

We all want to be fantastic, beautiful and successful, and it's damn painful when we aren't, if we compare ourselves to those who apparently are, and I use *apparently* for sound reason. To be successful is no guarantee of fulfilment, neither is being beautiful or idolised by millions any measure of success. Success can only be achieved by a sense of fulfilment; without it, the feeling of failure is never far behind.

Do you believe that those we look up to in the celebrity world or those we aspire to be like have it all figured out... that wealth and fame can somehow buy happiness, joy and peace of mind? Ironically, I would wager that the opposite is far more likely and that the emotional pain levels of those who have everything that you aspire to have often supersede your own.

If you have never had fame and monetary wealth, then you cannot know how it is to have anything you want and still feel empty. If you live in a studio, then aspiring to move in to a one-bed apartment in the future is a reasonable ambition that can keep you motivated.

But what if you already live in a huge mansion and have all the cars, boats, planes, bells and whistles – what then? Where do you go from there, and what then motivates you when you have the money to buy anything you want? Remember, we must make progress to feel satisfied, regardless of financial or social status; because of the law of diminishing returns (which I mentioned earlier), even the best of the best experiences become mundane and boring very quickly, and thus begins the quest for anything that staves off the treachery of apathy.

Apathy is little spoken of, yet it's one of the most perilous and debilitating emotional states we can experience. When life becomes indifferent, without passion and without energy, and we lack appreciation of life's simple joys, it can get dark pretty quickly, especially when we rely on a never-ending list of external experiences to stave off the growing emptiness. This can often lead to panic attacks, insomnia, violent outbursts, substance abuse, eating disorders, sex addiction, deviant sexual behaviour... and on it goes.

It's no surprise that suicide rates, depression and general anxiety among high achievers and celebrities is growing faster than ever. Instead of bringing them happiness and freedom, being sought-after, rich and at the top of their game leads, for many, to an identity crisis and ruminations on their self-worth. The solution to this problem, I believe, lies in the cultivation of gratitude and the act of service to those worse off than themselves. You may have noticed that I repeat certain things intermittently in different contexts throughout this book; that is both deliberate and necessary. The human mind needs repetition in order to function at its best. By bringing to your attention that which I deem imperative for radical change, you are training the brain at an unconscious level to assimilate the information and pay it the rightful attention.

But for now, stop comparing yourself to others and focus on becoming a better version than who you were yesterday, than who you were last week... If you wish to compete, then compete with yourself. Believe me, you have more than enough work and a lifelong project to keep you occupied.

We fail to recognise our individual beauty when we are too busy comparing ourselves to others. From the cradle to the grave, comparisons are rife; we were taught as children to compare by parents who were taught the same way by their parents, and theirs before them. Life stays a bittersweet affair if we continue to run comparison software. When we compare, the saplings of jealousy and envy are close to hand, neither of which produce healthy fruit. Learn to run this race at your own pace. You are unique, like no other being ever created since the beginning of time. You really are incomparable to anything or anybody. Isn't it time you realised?

Comparison programmes uphold the illusion of separation, superiority and inferiority. Neither are you superior nor inferior to anybody else. Whether a king, an emperor, a prime minister, a billionaire, a president, the pope or an oil-rich sheikh, you are no different from those who pick up litter on a beach, scrub toilets in a mall, pick fruit from the vineyard or perform manual labour.

It is understood that some of us will be rich, some of us poor... some black, some white... some tall, some short. Some will excel academically, some will not. Some will hold positions of power and some will not. Some will be more aesthetically pleasing to the eye than others, thanks to a favourable roll of the genetic dice. All of this can only magnify a lack of confidence or stimulate a sense of false superiority, depending on the object of scrutiny.

To illustrate, it is safe to say that comparing yourself with someone who, on the surface, appears to be more successful, intelligent, famous, wealthy, good-looking, pretty or well liked will have you believe that you are inadequate or inferior to that person. On the other hand, if the object of comparison, in your opinion, has lower self-esteem, is considered unattractive, lacks confidence and struggles to find success, either in the workspace or in relationships, then your 'software programme' will convince you of superiority over them.

These egoic and mistaken beliefs cause (and will continue to cause) a disturbance if you believe them to be true. The only place that superiority/inferiority exists is within the unhealthy mindset of the individual or in the collective mindset of a society which fabricated and sustains this false paradigm.

Try looking at events, circumstances, opinions and other people with neutrality. Don't be confused with the word 'neutrality', associating it with the lack of passion or intensity. What it means is to look at others and events without judging them on the basis of your subjective reality. Neutrality enables us to retain our centre; it tethers us to the present moment, not allowing the anchor to be ripped from its moorings whenever a situation arises that creates discomfort.

Staying centred and neutral in situations that formerly irritated is a sure-fire sign of emotional evolution – an emotive barometer that gives feedback on where you are on your evolutionary journey of self-discovery. This is not to say that when unfavourable events crop up and you have the power to change them, you remain passive. No, neutrality is a state of awareness that allows the individual to observe any situation and act accordingly, without the troublesome ego directing proceedings.

If evolution is your goal, then knowing the difference between what you can change, the acceptance of that which you cannot, and the wisdom to know the difference cannot be understated; in fact, it is pivotal.

THE PURSUIT OF PERFECTION

*The pursuit of excellence is gratifying and
healthy. The pursuit of perfection is frustrating,
neurotic, and a terrible waste of time.*
– Edwin Bliss

The antithesis of neutrality is obsessive idealism or perfectionism. A great deal of personal and collective suffering derives from chasing this emotional apparition, by craving things to be a certain way in a world that is anything but certain! Perfectionism creates tension and disturbance when things are not as we want them to be.

Do not confuse perfectionism with a striving to be your best. Perfectionism is not about good accomplishment and growth; it is a shield, a protective mechanism, created from shame. This shame was born from past experiences where perceived failure was confirmed, either consciously or unconsciously, by those we respected as caregivers. The subtle glances of disapproval when falling short of expectation weighed heavily on the shoulders of the child, and have got heavier ever since. The underlying message was loud and clear: if you want to be loved, then you had better be successful and a perfect achiever.

Any type of failure or shortcoming therefore immediately equated to rejection, and voila, the perfectionist was born, an impossible archetype created to avoid the heartache of disapproval. There exists a voice in our head telling us if we are perfect in all that we do, then nobody can criticise, disapprove or, heaven forbid, reject us. It's that same erroneous voice which has convinced us that perfection means a painless life in which shame or inadequacy does not exist. Sadly, this is a myth-filled concept which inflicts much pain on those who submit to it. Genuine fulfilment becomes impossible when perfection is non-negotiable. To be human is to be flawed. Yet the perfectionist is so busy hiding flaws that the reality is lost while chasing this impossible obsession.

It is understood that we rightly enjoy the rewards that come from a task well done: a project finished on time that has the commentators singing our praises... the look of acknowledgement for a fine effort that brings a distinct inner glow... the external affirmation that tells us we are valuable conscientious human beings. All are perfectly normal and healthy emotional responses to our best attempts.

The perfectionist, however, is concerned with the details of a task to the point where they spend obsessive amounts of care to get the details precisely right. Obsessive perfectionists are so concerned with perfection that they are seldom satisfied with the outcome of any work they do. This can, of course, be beneficial. A specialist surgeon needs to be meticulous in all that he or she does when performing delicate operations on those whose lives are at stake. There are many other examples I could use to prove the importance of paying close attention to detail, but I am highlighting for your consideration the negative connotations that arise from the need to be perfect, and the accompanying emotions that chasing this impossible dream brings with it. Perfectionists produce work of the highest standard, of that there is no doubt, but this book is about seeking contentment and as much happiness as possible, which the perfectionist rarely touches.

The difference between the pursuit of excellence and the pursuit of perfection is thus. The pursuer of excellence understands the fragility of being human, and the inevitable mistakes we all make.

They understand that giving their best efforts is always enough, regardless of the outcome. They are mature enough to understand that their best will sometimes not be good enough, and to not fall apart when the inevitable happens. Perfectionism, on the other hand, is not the pursuit of the best in ourselves, but rather the search for the worst in ourselves, the part that tells us that nothing we do will ever be good enough.

Perfectionists often display symptoms of obsessive-compulsive behaviour but seldom recognise it, thinking that they are behaving in a way that everyone should or needs to. In my experience, rarely do I meet a perfectionist who is neither anxious nor unreasonably concerned with their lives and what they have or not achieved; on the face of it, this sounds healthy and a sure-fire method of always striving for growth. But the obsessive perfectionist is never satisfied and doesn't understand the word 'balance', yet balance is a key component of overall happiness and contentment.

For the record, regardless of who is reading this, you are not and never will be perfect, and unless you abandon this quest, whatever you achieve in life will never be good enough. So, how do we loosen the vice-like stranglehold that perfectionism places around the throats of its victims?

Can you identify the cruel inner critic by its harsh tone and delivery? It's the same voice which has been beating you black and blue whenever the feeling of failure, or the perception of not being good enough, surfaces. Whose voice is it, and what or who does it look like? Does it belong to you, or to a family member?

I am confident that the identity of the critical voice is not yours and neither does it look like you. Like most people, you have lived with it for so long that you have wrongly assumed it to be part of who you are. Not so. It was given to you – a psychological imprint based on the unattainable levels of perfection a particular person (or persons) strived for but could not reach, so those unrealistic expectations were projected on to you. And you have been carrying that burden around with you ever since. How many times have you wanted to do something, but didn't attempt it for fear of failing? How many times have you procrastinated and with it forgone the chance to blur the edges of perfectionism?

Perfectionists are often good at a few things, and they spend their time trying to be perfect at them. They seldom step outside of their comfort zones, for to do so is to run the risk of perceived failure and ridicule, something they must avoid at all costs, for it conjures up something much more painful. To try and then fail means not being good enough, which equates to not being worthy of love, and love is the one thing we cannot do without, regardless of whether we understand it or not.

Ironically, the love we need in order to feel safe can often be the thing we run from when perfectionism runs our lives. We fear that anyone who gets too close will see behind the armour how flawed we are, so we run for the hills and sabotage the relationship before it has a chance to grow. This is a very common pattern, especially when we meet a potential partner who appears to be good to be true. It starts off wonderfully, but soon enough the doubts appear: 'What will happen if they find out I'm not perfect. They are going to leave me and with it a trail of destruction, so I had better take evasive action and end it before they do!' This leads from one casual and short-lived affair to another, following a similar pattern. Just to be clear, that person who appears too good to be true... they are flawed, just like you are. The reason we attract them confirms this. Neither of you, nor anybody else for that matter, are, have been or can be other than flawed.

Those impossible standards you hold of yourself, and of others too, are just that – impossible. And unless you abandon the belief that perfection is attainable, buckle up nice and tight because life is going to toss you are around like a rag doll. Nobody leaves this place without realising first that perfection was never accessible nor attainable, regardless of any attempts to convince themselves otherwise.

IN A NUTSHELL

Perfect, you can never be. You can, however, be the very best version of yourself. Being human is to understand that imperfection is an integral part of the journey. Perfection is a disguise for insecurities you wish to remain hidden. Dare to be vulnerable. Dare to be your true authentic self, and see how life begins to change for the better.

REJECTION

Adversity, pain and hardship come with the package of being a human being, and nowhere are afflictions more prominent or frequent than in the sting of rejection. Unless you realise that everyone must experience rejection multiple times in life, and that it's a natural and essential part of human existence, you are going to come undone at the seams repeatedly whenever the inevitable pays you a visit.

Rejection is painful, of that there is no doubt. It is one of the most potent instigators of low self-esteem, yet it is hardwired into the psychological fabric of Homo sapiens. To understand why, we must venture back in time and visit our ancestors.

Evolutionary psychologists claim that rejection served a vital function in our evolutionary history. When we lived in small communities as hunter-gatherers, being excluded from our clans was fatal. Back then, when food, water and essential materials were in short supply, the necessity to be a valuable member of the tribe was of paramount importance. It was so important, in fact, that we believe that those not pulling their weight – or better said, not adding value to the herd – were ostracised and left to fend for themselves, which was tantamount to a death sentence. The psychologists believe, therefore, that the brain developed an evolutionary and cautionary warning system to alert us to the risk of abandonment or rejection.

At this juncture you may well be assuming that if that be the case, then you can't help behaving and feeling as you do. It's a sound observation, but no cigar I'm afraid. Many aspects of the human journey, including our own ability to evolve, have radically changed since the days of our ancestral wanderings and running down mammoths for food and clothing. Gone are the days when extreme vigilance was needed to outsmart quicker, stronger and hungrier predators whose fondness for human flesh is well documented. Today, it's pointless fearing that a ravenous sabre-toothed tiger may appear from behind a tree as we ramble through the countryside... nor does it make sense that the fearing of any kind of rejection will lead to a premature demise. Life has moved on, yet it appears many of us have not got the memo.

The fight-or-flight mechanism is forever being initiated, but rarely for justifiable reasons. The fight, freeze or flight response is a reactive process we can access in times of great peril to save our lives. It wasn't designed to be triggered every time a partner raises their voice, somebody flips you the middle finger in rush-hour traffic or pushes in front of you while at the bar on a night out, yet this is what is happening.

In the same way, rejection no longer means an early grave; rarely is it necessary to prepare to run for your life, freeze like a rabbit in the headlights or prepare to fight like Genghis Khan while jostling for a beer at your local tavern. We must understand what it is we are doing when we initiate any of these first-response mechanisms out of context. I will cover in greater detail the fight-or-flight mechanism further on, and how important it is to understand the mechanics and what we need to do in order not to trigger it repeatedly.

Learning to deal with rejection is vital, and as painful as rejection is, it's an integral part of being human and an experience nobody escapes. Rejection can be so painful, in fact, that it replicates physical pain in the brain; research shows that the areas of the brain triggered when we experience rejection are the same as those when we experience physical pain. The brain responds so similarly to rejection and physical pain that medication for physical pain works in the same way as for rejection. That would go some way in explaining as to why many people lean on painkillers, though few understand the mechanisms that drive the need to take them.

The experience of rejection, if not properly understood, can lead to several adverse psychological consequences, such as loneliness, low self-esteem, aggression and depression. It can also lead to feelings of anxiety and a finely tuned sensitivity to ultimate rejection, unless it's reframed and the perspective is altered. Every person who has ever lived has felt the sting of a failed relationship or has been rejected in any number of ways. Nevertheless, we are not taught in schools or colleges how to process or cope with this sledgehammer event or with the amount of discontent it creates.

Handling Rejection

The good news is, rejection is not an unchanging condition, and you can take steps to reduce the stranglehold it has over you by applying some common sense and asking some pertinent questions.

What Is Going on in My Head?

Any time you feel the emotional response to rejection, start by questioning the thought process that is going on in your head. Just because an idea about yourself has been triggered and it feels familiar, it does not make it a fact. An idea or thought is just that, without a definitive truth.

For example, is it true that your ex-partner not wanting to be with you means that you are now unlovable? Absolutely not. Let us examine the facts...

One person no longer wants to be with you... Does that really make you unworthy, when so many in the past have and will do so again in the future? Do your friends no longer love you, or your parents, siblings, pets, etc.?

Not worthy of being loved. Really? Is that a fact or an assumption? Is your ex-partner's opinion more valid than somebody else's? Does it exist as a truth that you are not good enough or worthy of love and attention? Or is that just a thought... a story you have running in your head? Of course it is a thought, a story, a thinking process, created way back in time when you were too young to remember... when any type of rejection meant the same thing: 'I am not worthy of being loved or good enough.'

The truth is, your ex-partner leaving has taken the air out of your balloon, and you believe that the only way to inflate it again is to bring him or her back into your life to blow it up again. When we are hurting, we lose sight of the facts and focus on anything that we believe will mitigate the pain... in this case an ex-lover who we believe responsible for our suffering. The truth, however, is something else: the relationship ended because it was not working, and bringing that person back, even as a possibility, means that you bring everything back, including why you broke up in the first place. When we remove the rose-coloured spectacles and see the situation for what it is, a gap appears – a gap that suggests that what we are feeling is not a true reflection of the current situation.

The pain is not being caused by the ex-partner's absence alone, although this is a contributory factor; the real pain is how this separation has made you feel about yourself. Your self-image has been punctured. All self-identities built around external validation are flimsy at best, and so any type of sabotage from an external source will create panic, suffering and a sense of uncompletedness.

When we lack self-love, which most of us do, we must extract it from an external source... in this case our ex, who we labelled as our pleasure dealer when we were together. The moment they walked away, they became our pain dealer, and, in our ignorance, we believe that getting them back under any circumstances will take away that pain, but not so. You do not need this person back in your life to inflate your balloon. How often did they deflate it when you were together? Hundreds of times, I would wager.

You don't need their validation for you to feel worthy, and neither must you convince them of your lovability to feel complete again. Divorce your story that's running in your head and marry the truth. You survived before you met them, and you will survive (and dare I say thrive) in the future, if you can learn from the painful lessons that have presented themselves.

I promise you – you are worthy, complete and good enough with or without your ex, and you will continue to love and be loved by many others throughout your life.

2. Why Do I Feel This Way?

Understand that rejection has triggered an age-old programme from humanity's distant past, and that the circumstances in which the programme was created do not apply to your present situation... unless you happen to be a hunter-gatherer, wandering the savannahs alone, having been ostracised from your clan!

3. How Can I Settle My Nerves After a Rejection?

One way to settle the nerves after a rejection is to reach out. Reach out to your own tribe – your friends, colleagues or family members – to obtain the necessary emotional support and to remind yourself that you are appreciated, loved, wanted and above all safe.

It's in times of woe and hardship when a faith in something greater than yourself is invaluable. I have a secret admiration for those with an unwavering faith in an interventionist creator that truly cares and whose love for them is unconditional. When one is sad, low and dejected, it can be very comforting to have a spiritual practice to turn to. If praying helps you cope and overcome the hurt, then I encourage you to do it as often as possible.

4. How Do I Restore My Self-esteem?

Now is the right time to remember who you are – your skills, abilities, positive characteristics and value. Write down a list of qualities you have, and next to each one, add a section describing in detail your strengths. For example:

I persevere: When I start something, I am disciplined enough to finish it.

I am reliable: My word is my bond. If I say something, I deliver on it.

Trustworthy: I value honesty and trust primarily, which installs confidence in those who know me.

I am faithful: I am loyal in intimate relationships and consider infidelity a deal breaker.

I am intelligent: I enjoy having deep and meaningful conversations. I am a good listener and love to learn new things.

I see the glass as half full: My default emotional home is to be happy, and that reflects in my attitude towards others and towards the world in general.

These are just a few examples, so write about your *own* strengths, to remind yourself of what *you* bring to the table, which will bolster your self-esteem at a time when it needs it most. Keep writing as much content as possible, and then read and reread it whenever you feel arising within you the emotions that accompany rejection.

PLAYING THE DATING GAME

Life often throws up puzzles to keep us learning and on our toes, as long as, of course, we are awake and vigilant enough to recognise them. And in no area is life more problematic or potentially confusing than in the dating game.

Who we think we deserve and who we get are often polarised. I have described in detail in earlier chapters why and how we attract certain types; if you need a refresher, I suggest going back and read again the relevant text that explains it. When you are ready and have time, grab your trusty notepad and pen, as it's time to get busy. For most of us, the dating game is a guessing game, but when we get strategic, we can remove much of the guesswork from the equation. Write down the following quality categories in separate columns:

1. Emotional. 2. Physical. 3. Intellectual. 4. Material. 5. Spiritual.

Let's first examine the positive traits in a partner.

Positive Traits

Under each column, now list as many things you consider favourable. For example, if I were to write down the positive traits in a woman that were appealing to me, then the corresponding lists would be as follows.

1. Emotional

Kind, empathic, caring, giving, honest, tolerant, funny, laughs a lot, confident with healthy self-esteem, light-hearted, speaks kindly of others, good listener, independent, consistent, good communicator, respects my freedom, non-jealous, comfortable in silence, does not invade my privacy.

2. Physical

Height (a minimum/maximum), fit and healthy, no large visible tattoos, sporty, attractive natural face, nice teeth, warm smile, minimal make-up, as happy barefoot in board shorts as in a dress and heels.

3. Intellectual

Bright, good conversationalist, problem solver, pays attention to detail, reads a lot, studies, understands subjectivity, practices self-improvement.

4. Material

Decent job, self-sufficient, ambitious with strong self-belief, own car, own home.

5. Spiritual

A non-believer in a punishing god, understands we are all one, does not think of herself as superior/inferior to anything or anybody, works on herself beyond the physical avatar, enjoys meditation, practices yoga, understands the nature of the universe and who we are, believes death is a transformation of form, a nature lover, loves the ocean, forests, lakes, parks and wildlife.

Impressive lists, no doubt, but we are just getting started. Let's now look at negative traits.

Negative Traits

Take those five quality categories again and underneath each one, write out the traits that you deem detrimental to your ideal. Once again, here are my lists, as an example.

1. Emotional

Selfish and self-centred, greedy, clingy, miserable, heavy-hearted, rarely laughs or smiles, judgemental, critical of self and others, a lousy listener, speaks too much, controlling, jealous, insecure, envious, bitter, cannot be trusted, lousy communicator, a heavy drinker, smoker, promotes idealism, doesn't understand subjectivity, values IQ over EQ.

2. Physical

Very overweight (lacks discipline), bad hygiene, heavy make-up, obsessed with beauty treatments and cosmetic surgery.

3. Intellectual

Poor conversationalist, doesn't work on self-improvement, a believer in the mainstream narrative, has a 'I am right' attitude, watches mind-numbing reality TV shows, spends hours on social media, gossips, judges, rude, has a superiority complex, feels entitled.

4. Material

No job, wants to be kept woman, no ambition, no savings or financial stability, does not own a car or a home.

5. Spiritual

Dogmatic follower of theistic religion, does not agree with or understand the spiritual path, 'we are one' is a foreign concept and believes that humans are the superior species on the planet and that animals, fish and birds are here to amuse or serve us, has no interest in the universe beyond planet earth, cares not for quantum physics, the law of attraction or anything that cannot be explained by mainstream science or the mainstream narrative.

Once you have finished both of these lists, go over them carefully and determine what your deal breakers are... which qualities and non-qualities are non-negotiable. What remains on paper is then a representation of your ideal partner. Look at the lists closely – spectacular, no doubt. Now the wake-up call: who must *you* be to deserve such a person entering your life?

In the same way you highlighted a partner's strengths and weaknesses which either appealed to you or repelled you, you must do the same with regard to yourself. This process will be useless unless you are prepared to do so with brutal honesty in order to show the truth of who you are. Who we think we are, or who we portray ourselves to be, rarely aligns with who we really are. We can contest that vigorously, yet the truth is often revealed to us by the people we continue to attract or we remain attracted to.

Look at the list of positive traits that you have and then do the same with those considered unfavourable or need attention. If you have been sincere, I will wager that the ideal partner's traits you have highlighted as favourable or must haves may clash with those you have highlighted in yourself as undesirable.

Remember how we create our individual reality and that nothing exists outside a projected perception? Well, in simple speak, what we like about others we will like about ourselves, and what we don't like about others we won't like about ourselves.

The signs may be subtle or they may glow like a beacon, but I assure you that whatever you both like and dislike about others is what you both like and dislike about yourself. Sure, there are levels, as there are with all things, and what you loathe in someone else may be a hugely exaggerated trait you carry in yourself, or it was a trait you used to, but no longer, express. I can't tell you how many clients push back against this until I show them how subtle it can be, and that somewhere hiding in the shadows of their own psychology sits the very thing which replicates the behavioural expressions of those they critique. This is why we continue to attract similar versions of those we have spent our lives involved with. We say we want something better and deserve better, yet our inability to change means a replicated pattern is guaranteed alongside the repeated triggers that cause us to suffer.

This is why being rejected can be the catalyst for real change. Use this pain to analyse who you are and what needs to be worked on. Only then will a difference in your circumstances be forthcoming. Only then will a person with the favourable traits you want show up and stick around. Use pain to transform, raise your standards and push through previous barriers, in the knowledge that what awaits you on the other side is something more significant than what you were before.

What is Your Tequila Moment?

Some years ago, while living in the UK, I was a frequent visitor to the London clubs, where I would go with a friend to have some fun. A particular pastime was enjoying a tequila shot or two. I loved tequila, or, better said, I loved how tequila made me feel and was part of my weekend routine...

One particular evening, however, some friends and I decided to have more than usual and, to cut a long story short, I consumed more than 10 shots in 30 minutes. The fallout was catastrophic: I found myself an hour later in the toilets, collapsed and unable to stand up. The security managed to get me into a taxi with my girlfriend at the time, and she took me back to hers, where I spent the next five hours vomiting anything and everything I had inside me, including parts of my stomach lining, as I lay there on the living room floor. I thought I was going to die.

The suffering was so intense and so painful that I decided that, while lying there in agony, I would never drink tequila or any other short again. To this day, just the slightest whiff of tequila takes me back to that night and the horrors that unfolded. That was over 18 years ago and never again did I (nor will I ever) go near tequila again... Why? My brain's neural associative conditioning process assigned massive pain and suffering to an event on the basis of my very real feelings that aligned with my words.

The reason most people don't change is simple: they have never experienced something so painful that they couldn't take another day, minute or second of it any longer. They have not experienced their tequila moment.

Look back over your life and try to remember when you made real changes, real breakthroughs. I am not a gambling man, but if I were, I would wager that the shift happened when a line in the sand was breached... when an event so painful arose that even to contemplate a moment longer of suffering became impossible.

It's those events which shape destiny and it's those people and circumstances we attract which show up and shake us to our very foundations. It's then that we know what we want, and most definitely what we no longer can or will tolerate. Suddenly we figure it out, and the thought of leaving behind the source of our suffering becomes joyful.

I can't tell you how many times I have to repeat this to people who sit with me and tell me how much they are hurting, yet are still unwilling to leave behind that which causes the pain... a toxic relationship... an unproductive bad habit... an unhealthy addiction. When I suggest that their pain levels are not significant enough, the anger is evident because everyone likes to believe that their suffering is immense and intolerable... but not so. Until you have crossed that line where another second of pain is out of the question, then on it will continue.

Speak to anyone who has made a massive transformation, and behind it will be a history of immense suffering. They took their pain and made it work for them, and I encourage you to do the same. When it arrives, and you can be sure it will, don't be in a hurry to escape it by distracting yourself. It's there for a reason, and the sooner you embrace it, acknowledge it and work with it, the greater your growth will be.

Looking for joy as soon as possible doesn't help you find closure on your past. Use this time to connect to who you are at your core. Utilise those emotions and thought processes to make some much-needed healthy changes in your life. Take your time and really understand what is happening inside of you and what you will and will not tolerate in your life. It's times like these we get the chance to raise our standards, and by raising our standards, our lives improve.

Once you know who you are, what you want and how to value yourself, the highlighted deal-breaking traits that you have declared will remain so. However, if you attempt to short circuit the process and get back in the game too quickly as a diversion, then the chances are you will continue to attract the same characters who indulge in the same patterns of behaviour that caused the pain, take you down the same path and, most probably, lead to the same outcome.

A simple method to train the mind not to view rejection as catastrophic is to go out and find ways to be deliberately rejected. No, I am not a masochist nor do I have sadistic tendencies. Rejection therapy is a very real and powerful modality that one can use to bring this monster under control. On top of that, it can be fun.

So, do you want to play? Of course you do! Great – let's GET REJECTED.

Rejection therapy has one rule: to be rejected daily by someone at least once for 30 days without a break. This practice is designed for anyone who wants to build confidence and overcome the fear of rejection... Read that again! Growth via rejection.

Rejection therapy will show you how rejection can be an exciting and positive experience, and here is how is it done. You must put yourselves in a situation in which you will be rejected – you ask something of somebody, and they refuse your request. If you get a positive response, then that, of course, does not count.

Be creative with your requests. You will be surprised how easy it is to be turned down, and that is precisely what you want to happen… to be faced with a negative response and be ok with it. Ask a stranger if you can borrow some money, or solicit random people in the street to pay you compliments. Remember, if they agree, it doesn't count. Ask someone at the petrol station to fill your car, or the waiter in a cafe if you can have a free coffee. Ask if you can buy that girl or guy a drink. Ask to borrow some money.

Phone a random stranger and ask them to buy something from you. Smile at everybody you see and count the number of times you are ignored and rejected. If others smile back, which they usually do, then fantastic – it makes you feel great. If they don't, we get the chance to embrace rejection. Ask a stranger to tell you a secret. Knock on a door and ask if you can take flowers from their garden or fruit from their trees.

Rejection and abandonment are pandemic in today's world. These programmes are non-specific to gender, race or religion; they will screw you up in any language and will continue to do so unless addressed. Whole lives are ruined because of the inability to handle rejection… Rejection therapy, as outlined above, is a fabulous way to break the stranglehold which refusal places upon us.

The theory behind this is that life is much more open-ended that most of us think, yet we allow our fears of rejection to control our ability to ask or do something that may result in perceived failure. What we learn through rejection is the following. People often reject us not because there is anything essentially wrong with us, but because they just weren't interested in what we were offering at the time.

The rejection therapy technique above is an updated version of the approach initially created, I believe, by prominent psychologist Albert

Ellis, who developed his now well-known model of therapy called 'rational emotive behaviour therapy' as a way of overcoming the fear of approaching women. Like all concepts and ideas, the model has morphed into differing versions as we have evolved, but the hypothesis behind it remains the same. How irrational social fears control and restrict our lives in ways we are not really conscious of, as they come so naturally…

Get back on the dance floor and enjoy life. Some dancers are going to stand on your toes; some will flow gracefully around the floor with you, and others will reject your hand altogether. That's the beauty of life. What are you going to do… sit on the side-lines forever and berate life and those who didn't or won't dance to your tune? Remember, you are going to have to kiss many frogs before finding your prince or princess, so pucker up those lips and embrace the uncertainty and the growth that arises from rejection.

By experiencing controlled versions of rejection, we learn how not to be attached to outcomes we perceive as necessary for acceptance or happiness. We permit ourselves to learn from the feedback and even enjoy rejection in a way considered implausible by our former selves.

To sum up… Don't let the fear of rejection paralyse your decision making. If you have an idea, try it. If you have a question, ask it. If you have a path, pursue it. If you like that person, then ask them out. The downside is low, but the upside is enormous.

Try the rejection therapy for 30 days; at least once a day, you must be rejected. Write your experiences down and note your progress, but enjoy the experience. I know that sounds a little masochistic, but it's not. This tool is handy for overcoming one of mankind's greatest fears.

There's one caveat I must be clear about: do not do anything that could land you in trouble or put you in harm's way. Other than that, have fun, get creative, and enjoy being rejected and who you become a month down the line.

IN A NUTSHELL

Life is not predictable and neither is it possible to avoid rejection. Life is not just about beauty and pleasure. Are you going to miss out on the fragrance of the rose because you fear its thorns?

TRAFFIC CONTROL 2

---◆•◆---

Take time out.

It's that time again... when we take a break from our busy schedule to stop and just be. So, get comfortable and bring awareness to the moment.

Close your eyes and breathe deeply through your nose via the diaphragm for four seconds. Hold your breath for a count of seven seconds and become aware of how it feels to focus on holding the breath. Now breathe slowly out for eight seconds through the mouth, as if blowing through a straw, making a subtle but audible whooshing sound. Then hold for two seconds with empty lungs, before repeating the cycle. Continue until five minutes have passed; you can extend this time, but make five minutes a minimum.

The above breathing technique is an elaboration of the original traffic control routine I shared with you earlier in this book. It has been proved to be an aid to relaxation, a superior coping mechanism for anxiety-related conditions, and a real bonus in helping those with insomnia if practised when in bed at night. Breathing actively influences the physiology and thought processes, including our moods. Bringing our attention to our breathing is a powerful way of shifting our physiology, being mindful and, dare I say it, dropping us into a meditative state.

You cannot pick up a book, newspaper or magazine these days without an article extolling the virtues of meditation and mindfulness. The reason for this is that these techniques have been scientifically proved to work: they reduce stress, improve concentration and in fact enhance all aspects of human life.

Anybody new to meditation needn't be alarmed – it's the most natural thing in the world. It isn't part of any religion, and neither does it belong to the stereotypical new-age hippy archetype, sitting cross-legged with a long ponytail and round coloured sunglasses and chanting in unknown languages. (No offence if you happen to have long hair, round tinted specs and enjoy meditation this way.) It won't judge you, shout or scream and never will it let you down. Practised regularly, meditation will enhance the love, compassion and awareness we desperately need in today's world.

MEDITATION 101

Through mindful meditation, the ability
to concentrate improves.

Dedicating time to meditation is a meaningful way of caring for yourself that helps deal with the pressures of life; as life gets ever faster, the pressures become ever more intense. As this skill develops and the mind grows quieter, we begin to see self-defeating and harmful thought patterns for what they are – mind constructs.

Through meditation, we can better understand the behaviour patterns and emotions by becoming the observer and not the absorber of them. The increased clarity, which stems from reflection, enables healthier options. As stated previously, anything that elevates our emotional state provides access to better solutions, and the calmer the mind, the more resourceful we become.

Meditation helps us better understand our worries, our fears, our anger and all our emotions. Hence, I want you to include the practice of meditation in your new daily routine. Just as you wouldn't leave the house without brushing your teeth, neither should you go out of the house without meditating for a few minutes. So as not to rush into it, I suggest starting off with three minutes. If three minutes sounds daunting, then just a single mindful breath is a start.

Wherever you are now, if safe to do so, stop, close your eyes and take one large breath in and become mindful of the lungs expanding. Hold that breath for a few seconds and pay attention to your body. Next, exhale slowly, letting go as the air leaves your mouth while focusing on the falling of the body as you do so. The awareness of the rising and falling of the chest and abdomen will become your points of focus while meditating. Now, please open your eyes and take another slow, deep breath and become aware of your surroundings – the smells, the sounds, the sights, the texture of life itself.

Congratulations, you have just taken a fully conscious breath... a breath anchored in the present moment, the only period that has, can or will ever exist. Don't underestimate the power of a single conscious breath; it can be the catalyst for massive transformation.

So, what is meditation? Unless you have been in a coma or living under a rock for some time, the term 'meditation' will not have escaped your awareness, but what is it? Meditation is an approach to training the mind, similar to the way that fitness is an approach to educating the body. But how does one learn to meditate and keep it simple? It can be challenging for somebody to sit still and think of nothing, or to have an 'empty mind', when they are used to a mind full of content. I can't tell you how many people say to me that they are unable to meditate because they have active minds, which makes me smile since all minds are engaged. That is what a mind does – it thinks, endlessly, unless some form of training is followed.

Meditation is not intended to eradicate your thoughts, but for you to become better acquainted with the nature of your mind, and be more able to disengage from your thoughts, than to be captured by them. If you start out believing that you can empty the mind, you will quickly give up, labelling yourself as a poor meditator and another reason to think yourself not good enough or a failure of some kind.

The average human being has between 60 and 70 thousand thoughts a day, which equates to about 250 ideas in a five-minute meditation session... like a bunch of monkeys, jumping around, screeching, chattering and carrying on endlessly, all clamouring for attention. But – and this is very important – you cannot fight with your thoughts or try to eliminate them from your mind; this will not work and will only increase the tension. 'That which resists persists' is an easy-to-remember mini-mantra to use when trying to eliminate anything by focusing on it. 'What you focus on, you will get more of!' is another powerful reminder.

By understanding and calming the mind, one can learn to tame, not eliminate, through meditation the constant chattering monkeys. Thoughts become more peaceful if we tenderly bring them into submission with consistent practice. Only when we focus and re-focus on them do they hang around for longer than necessary. It's worth noting that it's not emotions which cause pain or suffering, but the stories we attach to them. Bear this in mind as we proceed – it will be invaluable.

Begin with mindful breathing, a tried and tested approach, and the most comfortable form for those new to meditation. There is no destination, nor any goal, so there is nothing to win or lose. We often define ourselves by winning or losing; with meditation there is neither. Just keep returning to the breath, with tenderness and tolerance, noticing what is happening, without making judgements, and seeing the experience as neither positive nor negative.

Be gentle and remain calm if what ascends is overwhelming, which can happen as you pay attention to the emerging feelings. We often try to push uncomfortable feelings away, so sitting and welcoming them may feel strange. Remember, there is no destination to reach and neither is there anything to achieve or feel. We are merely teaching ourselves to observe the mind and any arising thoughts or emotions that emanate from the ideas in our head.

Observe the feelings, without attaching a story to them; the key is to observe, not to absorb. Imagine yourself as the watcher, looking on from the corner of the room as you meditate... Using myself as an example, if I were feeling anxious, I would say: 'Darren is feeling anxious, Darren is feeling nervous or Darren is thinking about paying his telephone bill.' By looking on as the third person, I create distance between my true self, the infinite self, and the physical avatar whose name is Darren and who is having these human emotions and feelings.

Whether you believe you are an infinite consciousness or a one-time physical entity matters not. Creating distance between yourself and the arising emotions by looking on as an imaginary third person can often take the edge off powerful feelings and emotions that can surface. *Disassociation* is a powerful practice that can be applied to any painful or hurtful memory or event.

I had a client who was involved in a minor motorbike accident and was having a hard time coping with the troublesome memories that were being magnified by his constant focus. I instructed him to step out of his body and float backwards and upwards, looking down on the event from a third-person perspective. I then asked him to freeze the movie running in his head and create a still picture of the event. Next, I asked him to drain the colour from the image and make it even smaller as he floated further back, using his imagination to reframe and change the perspective of the accident. He immediately felt relief as this new and powerful internal representation suggested a new reality. I am happy to report that, after a few days of repeating this technique, he no longer experienced the hardship associated with the accident.

On the flip side of the disassociation coin is *association*, which one can use to enhance the feeling of well-being. Go back in your memory or project yourself into the future to an event which creates a feeling of positivity. Imagine your desired outcome. Now, step into the event and see it through your own eyes, and use your powerful imagination to enhance the feelings. Make the colours brighter, the sounds clearer and the smells more intense as you programme your mind to produce heightened feelings of well-being. Try it for yourselves – it's simple, but very powerful for shifting internal states of being, and, lest you forget, the quality of your life is directly correlated to the state of your emotions. Remember, we are forever feeling our thinking; therefore, change how you think and you change how you feel.

IN A NUTSHELL

To reduce the intensity and feeling of an event, use *disassociation*. To enhance feelings, use *association*.

MEDITATION ROUTINE

This simple daily meditation routine is a powerful tool which one can use to bring order out of chaos to a mind that jumps continually from one thought to another:

- Sit down or lie comfortably somewhere quiet where you will not be disturbed.
- Close your eyes.
- Make no effort to control your breath. Simply breathe naturally from the area of the body that you autonomously breathe from; for some, this will be from the diaphragm, for others, from high up in the chest. It's worth noting that breathing from the diaphragm has been proved to be the healthiest and most productive way for us to breathe.
- Focus your attention on your breath and on how your body moves as you inhale and exhale, opening your awareness to body sensations as they arise. Beginners can state in their heads 'I am breathing in' on the inhale, and 'I am breathing out'

on the exhale; this can be dropped later as you become more skilled in breathing meditation.

- If your mind wanders, recognise and acknowledge the emotion and return once again to the breath. For example, if you are distracted from the breathing process by a thought, simply state: 'I am thinking.' Stay with the thought that has arisen until it dissolves naturally, which it will, as quickly as it arose, if you don't ruminate unnecessarily. Apply this informal process to anything that enters your mind. If it's a sound, state 'I am listening' and let it go. 'I am singing', 'I am hearing'... state it, let it go and come back to the breathing.
- Maintain this meditation practice for two to three minutes to start with, although this can be longer if you feel comfortable.

This practice of mindful meditation teaches us to connect to the present moment, by connecting to the breath. Everything in life is dependent on the breath, and breathing only ever occurs in the present moment. By using the breath as an anchor to which you return whenever the mind wanders off, presence is resumed.

Be kind to yourself when trying this for the first time. It's almost inevitable that the mind will repeatedly scramble the process. Do not worry or become agitated – it is entirely normal and to be expected. Just name in your mind what it is that has come into awareness, and let it go. Return gently to the breath and start again.

Breathing meditation encourages you to observe wandering thoughts as they drift through the mind but to not attach to them. The intention is not to get involved with the thinking process or to judge, but to just be aware of each mental note as it arises, name it and let it go. A further layer of labelling can be applied as you become more accustomed to the practice of meditation, but for now, start with the above. I will discuss and expand upon meditation and different techniques as we proceed.

As you sit quietly, you will learn quickly how thoughts and feelings tend to move in regular patterns. You will become aware of the tendency to judge experiences, labelling them as good or bad, or pleasant or unpleasant, when they need not be marked but merely regarded as different encounters.

The health benefits of meditation have been scientifically proved beyond any doubt. Just a few of the verified benefits that meditation provides are: reduced blood pressure, improved blood circulation, lower heart rate, less perspiration, slower respiratory rate, less anxiety, lower blood cortisol levels, improved feelings of well-being, less stress and more profound relaxation.

I will reiterate the benefits of meditation, and how important it is as a practice to master the thoughts and constant chatter that infects the mind. The mind is the greatest servant or the most miserable master; how you train it is directly proportionate to the quality of your life, so choose wisely.

IN A NUTSHELL

Meditation is a sure-fire way to increase concentration and decrease stress when practised consistently. When we meditate regularly, we become less bothered with minor problems and are better equipped to handle the bigger issues that life throws at us. In consequence, we better understand our minds, making everyday tasks easier to perform.

IT'S TIME TO LEVEL UP

*Honesty is like a disease that pollutes
everything it touches. Be honest, and those
around you start coughing up bits of sincerity
all over you. It's amazing.*

How did you get on with meditation? I am hoping it's the start of a beautiful relationship between yourself and your blossoming mind.

But for now, it's back to work and time to dig deep again for those golden nuggets... to unearth the hidden gems which lie unseen in the catacombs of your psyche, awaiting your arrival. That can prove difficult when trying to level up, especially when the ego has a vested interest in maintaining the status quo. I am as guilty as anyone in this department, and it took me many years of trial and error before reaching a point where I became far more aware of how I was being, who I was being and who I wanted to be.

ALIGNING THE PARTS

Until the above components align, confusion and a lack of productivity are guaranteed. And never are you more confused than when you try to convince your heart and spirit of something that your mind knows is a myth. So how does one expose these parts and align them with authenticity? Start by asking some insightful questions about yourself; my personal responses to the questions are included here, to give you some idea.

1. 'Who do I want to be?'

Honest, reliable, helpful, successful and growing in my chosen field, but above all happy.

2. 'Who do I not want to be?'

A paycheck guy, working for others in a nine-to-five job. Someone recognised for starting but not finishing projects or undertakings. A liar who cannot be trusted. A selfish man who takes much and gives back little in return.

3. 'Who am I right now?'

Not totally honest. Too comfortable. If I continue learning as I am, my knowledge will grow but my wisdom not so. Not trying hard enough to achieve the success I say I want. I'm stuck in routines that do not help me develop. Not someone that I can be thrilled about, which suggests, if this continues, I will be in the same position a year from now... one year older, yet no further forward.

POST-ANALYSIS

After asking myself the above four questions and answering them, I sat a while and projected into my future, five years down the track. I didn't like what I saw... more of the same, but tired, grumpy, five years longer in the tooth and unfulfilled. Something had to change. I had to find something – a catalyst – that could ignite a spark inside me. And there it was, my second tequila moment: the free-diving accident I spoke about earlier which had left me deaf in one ear and with crippling tinnitus in both. The pain and suffering were so intense, so all-encompassing, that I radically altered everything which defined me as a person in an attempt to defeat the howling demons in my head. I drew upon that experience as the trigger for the changes I had to make elsewhere in my life.

It was so painful, so fundamental in my life, that I made a decision right there and then that I would do anything to change the circumstances and the pain. *And in that moment*, my life changed. Instead of sliding and falling (as some do) when severe adversity calls, I used the hardship to climb out of that hole, defeat the negative self-talk, catastrophising and victimisation, and began to walk a new path. I found a silver lining and a way to reframe massive suffering and use it for constant and never-ending improvement, thus creating a better version of me.

Winners use experiences, regardless of the pain, as lessons, whereas losers believe that life has a grudge against them and give up. What sets the coward and the hero apart? They feel the same emotions, the same fears and the same uncertainty when faced with the dilemma presented to them; however, the heroes act, they do what is necessary or, better said, they do what is right. I implore you to do what is right, do what is required and make those necessary changes. I am not asking you to enjoy the lessons, but certainly learn and grow from them!!!

From the moment the decision to change is made, life can never be the same. You have levelled up and it's onwards and upwards from there to the next level, and then to the next, until you depart the video game we call life. Use that defining moment, use that event or circumstance to facilitate a better life for yourself. Get yourself together and make some real life-changing plans. If you want a compelling future, then list some possible and persuasive intentions and give them a score from 1 to 10. Any target that does not have a 10 beside it should be discarded immediately because it lacks total commitment, and total commitment is what's needed.

Time is precious, so stop wasting it on plans and half-arsed aspirations that will fizzle out and come to nothing. Your time will be better served on projects and goals that light you up at a 10. Remember, every time you start something and give up or don't finish, you are strengthening a limiting belief and cementing a negative self-image about yourself that you are not good enough and a perpetual failure. That will cause unhappiness and another reminder of your past and that which doesn't serve you. It's either 100% or nothing.

In reference to his entire sailing battalion being set alight before engaging in combat with the British 2,000 years ago, Julius Caesar is attributed with saying: 'If you want to take the island, burn the boats!' By doing so, he left his men no choice but to win the battle and take the island and all the spoils that would be theirs in victory. Another way of saying the same thing is: forget a backup plan or a plan B. Safety nets and insurance policies present too much wiggle room. Know what you want and keep going until you get it.

If you are anything like me, then my intentions, although admirable, lacked essential ingredients; for example, I wanted to write a book but had no idea how to go about it, other than sitting down at my computer to pour my thoughts into a Word document. But that is just a small portion of what one needs to do before it becomes a finished article and ready for public consumption. I had to find someone who had already achieved this ambition. You've heard me mention this before, but I had to find a role model – someone with the capabilities and know-how that I needed in order to take my dream to the next level of productivity.

Role modelling is the best and easiest way to replicate and create exponential growth. You can attempt to do it all on your own... that's a given. But without a coach and the necessary training, courses and advice from mentors and role models, and unless you are an absolute natural genius in your field, it will be damn difficult.

So, I found a writer who had been published multiple times, and I spent the necessary time with him until I was clear on the process. In fact, this writer introduced me to his publisher, who decided to give me a contract for my first book... the one you are reading now. That would never have happened had I not reached out in the first place, believing that I could do it all on my own.

I cannot emphasise this strongly enough: learn from the best, in every sector of life. If you want the best body, then get the best trainer you can afford. Do you want a mind that's sharp, clear and energised? Then employ the best coach you know. If you want to enjoy the very best food, then hire a chef to cook it for you.

Would you like to know the immeasurable differences between a chef and a cook? A chef will take the same ingredients as the cook, but because of his passion, his rejection of the ordinary and, above all, his expertise, the chef will refuse to allow anything other than the best dish possible to grace your table! The moral of the story: learn from those who are where you wish to be and see how fast you level up.

Once you have all your ducks in a row, and have gained the necessary information or qualifications, it's time for action. Often the hardest part of any climb is the first few steps. We look up from the ground, contemplating what we may have to face before we reach the summit. It can be daunting, that's for sure. But remember, you discover who you are on the way to the pinnacle of the mountain, and not who you become while sitting at the zenith.

Put your best foot forward, followed by the other, and you begin. You do the math. You solve one problem, and then you solve another and another, until momentum is firmly on your side and now you are cooking. Now, don't ease off the accelerator until you have made a real breakthrough. This part of the equation, however, can be potentially troublesome.

What I did was to share my goals with people I trusted and respected. I asked them if they would hold me accountable while I attempted to scale my Everest. I clearly outlined what I wanted to achieve, including how many words I would write each day and any further work I needed to do. This extra layer of accountability can make all the difference. A man's word is his bond, or I believe it should be. For what is a man without it? Where is his integrity if he *says* some thing yet doesn't *do* some thing? By making a promise to those I respect, I wasn't about to let them or myself down. Each night I would send them my report and proof of my work.

I suggest you do the same when attempting to make a break-through of any kind. Recruit two or three people you love and respect and whose opinion of you matters; ask them to be your co-pilot for whatever it is you wish to achieve. Ask them to deliver the hurt, to deliver the tough love needed to help you when things get rough and you feel like giving up.

Make some real tough promises to yourself and keep them at any cost... promises that scare you, promises that have you coming face to face with the inner procrastinator, promises that challenge your fiercest inner critic and the self-sabotaging voices which accompany that swindling part of your psychology.

Commit to doing precisely what you say you will do, not only when working towards your specific goal, but in every walk of life. Telling the truth at all costs is bloody hard, but this is what I want from you: total honesty, absolute integrity and complete accountability. You can't imagine what it will do for your life if you see this through. If you ignore everything else I have written about, but commit to telling the truth and deliver on your word, you will create a wave of positive momentum that will carry you towards where you wish to be.

Ignore, or better still remove, anybody and anything that tries to dissuade you from your path or bring you down. You will not light up your life while shadows are being cast all over it by those who block out your sunlight. I heard a great term recently to describe those who indulge in the art of holding others back: 'dementors', characters invented by JK Rowling, of Harry Potter fame. Dementors suck all the happiness out of people, and you'll feel like you'll never be happy again when one comes near you. They drain peace, hope and happiness out of the air around them. Get too near a dementor and every good feeling and every happy memory will be sucked out of you. If it can, the dementor will feed on you long enough to reduce you to something like itself, and you will be left with nothing but the worst experiences of your life.

Do you have dementors in your life? If so, you know what to do!

So, what's it going to be? More of the same? Or are you ready this time to go for your win... to punch through the resistance and make a real breakthrough... to up your game once and for all? Listen. If this sounds too much hard work, that's ok. If you are not prepared to go all in and leave untapped potential on the table, then so be it. Admit to yourself you can't do it. You are not ready to play at this level of the game, and if that be the case, stop searching for solutions you are not prepared to implement and jump back into that boat, without a compass, captain, map or anchor, to be buffeted by the random forces of nature.

TRAFFIC CONTROL 3

—◆◆—

A chance to slow down again, pull back and
appreciate your surroundings.

Before moving on, I suggest you take another minibreak if possible and savour another chance to calm the mind and to appreciate your surroundings with a simple yet powerful form of meditation using a single candle as your point of focus. The mental focus needed for change is demanding, so balancing that out with recuperative time-outs is crucial; hence the need for regular traffic control.

By using a candle, we can harness the mind's ability to focus on one thing and remain with it for a short length of time. The breathing pattern we will use is a four-seven-eight tempo: a four-second nasal inhalation, followed by a seven-second hold at the top of the breath, and then a slow and controlled eight-second exhalation, as if you were blowing out through a straw. Set your timer for a minimum of seven minutes before you start. Place the candle around 2.5 metres from you, as close to eye level as possible, but don't worry if that's a problem; anywhere in front of you will be fine provided, of course, it's safe. Darken the room as much as possible, light the candle, take your seat or sit on the bed with your back straight, and start your timer.

Now bring your attention to the flame and with a soft gaze stare right at it. As directed in the above breathing pattern, draw in a long, slow breath through your nose and hold; as you slowly breathe out through your mouth, let the busyness of your mind drop away. As you continue to breathe, be aware of any tightness in your body by scanning down from head to toe, and internally check in with the quality of your bodily sensations, feelings and thoughts. If there is any tightness, direct your attention to that part of your body, and imagine breathing into it and relaxing it as you exhale.

Once again, draw in a long, slow, deep breath, all the way down into your belly. As you exhale through your mouth, ensure that your back remains straight and that your shoulders are not raised. Put a small smile on your face and enjoy this solitude. I am hoping that you learn to not only appreciate but look forward to rare moments of silence in a world that gets ever louder. Silence is a beautiful teacher, once you have trained the mind with a consistent meditation practice.

Continue to gaze softly at the flame... blinking when necessary. Don't strain your eyes in any way. Allow your mind to soften, but acknowledge, as before, any thoughts that enter your awareness. Name the feeling or emotion and let it go, without building a storyline around the thoughts; allow them to float out of your mind like passing clouds.

A powerful metaphor I like to use when teaching meditation is the following. Imagine yourself sitting in your city bus station, watching the buses come and go, each one displaying a different location at the top of its windscreen. There is no need to hop on any of them. Just continue to monitor the buses coming and going, and notice their respective destinations while remaining where you are. Jumping on a bus and leaving the station is comparable to climbing on a thought or a feeling and riding it to its final destination. If you find yourself doing so, gently catch yourself, note what it is, state it in your head and return to the exercise. Or, if you see yourself hitching a ride out of the station, stop the bus, get off, and make your way back to your seat in the station and continue noting the buses as they come and go.

Don't be discouraged if your mind is busy or beat yourself up because you are finding it difficult to stay focused. This is your meditation practice, and it takes time and patience to train the mind. Pay special attention to the word 'practice'. Great artists had to practise... sports stars had to practise... musicians had to practise. In fact, nobody achieves anything outstanding without the hours spent practising; meditation and training the mind is no different, so be kind to yourself when starting out.

Try not to get disheartened when your mind is pulling you in every conceivable direction, which it will at times. A busy life equates to a busy mind, and meditation is a wonderful way to pick apart the seams of the overthinking process, and to allow some much-needed space to develop in the mind.

Once the timer lets you know your practice is over, bring your awareness back into the room and back into your body. I like to express my gratitude for something greater than myself on completion of my practice: the miracle of life... the incredible universe we are part of... God, or however you wish to language him or her... or merely for being able to spend those few minutes in silent contemplation, before reengaging with the hustle and bustle of daily life.

There is a something very special about gratitude, yet it costs nothing; it improves psychological health, increases happiness, reduces depression, enhances empathy and reduces aggression. All those amazing positive benefits can be reaped simply by being appreciative and focusing on what you do have, instead of focusing on things you do not.

So, give thanks, blow out the candle and enjoy the rest of your day. Or if your practice is before bed, blow out the candle and enjoy a restful sleep.

NO TIME LIKE THE PRESENT

————◆●◆————

*Once you replace negative feelings with positive
ones, you will start to have positive results.*

Take a little while now to evaluate your life and the direction
it is heading. Where will you be in a month or two... or in
a year's time, if you continue as you are right now? Is that
appealing? Have you realised your full potential and honoured the
miracle that you are?

What is it going to be? The old you... the old ways, habits and rituals... the procrastinator that wants, but never does? Or the loving,
able you, who recognises the beauty and unlimited potential that life
has to offer and goes after it with the tenacity of a pit bull terrier?

One of the biggest mistakes you may be making is to think that,
because you are young and healthy at the moment, you can afford to
waste a few more days, weeks, months or years engaging in routines
and habits that add no lasting value to your life. I am hoping that
those who have got this far in the book will have already taken massive action and are feeling the benefits that support those who seek
it. If not, let me tell you a little story; this applies whether you are 19,
29, 39 or 69.

It happened that 15 years ago I met an attractive 20-year-old
woman, who I will call Nicola, whose primary goals in life were to
be married, become a mother, and raise a loving family equipped

to make a difference in the world. She was beautiful, full of life, invigorating and enchanting, and wanted to become a therapist to help those in need.

I was impressed with the clear picture of how she wanted her life to look. Surprisingly, however, she started putting off the necessary steps that would prepare her for the future she had outlined. Whenever she was challenged to be more responsible, her excuse was always: 'There is no rush. I have plenty of time on my side.'

So, she kicked back, fooled around and treaded water, instead of reading the necessary books, studying and taking the courses she required in order to facilitate her dreams. She did what many choose to do: rather than delay gratification and stick to her plan, she wanted it there and then. To be clear, I am not making a judgement here but merely relaying what happened to Nicola and others who lean towards instant gratification and continue to suspend working towards their specific purpose. Remember life's ultimate equation? Our choices create our circumstances.

A well-known cliché the Brits use is: 'time flies when you are having fun'. In Nicola's case, time was passing in a blur until she woke up one morning, looked in the mirror and realised that she was 33 years old and had achieved none of her carefully laid out plans.

The last time I saw her was when she came to see me for a one-hour consultation. She was now 35, single, unfit, diagnosed with an anxiety disorder and working as a secretary for a boss she despised, in a job she had zero passion for. She told me she hadn't educated herself to the necessary levels and sorrowfully had almost lost her will to live on more than one occasion. No less than four times during the session, she said to me that she didn't know where her time had gone.

And the moral of this story? Take care of your time and spend it wisely; live a life of purpose; find out what that purpose is and go after it, but go after it *now*. Don't wake up like Nicola one morning and wonder how life has passed you by.

Here are a few more reminders that can keep you focused, inspired and on track:

1. Take time every day to ask yourself: 'What's the best use of my life, and am I moving towards or away from that objective. Am I focusing on what I want or is my attention still very much on what I don't want?' Do this repeatedly, and you will gain a definitive insight into what you are here to do.

2. Safeguard your time and be careful whom you spend it with. Show me your associations, and show me how you spend your time, what you talk about and what you focus on, and I will show you where you are headed.

3. Be aware of the undertones of discomfort in your body, so that at the slightest onset of physiological dysfunction, you can initiate techniques to interrupt the patterns. Remember, emotions are feedback about the quality of your thinking and actions. Listen carefully to your body and do what is necessary to interrupt the pattern. Learn to recognise the difference between a destructive habit that craves unhealthy familiarity and a zero or nothing day, where the best thing to do is write it off and take some much-needed rest and recovery.

4. Listen to your conscience... that powerful inner voice which discerns morally correct and incorrect actions, and the differences between right and wrong. Some believe that God talks to us through our conscience, while others believe that it's an inherent quality taught to us by those who exert their authority over us, such as parents, the media and friends. It matters not what *you* believe, only that you listen carefully and trust your conscience when it's trying to guide you in a particular direction.

5. Feed your spirit; the best way to do that is to give. Find ways to regularly make a difference in the lives of others who are worse off than you are. Get this right, and your life will never be empty, regardless of what you do.

TRAFFIC CONTROL 4

*Keep it simple: if you can't explain it to a
six-year-old, you don't understand it yourself.*

We often look for rich experiences to define our lives...
expensive holidays, high-tech gadgetry, gourmet meals,
designer shoes, clothes, bags and watches, or any number
of things we buy or do to shore up the fragility and discontent of
everyday life. We really are biological weapons of mass consumption.

Yet, as with most things lacking substance, these 'pick-me-ups'
dissolve quickly, leaving us with that familiar empty feeling. From
there, the search is on for the next fix until we have an itch we just
can't scratch. Sound familiar? Well, let's try something different –
let's keep it simple and organic.

All around us there are simple opportunities abounding with happiness that won't cost you an arm and a leg if you shift your focus...
the smile of a child, unbridled laughter, a hot bath, a homemade meal,
a massage, hearing from an old friend, a 10-minute run, an email
from an admirer, or all green lights and no traffic on the daily commute to work. Perhaps it's your favourite song on the radio, singing
in the shower, a smile from a stranger, finding a bargain online or in
a charity shop, writing, reading a book, or sitting in the sun. It could
be a coffee in your favourite cafe, watching a good film with somebody whose company you value, a great conversation with friends,

an empty line at the supermarket, or cycling through the countryside with the wind in your hair.

The list is endless, and a whole book could be filled with everyday but compelling examples of simple pleasures which we overlook in the search for something grandiose. Make a list for yourself – write down the simple pleasures that bring a genuine smile, not just to the lips, but to the heart. Then look out for them, notice them, be grateful for them and indulge in them often, for these self-help remedies can work wonders, yet cost little or nothing at all.

HAPPINESS

———◆◆◆———

For every minute you are unhappy, you lose
60 seconds of potential happiness.

'Wouldn't life be wonderful if science came up with a mathematical formula that solved unhappiness?' is a statement that many new clients intimate. They may word it differently, but the underlying message is the same: if there existed a pill invented by science that stimulated perpetual happiness, they would happily take it.

When we are hurting and in pain, we long for the suffering to abate, but would everlasting happiness be a good thing? Absolutely not.[10] We need balance in every aspect of our lives, and the happiness/unhappiness puzzle is no different.

You may be wondering where I am going with this when this book is heavily skewed towards behaviour and thinking that stimulates happiness and actions which lead to positive outcomes. I am merely playing devil's advocate and warning you of the potential downside

---

[10] Scientist June Gruber concluded on May 18, 2011, after in-depth research and extensive case studies, that too much cheerfulness can make us gullible, selfish, less prosperous and more prone to taking unnecessary risks, and lead us to neglect threats. See https://www.washingtonpost.com/national/health-science/too-much-happiness-can-make-you-unhappy-studies-show/2012/04/02/gIQACELLrS_story.html?noredirect=on&utm_term=.45ef72c059b6.

of seeking out happiness at all costs and berating yourselves when you are feeling anything other than happy, which is going to happen.

But before you throw *The Journey Back to Self*, along with all your other self-help books, in the bin, take a breath and listen up. There are a host of benefits associated with changing your emotional states and negative patterns and focusing on what makes you feel good. Just refrain from keeping score on how happy you are, and stop believing that it's possible never to be unhappy, sad, miserable, angry or frustrated again, as that is never going to happen.

I won't bore you with Gruber's in-depth study that was used to prove that too much happiness can be destructive, but needless to say, it was concluded that three positive emotions (such as joy, compassion, gratitude or hope) for every one negative emotion (such as disgust, embarrassment, fear, guilt or sadness) was the equation we should strive for in order to maximise our lives. If we can experience three happy encounters for each unhappy occasion, then we have solved one of lives greatest conundrums.

But didn't I tell you that we, as a species, naturally lean towards fear and negativity? Furthermore, the human brain isn't designed to make us happy and fulfilled: it's designed for survival. Our minds are forever on the lookout for what is wrong, for whatever can hurt us, so that we can either fight it or flee from it. Indeed, I did. Hence, we must use strategy to rewire and reprogramme the brain to behave in ways that rejig those odds and stack them in our favour.

And no, this isn't a war of attrition or a complex modality that needs months of application. This is so profoundly simple, a child could grasp it... well, certainly the first part, which I will deal with initially.

If I asked you what sets apart the happiest people on the planet from the least happy, what would you say? I bet you are now racking your brains for elaborate and in-depth replies, believing that it must be something complicated and intricate, when the answer is so simple: the happiest people alive regularly do more of what makes them happy! And before looking perplexingly at your screen or book, and contemptuously ignoring what I just said, reread the following sentence and let it sink in:

*The happiest people alive repeatedly do more of
what makes them happy.*

Now ask yourself how regularly, or daily, do you engage in all the things you love to do? Before answering that, let me explain how this works. If I asked you what made you mad, sad, jealous, vengeful or angry, you would come up with things based on experiences in your life which align with those emotions. They would each have their own recipe in the same way that an apple pie has a recipe: to bake an outstanding apple pie, you first need to know the ingredients and then use them to produce the desired outcome. Well, happiness, fun, joy and excitement are no different and also have their recipes – it's not rocket science, just plain common sense.

HAPPINESS EQUATION PART 1

Now, I want you to write down everything you enjoy doing... anything that brings you contentment, however minuscule. Then, write down what you do on a typical day. Next, compare the two lists. If your daily routine consists of very few or none of the things which make you happy, you are giving yourself little chance of experiencing joy, wouldn't you agree?

To help you out further, let's get a little more tactical and specific by categorising areas in your life which are deemed critical. As an example, my daily list could look like the following.

Hobbies and Lifestyle

Euphoric dance or a body-based movement on awakening, for 10 minutes. A cold shower or a cold bath, time permitting. Studying

Spanish. Writing a blog, a gratitude journal or a book. Watching Ted Talks or podcasts with men and women that provide quality content for my mind. Reading books that help me grow in my chosen direction. Assisting as many people as possible through the day in any number of ways. Watching comedy each day on YouTube. Engaging with animals. Travelling.

Sport

Swimming in the ocean, a lake or a pool. Running on the beach, through the countryside or in a forest. Cycling. Weight training. Playing golf. Go-karting. Beach volleyball.

Relationships

Spending quality, not quantity, time with my partner. Engaging and growing with her by way of meaningful conversations. Reaching out to friends and family across the globe via Skype or FaceTime.

Work

Bringing as much value as possible to my work by improving my skill sets in my chosen career, to better serve my clients and the public. Enrolling in workshops or new courses.

Religious or Spiritual Aspirations

Daily meditation. Yoga. Prayer. Chanting. Self-hypnosis. Mindfulness.

Health

Drinking purified water. Preparing and eating healthy food. Wim Hoff breathing protocol. Walking barefoot on the grass, through a park or on the beach. Using a floatation tank to calm and soothe my nervous system.

Post-analysis

After you have completed your list, see how many of the activities you perform each day. You may have another eureka moment. How many of your chosen activities are you engaging with daily? How many could you enjoy if you wanted to?

I know life can be troublesome at times and there are not enough hours in the day, but find a big enough 'why' to do something, and you will figure out how to incorporate it into your life. I am assuming that happiness is the ultimate why; if not, why not? We often sabotage ourselves and allow those ruts we get stuck in to get ever deeper. Pick yourself up and go do what makes you happy – not tomorrow or in a week's time, *now*. Choose one thing you really enjoy and go do it.

The journey of a thousand miles begins with a single step... I invite you to take it! Go for that run or intense walk. Cycle somewhere, have a swim, skip, beat your chest, do some press-ups, chant, read that book, listen to a podcast. Dance, knit, cut the grass, hug a tree, volunteer, do some charity work, scream, call a friend, call all your friends, meditate, recite your favourite prayer. It matters not what you do, as long as you do something you like every day and begin to stack these activities one on top of the other. See what this does for your emotional and physical state... I promise you won't be disappointed.

The first part of the happiness equation is therefore clearly very much activity based... pursuits we can do physically to interrupt our stale and unproductive patterns, change our moods and retrain our brains by means of repetitious and favourable activities that produce feel-good hormones, such as endorphins, dopamine, serotonin and oxytocin. The more of these hormones we experience, the happier we feel, and happiness, like any other behaviour, becomes addictive. I know what you are thinking: any addiction is potentially damaging. Right? Well, in its purity, yes... anything which is unavailable that we come to rely on in order to feel a certain way is going to create a negative reaction.

A runner's body, for instance, is flooded with endorphins and a cocktail of feel-good hormones while clocking up the miles, producing what is known as 'runners high'. But what happens when an injury prevents the runner from hitting the tarmac or the treadmill for an extended period? They experience agitation, irritability, anxiety, frustration or, from my experience with working with runners, all of the above.

However, we must apply common sense here and make a distinction between an addiction to something harmful (such as smoking or drinking) and an addiction to something beneficial (such as working out, running, meditation or yoga). If we are to be addicted to anything, then we had better make it as healthy as possible – agreed? But we also need to have available to us other pastimes and hobbies that we can actively engage in if we are unable to participate in our primary source of enjoyment. That is the point of making a list of all the things you enjoy, and participating in as many of them as possible so as not to fall foul of the addict's curse.

Now, let's look at the second part of the happiness equation, which is a little more complicated.

HAPPINESS EQUATION PART 2

Healthy addictions aside, there is another recipe for happiness which we must explore if we are to tilt the scales in our favour. This level of happiness goes beyond the physical actions that we do, and addresses the psychology behind what we do and why we do it.

When discussing happiness with a client during a session, I will ask them: 'What part of your life is working for you, and why are you content in that domain?' They might say that they are happy with work or their relationship, with being a good mother or father, with their relationship with God or with how their body looks... or that they are happy for any number of different reasons.

I ask them to write down which parts of their life please them and create genuine contentment. When they have done that, I ask them if they can now explain why they feel that amount of comfort. The answers vary, of course, but the recipe is simple: whenever a part of your life is fulfilling and satisfactory, it's because your expectations in that particular area of life are being met. To illustrate, I will use a particular case study.

A woman in her thirties, of European descent, came to me for coaching because she felt unfulfilled and irritated with life. This client's response to my question 'What part of your life is working for you and why?' was 'I am very happy with my work life'. She was an HR director, having worked her way up through the firm; she earned great money and had lots of responsibility, which fed her need to feel significant and respected. Everything about her work life matched her blueprint or her expectations.

Where she wasn't so happy, however, was in her personal life. A failed marriage and a string of broken relationships which followed a familiar pattern had defined her private life. Why? Because her expectations or blueprint of what a relationship must be like did not match her experience. This woman wanted to control her partner the same way that she controlled her work environment, which had proved costly, as the men she had attracted refused to play that role for too long.

She also needed constant reminding of how wonderful she was and to be appreciated for the amount of money she was earning and her position in the firm, to the point where it became demoralising and ultra-heavy for the men in her life; ultimately, these men couldn't sustain that amount of hero worship, so the relationships failed. That led to multiple heartbreaks (her words not mine), yet her heart was not broken... it was her expectations that were broken.

Nobody breaks your heart... they break your *expectations*. The rules under which she lived her life had been violated, and that sabotaged her poor self-image, which had been built on external validation. The moment a man walked out of her life, not on her terms, the control she needed to feel safe, sure and significant was taken from her and with it her self-esteem.

She was clear that the relationships were over way before the men walked out the door, yet found herself attempting to bring them back... not because she had made a mistake and the relationships were worth saving, but in order to shore up her fragile self-image that had been punctured. The only way she could feel whole again was to bring those men back who she held responsible for her pain, and to convince them that she was lovable and worthy. By doing this, her punctured self-image would be fully inflated, and the levels of self-love she required above all else would be restored.

Her book of rules (remember them?) stated that she needed to have a man who continually adores her, worships her and props her up while she remains in full control. That was the common theme running through her life: her need to control her intimate love life to match her book of rules, where she decided who stays and who leaves. On her terms, there was no disgruntlement or heartache. But when that decision-making process was taken away from her, she fell apart, for reasons previously explained. However, beyond the need for control was something much more profound... something more fundamental that was driving this woman's behaviour.

The reason she wanted control in her life, including the micro-managing of her relationships, was the need to be loved... to belong and to feel that those close to her wouldn't walk away or reject and abandon her. Yet in her desperation to avoid this situation, she was creating the perfect environment for her most painful nightmares to manifest. We had two options at this point:

1. Change her expectations.
2. Change her perception. This means changing her core beliefs that were cemented in childhood, in this case a limited belief that, because her father walked out on her mother when she was six years old, men would continue to do the same throughout her life.

I started with her expectations by questioning the absolute truth behind her thoughts. Were they undeniable truths, or were they in fact just thoughts? Did everyone she loved walk away or abandon her? Absolutely not.

She had built up a circle of many friends since her teenage years, friends who were still very much in her life, were always there for her and loved her very much. Her relationships with her brother, her brother's children and her mother were stronger than ever. These we quickly established as truths and not thoughts. And if she wanted, she could apply the same level of unconditional love to her intimate relationships as she did to her healthy relationships.

This fundamental reframing blurred the edges of her damaging limited beliefs, but we needed to go deeper, way back into her formative years, to find the event which caused her to create this limiting belief. Using the technique discussed in an earlier chapter, I could have asked her to travel back in time and speak to her inner child, and then into the future to meet her wisest self. This is a very effective modality and usually adequate for unhooking powerful energetic charges that are attached to painful memories, but instead I decided to use another NLP technique called 'timeline therapy', or 'mental and emotional release therapy'.

Timeline therapy is a powerful and safe method of travelling back in time to deal with emotions that are not conducive to our highest and healthiest self. For this, I have the client close their eyes and relax with some deep, slow breathing. Then I ask them to imagine floating out of their body and drifting back into the past, either to a remembered early childhood event which carries with it an authentic emotional response, or to an event where the unconscious mind identifies and presents for resolution some unprocessed emotions.

The unconscious mind stores all memories in a linear fashion, and attributes to each emotion a unique folder; for example, all fear-based memories will be stored in their own unique folder, as will sadness, guilt, hurt, anger and shame. Now, the prime directive of the unconscious mind is to maintain and uphold the blueprint for optimum physical and emotional health; it therefore wants us to face these unhealed hurts, process them safely and let them go. Unhealthy emotions harm the body, and until we address them, they remain stuck in the nervous system at the cellular level.

Once the event had been recognised by my client, I told her to hover directly overhead, looking down on the incident, and notice the emotion, in this case her fear of being left alone, and where in her body she felt it. She told me that she felt the fear in her chest and throat. I then asked her what she needed to learn about that event for the emotions to dissolve. I instructed her to ask her unconscious mind what lessons she must hold on to before her mind was happy to unhook the emotional charge associated with the event. As before with Nicola (remember her?), my client began to retain the numerous powerful learnings that her unconscious mind needed for her to recognise and understand that particular event.

An entire reframing of the time when her father had left her crying in her tiny bathtub at two years old for what seemed an eternity was processed, understood and dissipated. When the learnings stopped, I then asked her to float further back into the past, before the event had taken place, turn around and face the NOW[11] with the event that was yet to happen below her and in front of her.

---

[11] The point at which she first drifted out of her body and up onto her timeline before starting her journey back into the past.

When she reached that point in the past in her mind, I asked her to notice the emotions in her chest and throat to see if they were still there, but they had gone. I then instructed her to float directly down into the event, where she was sitting in the bath as a two-year-old, and I enquired how she felt. Her feelings were now neutral, and the pain and fear had disappeared.

I asked her to return to the position she had just come from before the event had happened, looking back towards the now. And from there, I invited her to float back along and above her timeline, only as quickly as she could let go of all the fearful events in the past, all the way back to now. I told her that during this journey she was to pass slowly over each fearful event that her unconscious and now conscious mind presented to her, preserve the learnings she had just received, apply them to each episode, and let go of the fear all the way back to now.

When she opened her eyes, I gave her a few seconds before breaking the trance-like state she was in and asked her what felt different. Smiling from ear to ear, she replied: 'Everything!' I then put the question to her: 'Do you remember any event in the past where you used to be able to feel that fear and can you go back and notice if you can feel it?' She tried, but it had gone.

Next, I said to her: 'I want you to go to an event at an unspecified point in time in the future where you would have felt fearful, rejected or abandoned if it had happened in the past, and notice if you can find that old emotion.' Again, she could not.

I concluded by asking her if she sensed a feeling of calm, which might suggest that a healing state had been achieved. She had become tearful by now, which is very common, and stated that she felt lighter... that it felt like a heavy burden had been removed from her life.

I explained to her what had happened and that she was now responsible for maintaining this new state of being and that she was only one thought away from changing her reality, both good and bad. I added that if she wanted, from that moment she could change her old story and modify her approach to the impending relationships that were inevitable. Her blueprint had been radically transformed – no longer would she have to control the men in her life to feel safe. Her new belief was that the men she would meet would not be destined to leave her at all, and that the success or failure of her future relationships would not follow the same patterns.

We then proceeded to clear her timeline, addressing the emotions of hurt, guilt, sadness, anger and shame, one at a time, in the same way. I am delighted to tell you that at the time of writing, she is in a loving relationship and five-months pregnant.

NLP sessions are hugely influential, and for those struggling with resistant emotions and patterns of destructive behaviour, I strongly recommend finding a skilled NLP practitioner and exploring this healing modality.

APPLYING THE HAPPINESS FORMULA

We have discovered that happiness has a formula. A formula, if understood and administered, can help tilt the odds in our favour... and, boy, we need all the help we can get in a world that appears to be straining under the pressure of negative emotions. We live in an era where we have never been so safe historically, and never had so much, so readily available, yet we have never been more disgruntled and downtrodden. It's time to take control of our emotions.

The first part of the happiness formula is easily grasped by anyone with an IQ above a common house plant. Find out what you love and do more of it whenever you can. The second part is not so straightforward, but with careful application and a will to transform, we can assess our blueprint, the stories we tell ourselves, and see if they empower or disempower us. A general rule of thumb is as follows: any rule or story that you have running in your head that relies on the behaviour of others in order for you to feel happy, satisfied or content is disempowering. I am not suggesting that we don't need others and the ways in which they impact on us. We are relational beings, no doubt, but please distinguish between (a) relying solely on others and how they treat you or behave to meet your psychological needs and (b) setting the rules, to give you the best chance of sustainable happiness through self-fulfilment.

If, for example, your current blueprint for a happy relationship states: 'My partner must always be consistent with their feelings, never put me down and always be available to me when I need them. They must not raise their voice or criticise me in any way, and they must not look at or interact with members of the opposite sex, unless they do it on my terms. If they can do all that, I will be happy, content and feel loved.' What are the chances of your partner ticking all those boxes? How much of your blueprint is in your control? Zero... because your expectations hinge on others and how they behave or do not behave.

Instead, ask yourself, how else can I feel more love, contentment and happiness? What could I do? It could be reaching out and helping someone who is worse off than you are, and putting your life into perspective. Do some volunteer work at your local charity or animal sanctuary if animals are your thing. You could feel content and happy if you achieved your personal goals for the day, week or month. Call around your friends and family and express how much they mean to you, and thank them for their love and friendship.

This particular blueprint is a very different animal to the original: the first is all about how much you need to *receive* in order to feel safe, happy and content, whereas the second is all about how much you can *give* in order to feel the same way. Remember, the secret to living is giving, and what's more, when we are giving, we are growing – a fundamental psychological need that we must meet for our lives to mean something.

Here's another illustration using myself as an example. If I need the ringing (tinnitus) in my head to be at a certain level in order to be happy, content and fulfilled, but I have no control over it, what are the chances of me being happy? If I am continuously looking for ways to bring the intensity down, with a total focus on the problem, how do you think my life is going to look? Is my story of how life *should be* going to empower or disempower me? Is that a healthy or unhealthy blueprint?

Of course, it's very unhealthy. And, to be honest, I have been there, stuck in that loop of refusing to accept what was beyond my control and refusing to change my approach. If I can focus on what I can control, however, the story changes, and along with it emerges a new healthier blueprint. Instead of waking up and immediately tuning into the chirping crickets, the buzzing electricity field in my head and then ruminating over what I did, didn't do or could do, I get my shorts, T-shirt and shoes on, and head to the gym or put some music on and go for a cycle.

You have heard it many times, but emotions are energy in motion. E = motion, it's right there, hiding in plain view. If I want to change my state, the easiest and most reliable way is to move. Lying in bed checking my social media feed and berating my condition will not help. Remember, stagnation, anxiety, fear, uncertainty and frustration are physical realities, so the best way to deal with something physical is to *become* physical. After my workout or cycle, the buzzing noise is not any lower, but my mindset has shifted and I am now able to deal with it so much better, and therefore serve my clients better also.

If the gym is off the menu for any number of reasons, I listen to a Spanish podcast, or an inspirational audiobook, that puts me in a favourable state. I connect my headset and go about my awakening routine listening to someone or something that can change my emotional state. Try it. Write down a few of your favourite artists, speakers, authors, singers, etc., and each morning or whenever you get stuck, press play and change your state.

Listen, no one is at their best 100% of the time. I would wager that few reach the 80% marker... not even those who make people feel great for a living. Do you think that Oprah, JK Rowling, Joe Rogan, Wayne Dyer, Tony Robbins, Eckart Tolle, Deepak Chopra, Les Brown,

Michael Beckwith, Jim Carey, Will Smith, Beyoncé, Donald Trump, the Dalai Lama and thousands of others I could mention have life nailed? Not a bloody chance. They too are doing their best and have their own morning routines, which include listening to other motivational characters who help them shift their focus and their moods. And I know for a fact that most will have their own mentors, coaches and therapists to help them perform at their best and to help them navigate through the maze of life. That is the beauty of being human. We are all studying at the same school, and we can feed, learn from and teach each other... and I find that beautiful.

Depending on my daily schedule, I may choose to go to an animal sanctuary and play with the cats and dogs. Or better still, I will feed the strays that congregate around the park where I live. I search for ways to pay more attention to my clients and offer them even more value, or I look for more ways to serve others. I will write meaningful and transformative words and share them with the world. I check in with a WhatsApp community that I created for people to come together and share their thoughts, issues and how to become their best and strongest selves.

If you tell me you are bored and can't think of things to do, then you are quite simply not trying hard enough. I can assure you, it's not your ability to change, but your levels of motivation that are holding you back. If you can't motivate yourself, then pay someone to hold you accountable and light a fire under your life.

The most commanding force in the world is to be consistent with the thoughts, ideas and beliefs you hold to be true of yourself, and once you learn to control your identity through better choices, and by setting your expectations accordingly, you will continue to better manage the circumstances that show up in your life.

Make the rules work for you. If you can be satisfied by your own hand, by your own actions, then swing for the fences and indulge feverishly. If you want to take your life to the next level, you must: first, take direct control over that you can govern; and secondly, continue to raise your standards. Constantly raising your standards will keep your hunger alive for further progress, which we all need for our lives to make sense. The unconscious mind is always striving for new adventures and new experiences and always wants more. How you experience the new encounters that the unconscious mind demands will define how your future unfolds.

Creating a new blueprint where your choices are tangible will empower you. Keep asking yourself the same questions: 'What part of my life is or is not working?' Then look carefully at your book of rules to understand why it is or is not aligning with what you want or need in order to thrive.

The fact that you are happy or unhappy has little to do with what you have or don't have. If you are unhappy, your ideas of how life should be are not aligning with your reality. The pictures in your head are not matching what is going on in your external world. Change your internal picture with the tactics I have described, and your expectations will change along with it. That may require creating new aspects of your self-image. Remember how we are unable to outperform our self-image, and that everything we do achieve or do not achieve is associated with the limitations of that self-image and how we perceive ourselves?

I was listening to an Impact Theory podcast (which is one of my favourites) on self-image a few months ago, and the man being interviewed used a wonderful metaphor to explain how our individual identity is like an automated thermostat. He stated that the most powerful force in the world is to be consistent with the thoughts, ideas, concepts and beliefs you hold to be true to yourself! This is what your identity is made of! According to the man, your identity can be likened to a *thermostat*, setting the entire temperature of your life. And once you understand how to adjust this thermostat, you can adjust any area of your life you want to! The way he suggests to adjust your thermostat higher, to help bring it up, is to associate with those whose thermostats are set higher than yours... those already performing at the top of their game... those whose attributes you wish to emulate in every area of your life that needs attention.

We are the combination of the five people we most often associate with; who we hang out with, eventually we become. This is, of course, a reminder of the fundamentals of a concept already discussed, but it needs repeating: aspire to be like those who put fire in your belly, and drop those whose icy behavioural patterns cool you off.

Most of us do not have associations with successful people when we are growing up. We were never taught to think like a successful human being. Inevitably, and by default therefore, we associate with people who don't possess thermostats any warmer than ours. If we keep associating with the same people, then we will never be able to change our direction, and hence we will keep getting the same results.

However, we can change the thermostat by making new and better decisions. When we raise our standards, things begin to change, and with every new decision that yields improved results, our self-image begins to reformulate itself and automatically pushes up the needle on the thermometer a degree or two.

Remember, we are dealing with core beliefs here, and core beliefs arise from programmes stored in the unconscious mind. How did the unconscious beliefs get there? They were learnt through constant repetition until the neural connections in the brain created a habit. If you want new habits or rituals, new behaviours that empower your life, then apply the same process used to create your original core beliefs. Focus on behaviour that you can control and which serves you. Then, with strong discipline and repetition, cement that behaviour into the most powerful recording device ever created – the unconscious mind.

If you have tried your best and performed the tasks you promised you would, you will sleep peacefully every night. There really is no pillow as soft as a clear conscience, but if life remains complicated, and you feel you can't make a breakthrough alone, get a coach or see a good therapist and heal those past wounds. Because, if you don't, those wounds will continue to bleed over those who didn't cut you in the first place.

A JOURNEY INTO THE UNKNOWN

*The key to your behaviour is stored in a box
that you can't open using standard tools.
The unconscious mind often needs a different
key to the one you've been using.*

I am convinced that with application, coupled with a keen will to learn and evolve, you can have the life that you crave; there is so much within these pages which, if applied, can help you achieve it. But, and sadly there is always a but, there exists a certain percentage of people who are immune to therapy and coaching, and as hard as they try, they are unable to make any long-lasting changes.

I have thought long and hard about this, because I believed myself to be in that category for many years, and hence began my quest for healing practices beyond what society would class as typical. I grew up in a household that demonised any type of drug that wasn't prescribed by mainstream medicine, or that was not promoted or accommodated by the *Daily Mail* newspaper. So, you can imagine the surprise on my parents' faces when I told them I was planning on going to the Brazilian Amazon for six weeks to participate in shamanic rituals that included repeated doses of the most potent psychedelic known to man, dimethyltryptamine.

What I am about to propose is not for the faint-hearted, and neither am I advocating its use. There are also legal ramifications which require your attention in certain jurisdictions that outlaw and forbid the use of plant medicines, so please do the necessary research, and know your legal position before committing to using them if you hear the calling.

Please do as much research as necessary before working with any plant medicines, and always work with trained and experienced shamans or other human beings well versed in this arena, who will guide you on your quest to have the deepest and safest experience. Plant medicines used for healing are deserving of the utmost respect. They are incredibly challenging, or can be, yet they can offer profound and often life-changing experiences.

AYAHUASCA

It is challenging to verbalise the effects of ayahuasca. The words we use in everyday life do not exist in the dimension of ayahuasca or other plant hallucinogens. In fact, when you drink ayahuasca you can seldom describe it, as words cannot do it justice. Having said that, words are all I have to relay my experience, so I will do my best to share with you what happened in the Brazilian Amazon.

Many psychologists and psychiatrists who have worked with this strange brew have stated that it's the equivalent of 10 years of psychotherapy in one session. How accurate a statement that is, who knows? What I can tell you with legitimacy is this: for me, it was both mind-bending and mind-blowing.

So, what is ayahuasca? Well, it's a combination of two plants which contain the most potent hallucinogen known to man. But before you quickly turn the page in a cold sweat, let me first tell you that we produce this substance naturally in our bodies – primarily, every night during REM sleep, and secondarily, the moment we die and pass over.

The magical substance I am talking about is dimethyltryptamine, or more commonly known as 'DMT'. Scientific belief is that we manufacture this compound by means of the pineal gland, located on the back portion of the third cerebral ventricle of the brain. This tiny endocrine gland, shaped like a pine cone and hence the name, produces not only the magical DMT but also other feel-good hormones, such as melatonin, which is derived from serotonin and contributes to the feeling of well-being and our ability to sleep deeply and peacefully.

The more feel-good hormones we produce, the better we feel; the less we make, on the other hand, the harder it is for us to be on top of our game. That is why antidepressant medicines such as Prozac are so popular – they address the problems associated with low levels of feel-good hormones. I mention this, not to promote this type of medicine, but to point out that antidepressants mimic the malfunctioning glands that produce the needful number of hormones to enjoy life the way it was intended.

As you might have guessed, this is not my preferred method of healing. Nature has provided us, I believe, with a cure for every human ailment. With that in mind, allow me to be your tour guide when I take you on the wondrous journey I made in the forests of Brazil in 2012. But before that, let me first clarify the association between DMT and ayahuasca so as not to confuse you.

Ayahuasca is the name given to the combination of two different plants that, when mixed, produce a potent and long-lasting form of DMT. As stated above, we produce DMT during REM sleep, which causes us to have creative dreams. The psychedelic properties of DMT in sleep mode release us from the reality of the five waking senses and catapult us into a realm of heightened awareness and consciousness. This explains why we can fly, swim like dolphins, leap vast distances, hop across the universe if we so desire, or undergo any number of other experiences when we are dreaming. That is DMT doing its magic while we are unbound from our waking reality and liberated from the five senses that govern our daily lives.

DMT produced in the body when we are awake, however, does not affect us, because of an enzyme that we create in the stomach called 'monoamine oxidase', or MAO, which renders the DMT useless. The MAO blunts the DMT's ability to cross the blood-brain barrier and therefore nullifies any psychedelic experience. Science is unsure why this happens, and we may speculate on any number of reasons as to why this occurs.

There are two ways to overcome this: (1) DMT can be smoked, which produces a very intense DMT experience for 15 minutes or so; or (2) two combined plants can be ingested in liquid form, which provides a five- to seven-hour waking DMT experience. The latter is achieved by mixing the plant Banisterieopsis caapi, which contains a monoamine oxidase inhibitor, with the plant Psychotria viridis, which yields a potent form of DMT. Combining these two plants and cooking a particular way for a certain amount of time allows the brew to be consumed, albeit in a foul-tasting preparation; more to the point, it allows the active DMT to be carried intact across the blood-brain barrier and into the brain's receptors instead of being destroyed in the gut.

The shamans of South America have been mixing and using this magical healing brew for over 2,500 years, and possibly a lot longer, without any detrimental effects to their health. On the contrary, this exotic brew has been curing both physical and emotional problems since its discovery many thousands of years ago. The magic in the medicine comes from neither of its constituents alone, but rather from the mixture of the two and the synergy produced between them. Science is very busy today attempting to make sense of this, searching for answers within the mechanism that appears to interact with our consciousness when we participate in these extraordinary ceremonies.

For me, it comes as no surprise that global consciousness is growing at the same time that ayahuasca and other plant entheogens are becoming ever more accessible and ever more known to the many. So many shifts are happening on this planet, and as people look for ways to change their lives, more and more are finding ayahuasca and other psychedelics[12] to be an invaluable tool in their transformations.

---

[12] For further information on psychedelics and how they are at the cutting edge of all things mental health, please visit www.beckleyfoundation.org, and see for yourselves the remarkable results being achieved with controlled amounts of potent psychedelic substances. The Beckley Foundation, a spin-off from Oxford University, is a UK-based

Mention the word 'ayahuasca' a few years ago, and you would be met with a vacant stare and an 'aya-what-sca?' response. But nowadays, this is not the case. Now, when I mention this ceremony casually in conversations across the globe, a significant number of people acknowledge that it is something they have heard about, already experienced or have contemplated sitting in on a ceremony to undertake a journey for themselves. This is fantastic news for humanity, as this plant and many others have the power to reset our damaged psychological systems. Through these powerful plant teachers, we can become the loving, compassionate beings we were born to be.

Is this a pipe dream? Well, I do waiver occasionally from my beliefs that we can find peace and unity as a collective species, but I quickly dispel the uncertainty. The reason I am so excited about ayahuasca and other plant teachers is the following. There exists between humans and plants a very distinct botanical-glandular bridge where the magic happens at the molecular level. In case you weren't aware, we obtain the majority of mainstream medicines from Amazonian plant life. So far, thank goodness, no major pharmaceutical company has been able to patent and control ayahuasca... long may it continue that way.

There are many objections to the use of plants for healing, especially those plants which induce a hallucinogenic state, but this objection is based on ignorance, fear, a lack of understanding and a need to control the consciousness of humanity. Yes, I know that sounds conspiratorial, but having spent decades researching and understanding how the public are corralled and brainwashed by their respective governments, I will state with confidence that psychedelics are illegal because they are dangerous – not to people when taken in controlled environments, but to governmental structures.

Terrence McKenna, a brilliant ethnobotanist, writer, philosopher and activist, claims that psychedelics are illegal not because a

---

think-tank and NGO; its purpose is to pioneer psychedelic research and drive evidence-based drug policy reform.

loving government is concerned that you may jump out of a third-story window. He maintains that psychedelics are illegal because they dissolve opinion structures and culturally laid-down models of behaviour and information processing, and because they inhibit our hippocampal censorship mechanisms, which means they allow us to see things as they really are and not as we have been told they are.

Another reason why psychedelics are dangerous to the government is that they often create a feeling of loving unity, and organised groups of loving people are far harder to control than those who have become addicted to the fear-filled news channels and articles widely distributed and piped into their heads 365 days a year.

I could fill a whole book with conspiracy theories, or with the many that turn out to be conspiracy facts, but that will have to wait. That said, it is vital that you are aware of how governments, big pharma and major corporations are forever shaping and manipulating policies behind the scenes to centralise their power while eradicating your own.

I will make an outlandish statement right here. If every politician, Member of Congress or Senator were to participate in five ayahuasca ceremonies before pursuing a career in politics, the world would be a very different place. There would be a world with less conflict. The need to control others would melt as love and freedom became the predominant emotions. The idea of a species uniting in love and compassion terrifies those who have built their empires of incomprehensible wealth on fear, diversion and bloodshed, which is why you seldom hear about this anywhere on the mainstream news, other than to demonise or outlaw its use, for reasons already outlined.

Ayahuasca channels love and light and vital energy into our emotional and physical meridians to bring about a profound level of healing, yet the mainstream media warn you only against the inherent dangers. There are known cases of ayahuasca being responsible for the deaths of five people, yet the circumstances leading up to the ceremonies and what these people ingested before, during or after the ceremonies alongside ayahuasca are conveniently omitted.

To give this some perspective, 150 to 200 deaths a year are attributed to peanut allergies. A similar number lose their lives to falling coconuts; hence you are more likely to be killed walking through the jungle on the way to an ayahuasca retreat by a falling coconut than ingesting the brew itself.

Compare that with recent findings on healthcare in mainstream America. Every year in the USA there are:

- 12,000 deaths from unnecessary surgeries
- 7,000 deaths from medication errors in hospitals
- 20,000 deaths from other errors in hospitals
- 80,000 deaths from infections acquired in hospitals
- 106,000 deaths from FDA-approved correctly prescribed medicines

The total number of medically caused deaths in the USA every year is 225,000 and growing. Yet, how well known is this? Unless you specifically search for this information, you will go to your grave believing all is well in mainstream everything. And there lies the problem. Mainstream media do not report such findings and for good reason: big pharma creates billions of dollars for the mega-wealthy, and they don't want anyone spoiling their party or muscling in on their action.

Please read the book *Death by Medicine* by an author named Gary Nulls, who presents statistical evidence of hundreds of thousands of injuries and deaths every year due to conventional medicine. He looks at the pharmaceutical industry, drug reps, medical schools and medical journals, and at the absence of real medical science. Additionally, he highlights the lack of oversight of regulatory agencies and private insurance firms and the influence of lobbyists on legislators, who are in bed with a labyrinth of interlocking corporate, hospital and governmental boards of directors infiltrated by the drug companies.

What's even more disturbing is that Nulls reveals how drug company representatives are paid to write glowing articles about pharmaceuticals, which are then signed by physicians paid handsomely for their cooperation, though they may not know the adverse side effects of the drugs they promote. The most toxic substances are often approved first, while milder and more natural alternatives are ignored for financial reasons. Talk about an evil and malevolent agenda... putting profit before the lives of our brothers and sisters across the globe! This insanity must end, and plant medicines may just be the vehicle that builds enough momentum to light a fire under big pharma and their sinful conduct.

There exists a genuine threat to the establishment if plant medicines not patented by big pharma are allowed to weave their magic throughout humanity, and for this reason, those companies are doing everything in their power to destabilise its expansion. But I believe it's too late. The genie is out of the bottle. There is a global awakening taking place on planet earth. The shadows from which the global elite formerly operated and in which they were beyond reproach are now becoming illuminated. Like a snowball building speed and momentum as it rolls down a mountain, it's beginning to reach a point where the volume and velocity are so prominent that no force can stop the plant medicine revolution. Sooner, rather than later, ayahuasca and all plant medicines will be an accepted part of the healing world, embraced by both the spiritual community and the general population.

I openly admit that when I first became aware of ayahuasca, I was apprehensive. Coming from a family whose knowledge of drugs was minuscule at best, I believed in the narrative propagated in the family home. I was raised with the paradigm: 'If it's legal, it must be ok; if not, it must be the work of dark and malevolent forces.' It mattered not that alcohol and cigarettes have destroyed and continue to end or ruin the lives of millions, while marijuana has killed no one. Anyone caught smoking or selling marijuana deserved the firing squad.

I can laugh now because these beliefs stemmed from a limited information supply, but one can see how misguided and outdated rhetoric becomes a dangerous combination, and how a willing public is brainwashed into believing anything the global elite wish it to support. I left behind this antiquated belief system many years ago, but when ayahuasca began to call me, parts of my old conditioned self would utter: 'Don't do it – it's just like LSD, and you won't come back from the experience and you'll end up in a mental asylum.' My ego sensed that if I made that trip to the Amazon, it would never have the same control over me that it once had.

And the ego was right! The experience blew the doors of my reality and my ego to smithereens. FYI, the insights and visions one often gleans during the work with ayahuasca (which I will refer to as 'she') have to be continued long after the ceremony, but what she does is open doors for you to walk through and highlight what needs your immediate attention. Every ceremony is different, with each person experiencing a uniquely personal exchange with the medicine. I cannot tell you how it will be for you if you decide to work with her, but I can tell you that she will give you what you need, not what you think you need.

THE AYAHUASCA CEREMONY

On arriving in Brazil, I was nervous but excited. I was staying with my ex-girlfriend Guna and her new boyfriend Gil, whom I had not seen for a couple of years, so I looked forward to sharing quality time with them. They had both participated in two ayahuasca ceremonies, and we had planned to go together for my first and their third.

After settling in, we sat for many hours discussing their journeys and experiences with this mysterious vine of the Amazon. I still had fears reverberating within me, not knowing what to expect or how intense the encounter would be. They detailed their experiences and what these had taught them about themselves. A current theme ran through both of them: the call of nature and a sincere desire to follow what Mother Nature had shown them and what man had forgotten.

They each stated that their experience with DMT had been a blessing, one that increased their sense of peace and morality and their capacity for love.

I resonated strongly with the underlying message they had received... an increased detachment from the direction in which the world was heading, and the remedy being unconditional love... a sentiment that something far more significant was ready to be discovered, not out there in the external world, but within each of us... an awareness that something was happening here on earth with a sense of inevitability. Whatever that may be, I was ready to walk the botanical-glandular bridge which I hoped would illuminate the divine spark that resides inside each of us. (To say I was not disappointed is a massive understatement.)

Before I could participate in my first ceremony, however, I had to meet with my 'madrina' (Brazilian Portuguese for 'godmother'), assigned to me by the head of the shamanic group. This meeting was designed to grade my suitability and whether I was ready to undertake the journey or just a psychedelic tourist, looking to get high on a potent psychedelic. Ayahuasca seems to know precisely why you are there, and I will repeat: she gives you what you need and not what you want. Go there to get high and nothing else, and you may regret it.

We continued our conversation, and I spoke of my fears and nervousness associated with working with this unknown plant teacher, and about the various rumours circulating the forum boards outlining hellish experiences with dark forces, sending people insane. She remained grounded and unaffected by the conversation, answering each question with radical honesty, while settling my nerves simultaneously.

The takeaway from the meeting was that ayahuasca is a plant of love and infinite wisdom, and that I would be experiencing something beyond words. I would be going on a unique journey that would be mine alone but practised within a group of loving human beings who work with the plant to promote love, peace, contentment and growth through deep introspection.

She was very clear that genuine intention and a precise purpose of why I was there would facilitate the lessons I yearned for and that the medicine was not to be taken lightly. She also stated that the setting and the shamanic group was of paramount importance, as we would be working with energy frequencies well beyond those we experience during our ordinary reality. And like the duality in all things, negative energies are forever surrounding us to balance out the spectrum of positive energy.

That is why the setting, atmosphere and the guardians who over-see the ceremony are so important. I cannot emphasise this enough. I would strongly recommend that anyone reading this and who has made up their mind to work with this powerful brew do it correctly. Do not order this from the internet or try to make it yourself. Do not go around to the house of a friend who has managed to procure some, have a couple of beers and a pizza, and then knock a full glass back and wait to see what happens while watching a movie.

Plan the experience carefully. Know why and what it is you wish to work on. Then choose a favourite ayahuasca retreat, with as many recommendations from as many ayahuasqueros[13] as possible. Prepare to disconnect from the modern world for as long as you are there: no mobile phones, no Wi-Fi and no TV. You are there to work, which is why the shamans call it 'el trabajo' (Spanish for 'the work'). It *is* work, because it is bloody hard and taxing on both the emotional and the physical body. Let your partner, family or friends know, if need be, that you will be non-contactable for a few days, then commit to the journey of a lifetime if you are able. Jump on a plane to the Amazon and prepare to never look at life in the same way again.

You can use TripAdvisor or any number of referral-based websites to do your necessary diligence work before jetting off to the Amazon or to any number of retreats around the world; this is vital when working with powerful plant medicines. My advice is this: if you are able to do so, travel to where it's grown to familiarise yourself with

---

[13] Those who use or work with ayahuasca or participate in the ceremonies.

the plants in their natural habitat.[14] This will make a huge difference. Some retreats will take you to where it's picked and harvested, and you can participate in the making of the brew itself; that adds another layer of intimacy to the ceremony as you engage in a personal relationship with the plants, long before you consume a single drop of ayahuasca. As with all things in life, the better thought out your plan, the better and more complete the experience.

I was now ready. My assigned godmother gave me the green light to participate in the upcoming ceremony called 'la ceremonia de la luna' ('the moon ceremony' in English), which all newcomers must participate in before proceeding to a heavier and more intense ceremony referred to as 'la intercession', which I will come to later. The ayahuasca ceremony would be taking place in five days from our initial meeting, in a ceremonial outhouse built among the jungle vegetation and where both plants we would be drinking grow in abundance.

She gave me strict instructions on what I could and couldn't eat leading up to the ceremony. I had to restrict my salt and sugar intake as much as possible. No alcohol and no hot spices or canned food were allowed. Certain medicines had to stop. There had to be no dairy or smoked foods... no heavy oils or fats... no meat or fish proteins, especially duck or pork... no computers... no sex, no masturbation, no make-up, no touching of others, no soap, no shampoo or conditioners, no lotions, no toothpaste and no bug spray.

What I could consume was a healthy choice of vegan or vegetarian dishes, lots of fresh water and fruit and the occasional coffee or tea. The lead-up to the ceremony was an exciting time for a variety of reasons. I was focusing on repetitive behaviours that hadn't served me and what I was going to ask ayahuasca in ceremony. I was going through a painful breakup at the time, and the loss of not just a lover but also a friendship was proving very difficult to grasp. We occasionally communicated while I was there, but the trust had long

---

[14] I am happy to share with you where I experienced my five ceremonies if you send me an email.

evaporated, with her words and actions seldom aligning. The pain from that relationship was and has been my best teacher thus far. In hindsight, I realised how dysfunctional I was and why I had attracted that type of personality in my life.

I have spoken openly about the mirrored universe and how others are a reflection of ourselves. Well, what I saw in the mirror was not pleasing, and I could no longer squint and look at myself through parted fingers. I came to the painful truth that I needed to begin living life from an entirely different perspective, and that self-love and honesty were essential ingredients missing in my life that I needed to find... not out there, but deep within.

I realised that my relationship status defined much of my life – I only felt happy and secure in a relationship on my terms, but the love I'd experienced in these relationships was hugely conditional and mostly possessive. This love was based on ownership, insecurities and control and very much on the pleasures of physical interactions, namely sex, which, don't get me wrong, is essential, but there is so much more to a loving, mature relationship than our primal desires.

Remember, our choice of partner is a direct insight into who and where we are and reflects back to us both our light and our darker sides. For a reminder of this crucial subject, please reread the chapter on the law of attraction and how we attract those who teach us the most. I needed to learn honesty and to know if I could love myself with authenticity; I could then learn to love other people solely for who they were, rather than for what they gave me. But before I could do this, I had to release myself from this failed relationship which had me questioning much about myself.

My ego was battering me and was enjoying the emotional roller coaster I had jumped on and showed no signs of getting off. I had tried different approaches to self-healing, including hypnotherapy, where the aim is to open the heart and let go of the need to understand a relationship based not only on powerful emotions but also on even stronger levels of deception and underhand agendas. I achieved small victories with various approaches, but the underlying programmes responsible for my suffering were still very much there. For this reason, I was looking forward to the upcoming ceremony, hoping that I would find the answers to questions that had so far remained elusive.

The night before the ceremony, I plus my ex-girlfriend and her boyfriend Gil went out to have something to eat and discuss our intentions, when the strangest thing happened. I had not paid full attention to the strict rules about what I could and could not eat before the ritual.

I ordered fish with vegetables, but this time was very different. When the meal arrived, it looked very unappealing – not because of the presentation but because of something I could not explain. I ate a few vegetables and then tried to eat a mouthful of fish, which I had difficulty swallowing. I thought nothing of it as I tried again, which met with the same resistance. The mouthfuls of vegetables in between posed no problem at all, but every piece of fish provoked the same adverse reaction, until I was forced to go to the bathroom and was sick until nothing remained inside me.

I came back to the table and explained what had happened. I tried again... the same thing... the same pattern. You need to understand, I was a regular fish eater, and had never, repeat never, experienced any issues with swallowing and digesting any foods. Looking back, I can only assume that my body and mind were already preparing for the ceremony to come, in a state of awareness way above that of my normal comprehension, and that I was rejecting the food dictated to me by my ayahuasca godmother as prohibited.

To be honest, that startled me, and I wondered what was to come the next day. I didn't sleep well, tossing and turning and staring at the ceiling for what seemed hours. I finally nodded off, but was awoken by my alarm at 5.55am in preparation for the journey into the jungle. The three of us met on the outside veranda of the villa where we were staying, and we had a simple breakfast of fruit and tea before setting off together. Not much in the way of conversation took place. We were deeply contemplative as we dialled into the experience of what was to come.

We arrived at the jungle retreat some two hours later, where we were greeted by a plethora of birds and monkeys way up in the canopy of the jungle, singing, calling and playing. I smiled as we climbed the homemade wooden steps through the trees, towards a majestic ceremonial hut where the ritual would take place. Many participants were already inside, singing and playing a variety of musical instruments. They were dressed in white linen and looked remarkably healthy... they glowed in fact. I smiled and immediately felt better as the tension began to dissolve. The singers invited me to join them, but I politely refused, sat down and observed.

The energy coming from the ceremonial cabin was beautiful, with genuine smiles and a welcoming demeanour. I wandered outside and sat on the grass with my two friends Gil and Guna. Guna teased me about what was to come which I laughed at, but inside I was nervous. All around were people sitting alone, a few in meditation, some in yoga poses and others reading. Next to us was a young Brazilian girl in tears and traumatised. I asked her what the problem was, and replied she was terrified, as she had heard so many horror stories attached to this work and had no idea what to expect. Gil and Guna did their best to assure her that there was nothing to worry about, but the truth is, nobody knows what type of experience you are going to encounter.

The retreat was beginning to fill up with more people who were either part of the shamanic group or there to work with the plant medicine. My godmother appeared and introduced me to the head shaman, a charismatic and very beautiful female; she assured me that there was nothing to worry about, that I was among family, and that Mother Nature loves us very much and would show me this soon enough. Her words calmed me as I went somewhere quiet to prepare for what was about to start.

I sat and meditated and tried to focus my attention on love and oneness. But what came up was a bad experience that I had gone through involving a cocktail of marijuana and cocaine 15 years previously. I had been at a friend's house on Xmas eve as we celebrated the release of his new album; he was a famous recording artist, and we were listening to the album from the recording studio in his home. We were sharing a strong marijuana joint and doing lines of cocaine while drinking Jack Daniels. I do not share this to glamorise or to shock, but to be brutally honest and truthful. I have no idea what happened next, but I remember panicking and struggling to breathe. I got up and looked at my friend as I collapsed into his arms. I awoke almost immediately, having projectile vomited across the studio. I thought I had been unconscious for ages, but in fact, it was only a few seconds. To cut a long story short, for around six months afterwards I had flashbacks of that event which were not pleasant. So, that was the event which was playing in my mind as I sat and meditated, which did anything but calm me. What if a repeat of that event manifested itself?

I got up and walked around as I saw the shamans bringing the bottles of ayahuasca, which had been freshly prepared on site and were now ready for consumption. Now was my last chance to back out and leave. I took a deep breath and blew out vigorously, then walked back into the cabin and took a seat alongside the rest of the people who were there. The chairs were placed in a circle around an altar, which housed a large blue crystal and a broad array of symbolic tools and artefacts. Above the altar was an even bigger crystal pointed downwards, suspended from the ceiling with a two-metre gap between them.

The lead shaman then instructed us to sit in certain positions according to our previous experience with the plant; this meant that I sat with the other ayahuasca virgins and away from my two colleagues, who had already worked twice with the medicine. Opposite me were the musicians and singers, who were a part of the shamanic group, around fifteen in number and equal in gender distribution. To my left sat the three head shamans, with the head female in the middle. To her right was a doctor who participates in all ceremonies, which gave me a degree of comfort, as I had no idea of what was to come. Surrounding the circular building, enclosed by thousands of plants and trees of different sizes, were the guardians, dressed in long robes and adorned with a variety of staffs and amulets, whose responsibility it was to manage the energetic field during the ceremony. There were no framed windows, so the view was unobstructed, full of greenery, majestic swaying palm trees, butterflies and beautiful chirping wildlife.

The head shaman began to speak in Brazilian Portuguese, which was a not a problem, as I understand Spanish and it's similar. She talked about energy, nature, the universe and the transformative powers of ayahuasca, and about how she is a medicine of love and revelatory power and there was nothing to fear. I must state unequivocally that the language barrier is not a problem... whether you speak the native language or not. Your whole system is operating on an entirely different level of awareness by the time you sit down and the ceremony begins.

She instructed the shamans to go outside in the sunshine and stand in a line. We then followed them out, one by one, and each participant stood opposite a shamanic worker as he or she performed an energetic exorcism, making bold gestures around different parts of our bodies, mimicking the removal of invisible objects and discarding them into the atmosphere. When this ritual ended, the participants took turns in walking to the back of the circular building to receive a full cup of what can only be described as a brown sludge which tastes like battery acid mixed with prune juice. The taste, for some at least, was so bad that they gagged repeatedly and struggled to hold it down. As for me, I did not mind so much; I have become used to strange-tasting concoctions over the years, with my experimentation and mixing of different spices and liquids. I drank the concoction in one, wondering what the hell was going to happen as I bowed at the entrance, as all participants must, and took my seat once again.

The music started up with a compelling mixture of drums, flutes, pipes, guitars and singers, who harmonised beautifully with the frequency of the instruments. The songs performed are called 'icaros', which the shamans believe are the spirits of the plants themselves, manifesting as sound. These songs are used to either bring on mareación (the visionary effects of the ayahuasca) or take mareación away if necessary. They are used to call in different plant spirits, to call in the souls of others or the deceased, to take away dark spirits and dark energies for protection, and to manage the ceremony. Experienced shamans can recite hundreds of icaros, and for this ceremony, they would be singing 38 different songs over five hours, in line with 'la ceremonia de la Luna', which required a particular frequency in order to maximise the experience.

All ayahuasca retreats provide buckets for vomiting when necessary, which I was warned as being an essential part of the total experience. This process is called 'la purga' ('the purge'), and you need to recognise the cleansing for what it is: the purification of body, mind and spirit. Ayahuasca is most undoubtedly medicinal first and visionary second; she pulls massive amounts of physical toxins from our bodies, as well as healing our soul and emotions. That is why vomiting is a necessary part of the work. Those who do not vomit are said to be the ones who suffer from 'emotional stuffing', which means, according to the shamanic group, the ones who suppress emotions and create many identities in an attempt to fool others as well as themselves. How true this is, I have no idea. We are all so unique and respond to different situations in different ways on the basis of a lifetime of personal and collective conditioning.

We were instructed to go outside or to the open windows to purge when necessary. We were also given directions to the toilets, which were vital, since many ayahuasqueros experience explosive diarrhoea to complement the vomiting. As you can see, this undertaking is not for the faint of heart, and fun it is not.

I remained with my eyes open and looked around the room and spoke briefly with the young man next to me, who wished me luck and I returned the gesture. The icaros were beautiful and powerful at the same time, as were those who performed them. A smile on every face stared at me from around the room, and I felt a tear arise within me. My journey had started. It was 30 minutes since had I drunk the brew, and a very subtle change was happening within me. The colours around me and especially outside had become far more lucid, with greater detail; somehow, they were outside the spectrum of my usual eyesight capabilities, with different shades of the same colours appearing more vibrant and varied. My emotional connection to everything was also beyond what I had previously experienced.

I took a deep breath, closed my eyes and relaxed. From nowhere, geometrical patterns and mathematical equations in various forms entered my mind's eye. Sacred geometry appeared to me as pyramidal structures, so real that I felt I could touch them. I had no idea why this was happening, but felt so blissful and content that I questioned nothing. The pyramids suddenly became turned on their sides and sliced into sections, as more complex equations streamed across the surface in the form of grains of sand. Fibonacci sequences[15] flowed into my consciousness. Plants, flowers, insects and trees became transparent as the same numbered sequences were revealed to me once again running through these expressions of life. Ayahuasca was showing me that everything is interconnected and separation is an illusion, and the language she chose to reveal this was through the universal language of the cosmos – mathematics.[16]

I opened my eyes briefly, which in hindsight I should not have done, and I regretted it. My need to micromanage my environment, a robust subconscious programme of mine, was stirred by my ego that was trying to regain power and bring me back into this limited state of reality we call our waking lives. I smiled and spoke directly to my unhappy ego and told it to relax, as something far more powerful and profound had taken the reigns.

I looked over at Gil and Guna, who was singing. I zoned in on Gil who had his eyes closed, and I remember the amount of pure love I had for him. I became him as the tears came up from my toes.

---

[15] Fibonacci numbers are nature's numbering system, and appear everywhere throughout creation.

[16] For a more concise explanation of this, see https://www.youtube.com/watch?v=kkGeOWYOFoA.

I was unsure whether I was experiencing his emotions or whether they were my own, but any separation between myself and Gil was non-existent. We were having our own subjective experience in different avatars, but we were one and the same beyond our human form. In that moment, I had my first tangible experience of being source energy from which all sentient beings are born and to which all sentient beings return. The frequency of love had enveloped me, and I felt my heart would explode.

The combination of the frequency of love and the melody of the music was incredibly powerful. The drums, the pipes, the voices... all were crystal clear, creating a spinning vortex of love and healing which entered and climbed through my body until it hit me between the eyes. I had no embarrassment, no self-awareness... no need for pretending or holding back. I sobbed like a child, my whole body shivering and heaving as the emotions streamed out of every pore.

As I closed my eyes once again, a colossal dragonfly then presented itself to me, its eyes the size of footballs, its wings, made of what appeared to be golden thread, fluttering before me. 'Let go,' it kept saying. '*Let it go*, Darren.' '*Stop trying to control things and accept things as they are.*' I understood what the dragonfly meant. I had spent my whole life trying to manage everything and controlling proceedings; instead of accepting things as they were, I was intent on seeking to bend and manipulate the truth or events to suit my own needs and agenda.

The futility of how people communicate, and the amount of emphasis we place on content or the perceived lack of content, streamed into my consciousness: the sheer insanity of losing my centre because my partner had not written what I needed to see or hear in order to feel secure and loved... not enough love hearts or kisses at the end of a WhatsApp message... no declaration of 'I love you' at the end of every interaction. I smiled as the emptiness we often feel is created by our insecure expectations, and not how others treat us.

Ayahuasca, in the form of this incredible dragonfly, then showed me the force of unconditional love, the nature of the universe and our place in it, while my obsessive control programme was trying to make sense of it all. The dragonfly was still hovering in front of me, showing me so many things as I asked her question after question regarding the waking reality we recognise as life. I asked specifically about my relationships, and in particular why I had attracted this woman into my life who had caused, and continued to cause, a profound disturbance to me. The vast insect with the golden wings and the whole universe in her eyes smiled and gently flew away. I complained that I had not been answered and realised what I had done again. I was not allowing things to be as they were and wanted answers and instant gratification. I wanted things to be according to my desires and wishes.

I laughed at myself as my ego popped into my head and shouted: 'Got you.' I just closed my eyes and said nothing. The geometrical shapes returned. The all-seeing eye appearing in the floating capstone of an unfinished pyramid, as depicted on a US dollar bill entered my awareness. I did not question its meaning and assumed that it was my subconscious creating an image out of my fascination for secret societies and Freemasonry, when a butterfly came into my conscious awareness. Stunningly beautiful and like the dragonfly that preceded her, she was huge.

I have always been fascinated and drawn to butterflies, and she told me why without asking the question. 'As you know,' she said in my voice, 'the butterfly suggests transformation and evolving from one thing to another, which is what you have been doing your whole life and what brings you here today... to continue your journey of transformation, growth and awareness.'

'The dragonfly deliberately did not answer your questions, giving you time to process them for yourself,' she told me. Another answer to a question I wanted to ask but hadn't.

She continued: 'The answers are in the acceptance as you create a new level of transformation within you... This is why I came to you. I needed to say nothing, and indeed I am saying nothing. I am just reflecting back to you the wisdom from your highest state of self. It is always with you. Just be silent a while, and it appears. In stillness all answers are present.'

I began to cry again, my whole-body convulsing as the emotions that I had been holding on to were released. As I took some tissues to dry my eyes and wipe my face, I opened my eyes and saw in front of me a shaman imitating different animals. Another was making shapes that appeared not to be human, his body taut and upright; he held his arms in positions and ways that seemed to be impossible and defy human physical capability. Yet another shaman was sitting on his knees swaying back and forth like a king cobra snake. Bent over and huddled, the head shaman was shuffling around the room like an old crone, with a hood over her head, hissing and moaning like a possessed entity. On any other day, and not under the influence of the DMT in the ayahuasca, I am sure I would have run far and fast, but I merely smiled and watched like a curious child.

The drums had become louder and the music clearer, and the energy within the room had increased. Outside, the trees were now different entities, communicating with each other and with all things in and around them. The colours were so bright and vibrant that they appeared as if they had been painted by the most skilful artist on the planet. Was this real or was it a figment of my imagination? Had I entered a new realm of consciousness, or was this just a hallucinatory experience? It mattered not. For all intent and purposes, and as you know from my explanations throughout the book, the mind cannot distinguish between what is real and what is not; the mind only knows how to react to certain stimuli and act accordingly... It felt real, and the chemical reactions to this experience were aligning as if it was real.

My eyes locked on to a beautiful female member of the shamanic group, who was singing opposite me. She returned my gaze, but without any awkwardness usually associated with meeting a stranger's eyes for the first time across a crowded room. Neither of us blinked for what seemed an eternity, as a tunnel of energy and light joined us... She continued to sing as her eyes rolled back into her head, and she first became deathly pale and then bright green as her head appeared to transform into a black panther. Her eyes never left mine as I came face to face with either her spirit animal or my own. I still do not know to this day. Again, under normal circumstances, I would have been a little freaked out, but this was far from what is considered normal, and I did not question anything that was going on around me. Another victory for acceptance, it would appear.

I looked away and directed my gaze towards one of the guardians, stood up to my right, who purged and vomited very violently on the floor at that moment. A massive man with dreadlocked hair, he was an imposing figure. Our eyes met, but this time no animal spirits or anything remotely pleasurable transpired. His eyes became blood red as he continued to look right through me. I became nervous and looked away, but to no avail. I could feel this man's eyes burning through me, and so I looked again. His eyes had grown, still blood red, and I wondered what this all meant. Something inside of me spoke and said: 'Calm yourself, he is just a reflection of you and the different energies you carry within you, both light and dark and nothing more. He is you, and you are him.' I continued looking at the man, and he smiled and looked away as his eyes returned to brown. I thanked him for the lesson and closed my eyes again.

The journey continued. So many questions and answers... so many emotions. The tears, the memories from my life were coming at me from all angles. My consciousness was pristine and crystal clear, my mind a receptacle for all information at the highest level of understanding – like a super computer with a lightning-fast processor.

I was disturbed by a tap on the shoulder as 'the doctor' attempted to give me another half cup of this magical but foul-tasting brew. I declined, but he did not acknowledge my refusal; he placed the cup in my hand and gestured to drink it. I recall saying: 'You must be joking.' It was no joke as I swallowed my second helping of ayahuasca, as did everyone in the room. The intensity of the brew seemed to be building in my system, and I had just consumed another large dose. I looked at the guy next to me and remembered saying: 'This is intense.' He looked right through me and nodded but nothing more, either unable to speak or chose not to.

I checked my watch and two hours had passed in a heartbeat... I looked around the room. Some were crying, sitting as still as statues. Others were lying on the ground, writhing in what appeared to be emotional or physical pain, or both, asking for forgiveness or a release from the assumed suffering they were enduring, possibly? I remembered what the shaman had told me as I observed these people going through their ordeals: 'The plant will give to you exactly what you need and not what you want.' I wondered what these people needed, their faces and bodies contorted, in what appeared to be obvious displeasure. Whatever it was, it was intense and fascinating.

While this was going on an excessive heat was building within me... my chest, stomach and limbs all tingling with excitement never experienced before. Under normal circumstances, this might have caused concern, but not today. Everything that was happening had to happen as my healing on all levels associated with the medicine continued at a furious pace.

The process by which ayahuasca heals presumes an entirely different understanding of illness and medicine from that we are accustomed to in our modern worlds. But notwithstanding the benefits of Western medication and psychotherapy, it is clear that remarkable physical healings and resolutions of profound psychological difficulties or addictions can occur with ayahuasca. We have an awful lot to learn from these shamanic masters who have been practising these ancient methods of healing for well over 2,500 years and possibly a lot longer...

Three hours had now passed, and everywhere I looked there were people vomiting and purging as I sat very peaceful and still, hands on my knees, with my back very straight. We were told at the beginning not to cross our knees or feet so as not to block any energetic highways which would be carrying the medicine to the areas that needed physical healing. I became aware of how still I was, sitting comfortably for three hours on a usually uncomfortable plastic chair... no fidgeting, nor any need to stretch or change my sitting position. This is the real beauty of ayahuasca. In this altered state of consciousness, both body and mind are operating on a completely different level of awareness and function. The usual need to move and fidget was gone.

I was completely present and aware of all the things that were occurring within and around me. Yes, it's intense and can be very challenging. But I found that by opening my eyes, I was immediately transported back to a controllable reality. And for me, at least, I was never fearful or taken beyond my limit of endurance during either of the two ceremonies I participated in while in Brazil, or during three later ceremonies I attended in Europe. Now, I cannot promise you the same experiences, as we are all different and respond uniquely, but I will repeat: ayahuasca will give you what you require and not what you think you need.

It was now four hours since I had taken the initial brew, and the medicine was still as potent as ever. The doctor appeared once again at my shoulder and handed me another half measure of this unimaginable plant medicine. I took it from him, this time without objection, surrendering and letting go of any need to stay in control...

I looked around the ceremonial building. The band were still in full voice, their instruments appearing as extensions of their bodies. The sounds and the power of the icaros, combined with the brew, cannot be described, as my emotional state transformed from smiling and happiness to crying and sobbing once again. The image of my daughter, who was taken away from me and relocated overseas seven years before at the age of two and a half, came streaming into my consciousness. I thought I had healed that wound, but ayahuasca thought otherwise as she held her image in my mind's eye and assured me that she was loved, cared for and very happy, and that I had no control over the situation and should accept this... but to be ready if she ever comes knocking at my door. This powerful imagery, along with the vibrational harmony of the particular song that was playing, was the catalyst for my first purging, prompting that familiar feeling before any vomiting comes on like a tornado. And I purged violently.

I rushed outside between bouts of sickness and bent over with my hands on my knees as I vomited again onto the lush green grass between my naked feet. Again and again, I heaved from my toes as my body released the toxic emotions that I had been holding on to... my daughter... my failed relationships... my childhood programming... and so much more that being cleansed. The medicine ripped through all my defence mechanisms, gathering up as much toxicity created through emotional disturbance and dumping it firmly at my feet.

I eventually stopped heaving and stayed huddled over. Complete clarity hurried through me as I felt a huge weight lifted from my body. The grass was now communicating with me, moving around and through my toes, over my feet, breathing. It was the most sur-real experience thus far. The pretty girl transforming into the black panther was one thing, but this experience was somehow more profound.

A guardian who was watching over me took my arm as I looked up, beckoning me back into the ceremony. I said: 'The grass is alive, mov-ing and communicating with me.' 'I know,' he replied, as if it was the most normal thing in the world, and once again asked me to return to the ceremony. I wanted to stay there forever, speaking to the grass, but I stood up straight, walked back in and sat down on my chair.

I looked across the ceremonial tent at my ex-girlfriend who was looking at me, and we both started to laugh uncontrollably. It was a beautiful moment as we expressed unspoken unconditional love for each other... a pure love not experienced before, devoid of any type of sexuality or desire. On top of that, we were telepathically com-municating without effort of any kind. I asked her about it after the ceremony, and she stated that what I had been thinking and saying to her during the service had been received just as I had sent it... I know for some this may appear far-fetched, but I can only tell you the expe-rience I had. We have unlimited potential and use only a fraction of the inherent powers and gifts afforded to us. I believe that ayahuasca enables us to access and connect with those powers, which is why telepathy and many other forms of higher communication are often experienced by lots of ayahuasqueros while under the influence of this mystical and enchanting brew.

At this point, 36 of the 38 icaros had been completed and the ceremony would soon be coming to a close. Only two more remained, which would take 10 more minutes. I closed my eyes and realised that I was still heavily under the influence of the medicine and wondered how long it would be before the effects would start to wane.

The geometrical shapes and messages continued to manifest in my mind's eye as mother ayahuasca repeated her consistent advice to allow my obsession with control to dissolve and to live one moment at a time. The Christian serenity prayer came into my awareness, and I smiled. I love this prayer – it captures everything we need to embrace in three lines:

> *Dear father, grant me the serenity to accept the*
> *things I cannot change,*
> *the strength to change the things I can*
> *and the wisdom to know the difference.*

I thought to myself, wouldn't life be a breeze if only we could live that way?

As the singing stopped and the head shaman began to speak, my eyes remained closed; they were opened by a touch on my knee as a bunch of freshly cut flowers and plants from the jungle were presented to me. It was not yet 7pm and the evening moisture was glistening on every stem and petal.

I put my head into the wrapped bouquet and cried again, apologising for them having been cut and presented to me as an offering of sorts, which I had not asked for, and neither did I want. I wanted them back in the ground, growing, alive and vibrant… The very thing I love about flowers ceases to exist the moment they are cut and placed for our selfish needs in vases. This is why to this day I have never had cut flowers in my home. 'Why had they done this?' I asked myself, and a question I wanted to ask the shaman afterwards, but sadly did not get the opportunity. It was a bizarre moment as my distress became empathy and love for all forms of life. I felt the pain of the planet and realised that things had to change, or man and nature would be staring down the barrel of a destructive conflict sooner rather than later, which man would royally lose.

We were told to stand, step forward and make a single step to the right and then a step back to the left. Sounds simple right? Wrong! I made a complete pig's ear of it. My sensory organs were not receiving the signals from my brain to perform this simple procedure, as I was still very much immersed in a different reality. I tried again, but to my amusement and that of both Gil and Guna, who were watching me fail miserably, I just could not figure it out. We looked at each other and stood and laughed uncontrollably... It took me around 10 minutes before I could manage a step right and left without bumping into people on either side of me who had mastered it a lot quicker than I.

The purpose of this exercise is to bring one back into the body and this specific realm of conscious awareness that we live in after a considerable disconnect has taken place during the ceremony. The period for this reconnection can vary hugely with different people, ranging from seconds to many hours, according to an individual's own sensitivity, emotional and chemical make-up. To further accelerate this coupling of the senses and the signals being sent by the brain, we were made to stand in a circle as the band began to sing again and we took turns, two at a time, to perform capoeira...

Capoeira is a martial art that combines elements of combat, acrobatics, music, dance and rituals exquisitely and magnetically performed by two people. It is often called a 'game' that is played, not fought. Capoeira is always performed (or should be) with a smile on the face, symbolising that the capoeiristas are not afraid of any danger. However, the only way to truly understand the magnetism of capoeira is to see it and try it yourself... I was well aware of this sport having watched it many times but never tried it, and certainly not five hours after a rigorous and mind-bending ayahuasca ritual!

The results as you can imagine were comical, and I remember becoming self-aware as I fell over many times. Quickly my senses returned as my ego nudged me in the ribs and shouted in my ear: 'You are making a fool of yourself, you idiot. *Stop it!*' Usually, I would have listened and made a sharp exit, but not this time. I continued another three or four times, without any shame or embarrassment until my mind and body were firmly back on planet earth.

This lasted about 45 minutes before we all went outside to eat... fresh fruit, vegetables and salad. We were encouraged to eat, even though the majority were not hungry. Again, this was an essential part of reconnecting with the senses which govern our waking behaviour, a guardian shaman informed me. After eating and drinking lots of water, I felt very mellow and aligned with the senses that we use to interact with while awake on this particular level of consciousness. But they were heightened and sensitive to the information being processed. What I saw, heard, tasted, touched and smelled were all enhanced, way beyond that which I had experienced before the session. I spoke with many others about this, and most, but not all, were feeling the same thing.

We stayed another couple of hours, chatting, singing and, most important of all, replanting the two plants that were used to have this wonderful experience... Every member of the group was given one of each to take to a sacred place within the jungle to plant and say thank you for what we had just encountered.

My botanical-glandular bridge was very much aligned as I felt at one with nature, and I thanked mother ayahuasca one more time before heading back to where we were staying and back to what I know as 'normality' or whatever that was now. The journey back was contemplative, with little in the way of conversation. There were no uncomfortable silences, just a mutual understanding and respect for one another, way beyond the level of talking...

That night I slept very deeply with many vivid dreams unsurprisingly, which I remembered on awakening. I was vigilant on opening my eyes, and hopped out of bed and opened the shutters to my room, which looked across a sun-drenched valley and onto a steep bank of forested trees, sloping majestically from top to bottom with precision I had not noticed before. I went outside, made a coffee and returned to the sofa outside my room, facing the trees.

I took a few deep breaths and fixed my stare across the valley and onto the lush vegetation, trying not to blink, which is a technique I use when sun gazing at sunset and sundown. Within seconds, the trees came to life, swaying, contracting and expanding as if they were breathing, just the way we do. I rubbed my eyes and blinked, as one does when faced with something outside the compass of under-standing, and re-fixed my stare. It was no anomaly. Not only were the trees alive, but they also appeared to be communicating with me... like an orchestra directed by a skilled conductor. They moved with such precision that I became mesmerised as I felt the tears of hap-piness begin to well up again... I must state here for the record that I am not a prolific crier, but sometimes the heart speaks with tears when words are insufficient.

There is nothing wrong with crying – it's a natural mechanism essential for eliminating emotional and physical toxins. But, as a genuinely positive and happy person, tears for me were often many years apart. However, during and after the session I had cried rivers of tears, both of joy and of sadness. I did not question it then, and have not questioned it since, but felt that I needed to explain and highlight the power to move you that these plants possess...

I remained with my eyes open and began to breathe long and deep as I settled into my morning routine of meditation. The trees were still very much in my vision, and they continued their rhythmic dance, the wind moving effortlessly through the treetops, creating a display of pure exaltation. I laughed and smiled like an excited child on Xmas morning, and went to grab Gil to see if he could see what I was seeing. He looked across the valley and said immediately: 'They are moving towards us, visibly breathing in and out.' We smiled together and sat and chatted for a while, exchanging experiences from the night before as we watched the show, neither of us surprised or questioning the reality of what we each were experiencing – such a beautiful and pure moment, and one that is transfixed in my memory.

The shamans had told me that my teachings would continue long after the ceremony… boy, were they right. I was blissful, and the pain of my failed relationship was a million miles away. This heightened state of presence continued for at least four days, when a deeper understanding of what had transpired unfolded.

I had a mini-meltdown during the following week while watching a film alone in my room. In the film, a little girl of around the same age as my daughter at the time had just found out that her dad was not her biological father, and she wanted to meet him. For obvious reasons, this was very powerful and re-opened a healing wound, making me realise that I have further work to do in order to be free from this deep and buried emotional trauma.

I've summed up as best I can, hopefully without boring you or being overly self-indulgent, my journey into the Amazon to feel the healing power of Mother Nature first hand. Now for a reality check and a responsible caveat. Is it for you? Well, after my personal experiences with ayahuasca, and after some in-depth research, I will say this – I just don't know. There are a small number of you out there who are what I would term 'chemically incompatible' with some of the components of the brew.

Now, these are my own views, so please do as much research as possible, and ignore me if you hear the calling of ayahuasca. But those who have been diagnosed with bipolar or schizophrenia, I would suggest not using it; however, if you suffer from one of these conditions but want to sit in a ceremony, please do the necessary research to be free from doubt.

What I will state categorically, and I touched upon it earlier, is the following… and this goes out to all psychedelic tourists: ignore the required prior preparations at your peril, and be prepared to face the consequences if you act carelessly or arrive in the jungle looking to get high. If you are a regular drinker or an illicit drug taker, or participate in obsessive sexual conduct, and plan to continue this behaviour before and afterwards, not paying attention to the strict pre- and post-ceremony demands, then take full responsibility for your choices and the many possible consequences associated with this potent hallucinogenic...

There are a few who do not experience much at all from working with the plants, but this demographic represents a minuscule proportion of the global population. The vast majority are open and receptive to the magic of ayahuasca and the spiritual, emotional and physical cleansing which accompanies her. For me personally, it was my first encounter with ayahuasca that evoked the most significant leap thus far in my emotional and spiritual understanding, and opened the doorway for continuous exploration of who I am, why am I here and for what purpose.

To sum up in pop culture terminology... Working with ayahuasca is like pressing the control/alt/delete buttons simultaneously on your body computer, which resets the running system but leaves one remaining icon on your desktop called 'My old bullshit'. You can choose to ignore it, or you can click on it and start to re-engage with your old problems, bullshit and patterns and re-establish the thinking and behaviour which has plagued your whole life. One of my teachers once told me: 'Darren, you are only ever one thought away from changing your reality.' How true that is! Hence, leave that icon where it is and try not to activate it again, but if you do, click that X immediately. You have worked hard to transcend the suffering, so close that file down right away.

My personal take on psychedelics is the following. All psychedelic plants when used sensibly and under safe conditions can cut through much of the bullshit which imprisons the mind. Having said that, they are not a panacea cure all... well not for me at least, and certainly not for the hundreds of people who I know personally who have worked with the plant healers.

My life, however, changed beyond recognition after Brazil. I no longer see the world the same way since my experience with ayahuasca. My empathy or ability to see life through the eyes of others has become a default process, whereas pre-ayahuasca, I found that more difficult. I am a better listener and find myself intrigued by what others have to say, which leads me to ask more and more questions about those I spend my time with. It's the quality of a person's questions that defines them, not their answers, which now impresses me.

Increased gratitude is another positive learning I have preserved, and I naturally gravitate towards what's right in my life instead of what's wrong. On a metaphysical level, ayahuasca has taught me the interdependence of all things. People, animals, plant life – in fact, any life form – have instantly become part of an interconnected narrative with a common purpose: consciousness expressing itself subjectively.

There are many different types of plant medicine available, and there is no standard treatment for any one person. My advice is to thoroughly research any plant medicine you wish to work with and decide accordingly. The reason I have written extensively about ayahuasca is that I have worked more with her than with other hallucinogens, and like all other methods of healing in this book, I have repeated experience. I cannot overemphasise the importance of doing that which you claim to know. Remember, if you are not getting the results from any practice you claim to do, then you don't know it at all.

Authenticity comes from repeated experience, regardless of how much information is intellectually acquired. I encourage you to do the same on your journey through life... this will vastly improve your chances of becoming your most potent adaptation.

IN CLOSING

———◆●◆———

Our story may have any number of endings, but
its beginning is a single choice we make today.

The world is going through some monumental changes. The shifting consciousness is genuine, regardless of the narrative being displayed through mainstream media. Change is happening irrespective of the fear and negativity being peddled by those trying to hold on to the last bastions of control. Love will set us free from the lies, deceit and manipulation that has imprisoned humanity for too long.

You have learnt some powerful information and new ways to run your own life. The more you engage with this, the more powerful you will become, so I implore you to carry on and manifest more and more of what you want from life. By choosing to play along with me and to go all in, you have set yourself aside from the masses who prefer to follow the herd. By taking responsibility, you have become the agent of change and influence that I knew you could be. You are becoming a leader and a pioneer for change, and what you do from this point on will have huge significance, not only for yourself but also for the world around you.

But to be agents of love, to be the loving vehicles we were designed to be, we must first eradicate the obstacles that cause the obstructions. We cannot pour from an empty cup, and neither can we express with authenticity that which eludes us. The purpose of the content and the message of this book is to strip away the patterns of behaviour and limiting beliefs that suffocate our ability to express love for others, which first arises from loving ourselves.

People everywhere are hurting, and the world needs trail blazers willing to step up and be the example to others. Do not think for a second that your voice doesn't matter... that your influence is negligible.

It is often said that the planet is separated by six degrees of separation.[17] Think about that... from Donald Trump to the guy cooking fries at your local burger joint. We are bound together by a trail of six people or less. In 2016, researchers at Facebook disproved this hypothesis and reported that the social networking site had reduced the chain length of its members to three and a half degrees of separation: one and a half billion online users separated by no more than three and a half degrees of separation. Think about the possible implications of that statement and what that potentially means.

With social media growing exponentially we are only a click away from connecting with billions of people. Four billion users are expected to be online by 2020, with over six billion smartphone users; that equates to most of the world's forecasted population, according to research by the global telecommunications giant Ericsson. This continued growth will have a massive impact in more ways than one. We will have access to anybody on the planet. Facetime, Skype, WhatsApp and all the other video-enabled software means that we are just one click away from up close and personal with the whole world. Knowing this should empower you to drop the notion of 'What can little me do about anything?' Our voices, opinions, passions and determination have limitless implications.

Drop the idea that your voice carries little or no power... that your desire to help shape the world for the better is an impossible dream.

---

[17] Six degrees of separation is the theory that any person on the planet can be connected to any other person in the world through a chain of acquaintances that has no more than five intermediaries.

Your ability to speak matters. Think of your voice, your idea, as a stone dropped into a lake. As the rock touches the surface of the water, a ripple appears, becoming bigger and bigger. The ripple effect is much greater than the original impact shaped by the stone; the higher the force the rock hits the water, the greater the ripple effect will be.

It's the same with your ideas and voice: the water ripples that surround the stone demonstrate the effects or impressions of your ideas. There will be ripples created, however lightly the stone is dropped into the water, but non-comparable with the magnitude of ripples when determination and strength are used. We must believe in ourselves... we must believe that we matter. We must see that if we don't start something, then it will never happen. Throw that stone – no, scrub that – throw a handful of stones and encourage others to do the same. Become an activist for the world you wish to experience.

Humanity is waking up, however disjointed we appear to be. Across the planet, the shift is quickening. A loving consciousness is growing, and with it the power to heal and unite. Chaos is slowly being replaced by peace and cooperation. With greater authenticity and vulnerability, we become mirrors for each other, reflecting our infinite potential, while simultaneously dissolving the insecurities, fears and darkness.

Darkness cannot co-exist with light. St Francis of Assisi stated: 'Light is so powerful that all the darkness in the world cannot extinguish the light of a single candle.' He is right.

You may not be a single candle, but you can choose to be the mirror that reflects it.

Now, the essential reminders in a nutshell:

1. Own the first hour of every day and you will own your life. Get a morning routine that empowers you and stick with it. A new habit takes 66 days of repetitive engagement before it becomes autonomous.

2. Stop playing small. There is greatness inside you. Find it, follow it and flourish.

3. Keep your word, especially to yourself. Align what you say with what you do.

4. Tell the truth. Radical honesty is not easy, but it will set you free. The truth is one, lies are thousands.

5. We get what we deserve because we get what we tolerate. Raise your standards. You are worth it!

6. Stop believing that you have a predetermined genetic destiny. That is nonsense. A hardwired genetic blueprint, save for the tiniest percentage, does not exist. Your mind is fertile ground, shaped by the emotional and physical environments to which it's exposed. Whether you choose to plant and cultivate beneficial new seeds and ideas, or maintain old patterns of repetitive familiarity, is entirely up to you.

7. You are totally responsible for, and therefore able to respond to, the choices you make, including how you respond to painful events that appear to happen to you... your choices, your consequences.

8. Couple massive action with the required consistency in order to achieve what you want.

9. Continue to work on yourself to nourish your mind with quality content. Educate yourself to the level required. Being the best version means striving towards constant and never-ending improvement.

10. Take those courses, enrol in that workshop and learn from those who are playing at the level you wish to emulate. The better informed you are, the more confident and proficient you will be.

11. When doubts arise or limiting beliefs show up, stop everything and do something about it. Don't dwell and allow the emotional demons to take a foothold.

12. Surround yourself with like-minded individuals with prosperous attitudes. Energy vampires and naysayers will suck the life force out of you and need dropping like hot coals.

13. Remind yourself daily of what it is you want and who you wish to become. Sit for at least 15 minutes a day visualising in great detail what you want to achieve.

14. Embrace and practise gratitude day and night. By focusing on what's right in your world, gratitude naturally builds within you... and gratitude, my friends, changes everything.

15. Share your wisdom and do so with a loving and caring heart. Do not wait to become an expert. Do it now!!!!

16. Find your expression of existence according to your beliefs, religion and lifestyle. Practise that which serves the greater good, including: living in peace, practising non-violence, demonstrating higher tolerance, embracing subjectivity and celebrating life in all of its unique expressions.

17. Familiarise yourself with the inequalities of life and do your bit to eradicate them. Treat nobody as inferior, or as superior; instead, meet all at eye level. The world and her inhabitants can be harsh and challenging but equally beautiful and rewarding, worthy of our love and gratitude, and nothing feels better than contributing and serving others. Every act of kindness and loving gesture helps, however small.

18. Try to leave this world a little better before you take your final breath. You don't need to change the world, but don't let anybody say you can't, if that's your mission. Either way, moving the needle forwards just that little bit makes a huge difference. Knowing that you did your bit for evolving human consciousness and that your being here created a force for good is an act of real beauty.

19. If you can't do it alone, get a coach, therapist or mentor, and make that breakthrough.

20. And the most important of all: '*Love will set you free!*' The more loving and kinder your thoughts, decisions and actions, the higher your energetic frequency becomes, and the higher the frequency, the closer to unconditional love you become.

Enjoy this short time we have here. Nobody is leaving this place alive, so the only thing that matters is – how did you play the game and how did you affect others while playing?